'Triumph & Defeat: The Vicksburg Campaign
by Terrence J. Winschel

©1999 by Terrence J. Winschel
Maps © by St. Martin's Press and Theodore P. Savas

Includes bibliographical references and index

Savas Publishing Company
202 First Street, SE, Suite 103A
Mason City, Iowa 50401   1-800-732-3669

Printing Number
10 9 8 7 6 5 4 3 2

ISBN 1-882810-31-7

This book is printed on 50-lb., acid-free stock. The paper in this book meets or exceeds the guidlines for permanence and durability of the Committee on Production Guidelines for Book Longevity of the Council on Library Resources.

To my precious wife,

Therese Evans Winschel,

for whose love I live.

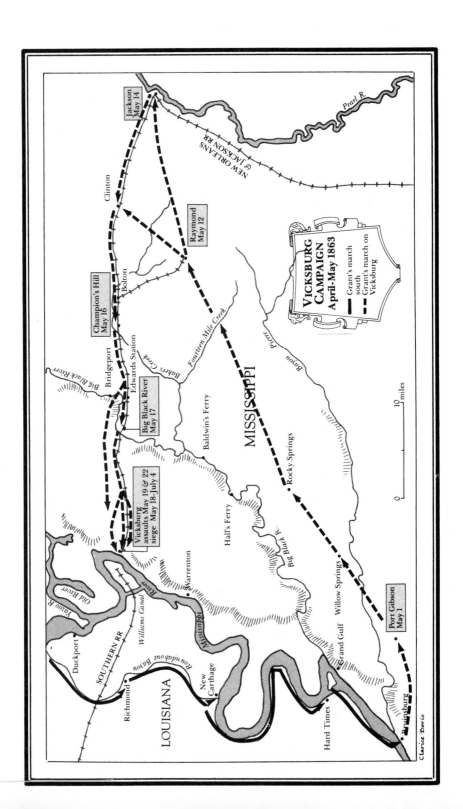

VICKSBURG
CAMPAIGN
April-May 1863

Grant's march
south
Grant's march on
Vicksburg

MISSISSIPPI

LOUISIANA

Pearl R.

NEW ORLEANS & JACKSON RR

Jackson
May 14

Clinton

Raymond
May 12

Champion's Hill
May 16

Bolton

Edwards Station

Bridgeport

Big Black River
May 17

Fourteen Mile Creek

Bakers Creek

Big Black River

Baldwin's Ferry

Bayou Pierre

Rocky Springs

Vicksburg assaults May 19 & 22
siege May 18-July 4

Hall's Ferry

Big Black R.

Willow Springs

Grand Gulf

Port Gibson
May 1

Bruinsburg

Hard Times

SOUTHERN RR

Warrenton

Mississippi River

Williams Canal

Roundabout Bayou

New Carthage

Richmond

Duckport

Yazoo R.

Old River

0   10 miles

Clarice Borio

TABLE OF CONTENTS

PHOTOGRAPHY & ILLUSTRATIONS

CARTOGRAPHY

FOREWORD

The words "Civil War Buff" and "Civil War Groupie" were two generations in the future during the harsh Montana winter of 1935-36. It was then that my father, a Great War Marine, rancher, and history enthusiast, introduced me to the Civil War. The conduit was John W. Thomason, Jr's. *Jeb Stuart*. This sparked what became a lifetime interest in "our war." Before graduating from Sarpy, a one-room rural school 40 miles from the nearest railroad, I read and treasured such books as Lloyd Lewis' *Sherman: Fighting Prophet*, and William E. Woodward's Meet *General Grant*. It was during these years that I named cattle on the ranch for Civil War battles. There was "Antietam," a part Guernsey milk cow, and her calf "Sharpsburg," and many others. At an early age I was covering both bases.

Visits to battlefields prior to my 1941 graduation from Hardin High School were dictated by distance and opportunity, and included no sites associated with the Civil War. Three of these battles--the Little Big Horn, Rosebud, and the Fetterman Fight--were associated with nearby Indian Wars, where many of the white participants had worn the blue in the years 1861-65. March of 1939 found me a freshman at St. John's Military Academy in Delafield, Wisconsin.

During the school spring break there was a field trip to Washington, DC, and to Hampton Roads, Virginia. Among the sites visited in the latter area was Colonial National Historical Park and there, not knowing of their Civil War association, I walked the British Yorktown earthworks.

September 1941 found me out of school and unemployed. Satisfied that the United States might soon be engaged in World War II, which had raged since the German invasion of Poland 24 months before, I hitchhiked across country. It was then that I saw the Shenandoah Valley and Manassas National Battlefield Park, my first Civil War battlefields.

The next four years found me in the U.S. Marine Corps. My first 20 months in the Corps saw my Civil War romance aborted by another and more immediate conflict. Then came 26 months in army and naval hospitals recovering from multiple gunshot wounds received at Cape Gloucester, New Britain, on January 2, 1944. This provided time to reflect and revive my interest in the Civil War soldier and his experiences. This was fortuitous because 14 of these months were spent at the San Diego Naval Hospital, with its excellent library. While there I read Douglas Southall Freeman's *R. E. Lee* and *Lee's Lieutenants*, the latter just off the press. I was enthralled, and since then life has never been the same.

After my March 1946 discharge from the Marine Corps, I matriculated at the Georgetown University School of Foreign Service. Although now in Washington, DC, the lack of a car prevented further battlefield tromping until my graduation and purchase of an automobile in the late spring of 1949. This, along with a job at the U.S. Navy Hydrographic Office, at Suitland, Maryland, enabled me to visit and walk those battlefields preserved as parklands within a day's drive of the nation's capital. These excursions, along with my readings, gave me a pronounced eastern and Confederate bias, and a belief in the greatness of the Army of Northern Virginia, its leaders, and its lean, mean rank and file.

In September 1953, I resigned my position as a "Geographer" at "Hydro" and headed for graduate school at Indiana University. While at Bloomington, I learned there were other armies. This led me to research and write my thesis, "Patrick R. Cleburne: Stonewall Jackson of the West." A research trip taken in July 1954 in support of my thesis saw me tromping western battlefields where Cleburne and his men camped, fought, suffered, and died. Sites visited included Perryville, Richmond, Stones River, Liberty Gap, Franklin, Shiloh, Chickamauga, Chattanooga, and places where Cleburne and his division saw action in the Atlanta Campaign. Until then, I was unaware of the importance of walking in the steps of history, if we are to truly understand and appreciate what manner of people these men in blue and gray were.

This was first underscored for me at Shiloh National Military Park by Charles E. "Pete" Shedd, the dynamic and knowledgeable park historian. He did this by leading me on a walk over the ground traversed by surging Confederates beginning in Fraley's Field and ending with their denouement in front of Dill Branch. He also told me that the National Park Service employed professional historians at most of its Civil War sites tasked to interpret the battlefields to visitors, regardless of their levels of interest. Until then, I had assumed that all those who wore the NPS green and smoky bear hats were law enforcement rangers or naturalists.

A year later, having returned to Washington, DC, and employed in the Department of the Army's Office, Chief of Military History, I chanced to be in Richmond, Virginia, and stopped at headquarters, Region One, National Park Service. At that time all the NPS Civil War parks, except Gettysburg, Antietam, and the units of National Capital Parks, were overseen by Region One. There I learned that there was a park historian vacancy at Vicksburg National Military Park. Seeing this as a chance to change an avocation into a vocation, I leaped at the opportunity.

I resigned my historian position at the Office, Chief of Military History, to take effect Saturday, September 25, 1955, and entered on duty at Vicksburg Tuesday, the 28th. This was done with some trepidation because heretofore the Vicksburg Campaign had commanded scant attention in my readings and none in my battlefield rambles. But, I thought, the Vicksburg position would be a point of entry into the NPS with the possibility of transfer at a future date to a eastern or an "Army of the Heartland" Civil War park.

As the weeks passed this prejudice changed as I challenged myself to learn everything there was to know about the Union campaigns to sever the Confederacy in two along the line of the Mississippi River and capture Vicksburg. This was no small matter as the Vicksburg Campaign commenced in mid-May 1862, when the blue water Union navy appeared below the city, and ended when Lt. Gen. John C. Pemberton surrendered to Maj. Gen. U. S. Grant on July 4, 1863.

Before I left Vicksburg, I had familiarized myself with most of the landscape embraced in a campaign that extended south from Memphis to Port Hudson, and east from Arkansas Post to Newton Station and Corinth. Indeed, a desire to walk in the "steps of history" became so consuming that my friend--the late scholar and Pulitzer award wining historian T. Harry Williams--introduced me at several meetings of the Baton Rouge Civil War Round Table as the "man who knew where every general's horse crapped during the Vicksburg Campaign."

The public and my interest in the Vicksburg Campaign generated a number of monographs published in scholarly journals and "slicks." In the years since 1962, I have authored two books—*Decision in Mississippi* (1962) and *Rebel Victory at Vicksburg* (1963) focusing on aspects of Vicksburg and the Civil War. Then in 1985-1986 Morningside published my three-volume set, *The Vicksburg Campaign*.

When completing my research for the trilogy I came to know a remarkable young historian—Terrence "Terry" Winschel. It was in the early 1980s when our trails first crossed. At that time I was the Service's Chief Historian, and Terry had recently entered on duty at the Vicksburg park. The association of the Pittsburgh native with the NPS began in May 1976 when he entered as a Licensed Battlefield Guide at Gettysburg National Military Park. He returned to Gettysburg the following summer as a seasonal interpreter and later worked in that capacity at Vicksburg National Military Park, Fredericksburg and Spotsylvania National Military Park, and Valley Forge National Historical Park, before becoming a permanent member of the National Park Service family in 1978 at Vicksburg.

My introduction to Terry came when he was on center stage of a living history program. Personable and polished, Winschel assumed the role of a Confederate captain in Company A, 1st Mississippi Light Artillery on July 3, 1863. His story of the campaign and siege gripped and involved the audience evidenced by expressions and a few tears. If Terry had been so inclined, I am confident he would have made it big on the stage.

As the years passed, I noted that Winschel's skills embraced other talents, as well. Both as Chief Historian and in the years since my September 30, 1995, retirement, I have reviewed many of the more than two score of articles Winschel has authored, as well as *The Corporal's Tale* and *Alice Shirley* and the *Story of Wexford Lodge,* book length monographs. In doing so, I discovered that Terry possesses first rate skills as a researcher with a flair for a graceful writing style that touches the reader's soul.

Meanwhile, in my travels during the early 1990s, I came to know Ted Savas, Civil War aficionado, attorney, Californian. Ted was then getting into the publishing business. He and his former partner, David M. Woodbury, soon made their mark in the highly competitive Civil War publishing trade. By 1996 Savas, now on his own as president of Savas Publishing Company, had established himself.

A happy combination thus came to fruition with Savas' decision to publish Winschel's *Triumph & Defeat: The Vicksburg Campaign.* This partnership will be applauded by Civil War scholars and buffs, as well as those of the general public who relish American history and appreciate quality in layout, maps, and typography. The superior quality of Savas Publishing and its corps of talented authors is apparent to readers of Mark Bradley's *The Battle of Bentonville: Last Stand in the Carolinas* (1996), and Chris E. Fonvielle's *The Wilmington Campaign: Last Rays of Departing Hope* (1997).

Triumph & Defeat is in the same category as Bradley's and Fonvielle's books, but is different in one major aspect: it is not a detailed campaign narrative. Instead, it consists of ten well honed essays. Five capture and encapsulate Grant's initial dogged and, once across the Mississippi River, brilliant campaign, that merits his inclusion as one of the great captains of western military history. The final five essays concentrate on the 47-day siege, Confederate failed efforts to relieve Pemberton and his army, and the surrender. The essay entitled "Shut Up As In A Trap: Citizens Under Siege," will enflame emotions and the reader's sympathies for the besieged civilians and soldiers alike. The essays are tightly drawn, fast moving, and convey the temper of the time. Terry knows when to let the participants speak, how to set the stage, and when to allow his narrative history to reign. If *Triumph & Defeat* had been on the shelves of the Park library in September 1955, when I first entered on duty at Vicksburg, it would have provided the missing one volume introduction to the campaign and siege that I craved.

Edwin C. Bearss
Historian Emeritus
National Park Service

INTRODUCTION

"Just give me a job," I implored. *"I will work for free."* After several years of rejection due to my age, I was finally eighteen, the required age for seasonal employment with the National Park Service. But even this offer was in vain, as there were no vacancies at Gettysburg National Military Park.

Growing up in western Pennsylvania, I was a frequent visitor to the many Civil War battlefields in that area that are protected as part of our national park system. My father was a Civil War buff, as was his father before him. Thus our summer vacations were spent touring Gettysburg, Antietam, Fredericksburg, Chancellorsville, Wilderness, Spotsylvania, and Manassas. My initial interest in these fields was to climb on the cannon and monuments, run through the fields, and, as my parents spoiled all of us, get a souvenir.

It was my older brother Tom who first developed an interest in the Civil War. I well remember him giving my Dad directions and reading from the guide book as we toured around Gettysburg one summer. "Who cared?" I thought. "Let's get out and run." But after a while, what Tom read began to sound interesting. Little could I or anyone else in my family have realized that the spark ignited that day by Tom and my Dad would become my life's passion and lead me toward a career in the National Park Service.

Several more years passed with the same response to my applications. However, the resilience of youth, coupled with perseverance and determination—characteristics received equally from the genes of both parents—enabled me to face the nightmare of completing another Federal job application in the fall of 1975. Returning home on Thanksgiving break from Penn State, I found yet another rejection letter from Gettysburg. But this one was different. It informed me that a test was being given (the first time in years) for those interested in becoming a licensed battlefield guide. I seized the opportunity as my chance to get in the door.

The notice gave me just a few weeks to study. I poured through my books and over maps, cramming as many details on the battle as possible into my head. My Dad drove me to Gettysburg the day before the test. I was too confident to be nervous, for I thought I was well prepared. The test, however, was vi

more difficult and longer than I had anticipated, and my hopes for employment at Gettysburg were dashed as I set my pencil down.

I spent the long winter focusing on school and contemplating what I would do come summer. To my great surprise, a letter came announcing that I had passed the written portion of the test and was invited back to take an oral examination. I set my school books aside and read everything I could get my hands on about the Gettysburg Campaign.

Once again, I traveled to Gettysburg with my Dad. The oral examination consisted of conducting a tour of the battlefield for one of the licensed guides and a member of the park staff. It was my fortune to tour Dick Fox and Nora Saum around the field. They were both very kind, and neither laughed or snickered at what must have sounded like gibberish. Rather, they listened carefully to what I said and asked a multitude of questions. Dick was shocked to find out that I was from Pittsburgh and had only been to Gettysburg a few times, mostly as a kid.

"How do you know the road network so well?" he inquired.

"From studying maps," was my reply.

Astonished, he asked, "You know all this from just maps and books?" He turned to Nora, "He'll make a fine guide." Her only comment was, "You do plan on getting a haircut before you start, don't you?"

Joy and elation hardly described my reaction. The door was finally open and I jumped through with both feet.

The summer of 1976 was the most exciting summer I can remember. Tours were two hours each and I conducted three tours a day, six days a week. The task never grew tiring. After work, I toured the park by myself or with others, reading every monument and tablet inscription, asking detailed questions of my companions, and listening intently to what they had to say. I quickly came to know every nook and cranny of the park.

I also went to all the park parties and let everyone who worked for the NPS, from seasonals to the superintendent, know that I wanted to be a park ranger. Years later when I related that to my wife, she said, "You were probably obnoxious." In truth, I probably was, but it worked. The following summer, after graduation from Penn State, I returned to Gettysburg wearing the gray and green uniform of a seasonal interpreter. What fun it was doing programs on Little Round Top and at The Angle. I especially enjoyed doing living history programs at Pitzer's Woods, and campfire programs at night.

Despite being in paradise, I knew that the only way for me to get on with the NPS in a permanent capacity was to travel around working as a seasonal employee—a summer here, a winter there— gaining as broad and diverse an experience as possible. Thus, toward the end of summer the grueling application process began anew.

Fortune smiled on me as I was offered a winter seasonal position at Vicksburg National Military Park in Mississippi. I cried when I left Gettysburg, but did so with the belief that I would return the following summer. Twenty-two years have passed and I still have not made it back to Gettysburg—at least not as a member of the park staff.

I later accepted a term position at Vicksburg as Crew Boss with the Young Adult Conservation Corps and worked supervising a ten-person crew clearing the park's boundary, painting tablets and cannon, pruning trees, and other manual labor. I did this in the hope of transferring back into a permanent park ranger position. Three months later, I learned that people in term positions did not have transfer rights within the NPS, so I accepted a seasonal interpreter's position at Fredericksburg and Spotsylvania National Military Park in Virginia.

At Fredericksburg, I had the privilege of working with Robert Krick, Will Greene, Chris Calkins, Ed Raus, and John Heiser—all of whom have molded sterling reputations in the field of Civil War historiography. It was at Fredericksburg that I learned the art of living history, which Ed Bearss refers to in his Foreword. After Fredericksburg I transferred on to Valley Forge, back in my home state of Pennsylvania. Going from the Civil War to the Revolution was quite a change, but a most enjoyable one. I remember my supervisor yelling at me, "Winschel, quit standing like a Civil War soldier! You're in Washington's army now."

In November 1978, I returned to Vicksburg in a permanent position. Years of frustration followed. Much of my time was spent manning the information desk and handing out folders, selling books, and giving directions on how to get to McDonalds. On really slow days I pitched pennies from the information desk into the 10-inch mortar on display in the Visitor Center. No matter how hard I worked or what I accomplished, transfers and promotions were non-existent—at least for me. To stay fresh and productive, I channeled my attention in other directions. I went to graduate school at night, taught school on my days off, and joined the local theater group.

The only pleasure at work was the pride I took in doing my job and talking with my co-worker, Al Scheller. Al is a remarkable man. A retired New York City fireboat captain, he came to the NPS in 1971 and worked as a summer seasonal at Vicksburg until 1988. Al and I worked the desk together and from him I learned the bulk of my knowledge on the Vicksburg Campaign and the Civil War—not to mention boxing, baseball, religion, and an array of other topics. Each day I asked Al a bevy of questions, and he knew the answer to each one. We discussed every aspect of the campaign until I became fluent with the strategy, tactics, and logistics of the complex operation. Al also took me to all the battlefields of the campaign, and we tromped every inch of them despite the snakes, ticks, hornets, heat, and humidity. Thanks to Al, I developed a fascination with this campaign and a deep love for the resources of the park where I serve. May my stewardship at Vicksburg be a testament to Al, his dedication, his kindness, and his friendship.

The promotion stagnation that plagued Vicksburg was not only frustrating, but crippling financially. I had married in 1981, and our first child followed in 1982, with a second in 1986. I was torn between my love of family and my stewardship for our national treasures. The former duty was paramount, of course, and I began looking for positions in the private sector. I was offered a teaching position in the Gettysburg school system and initially accepted the position, but after deep soul searching, I could not bring myself to leave the NPS.

My perseverance again paid off, for soon thereafter a new superintendent arrived at Vicksburg. Bill Nichols was unlike his two predecessors. Rather than working to maintain the status quo, he demands and expects productivity. With the bonds that stifle creativity broken, the floods gates opened. After years of frustration, dozens of ideas, recommendations, and suggestions bubbled out. I do not think Bill knew what to make of me at first, but he has the uncanny ability to size up a fellow's talents, skills, and abilities. Two years later, I was made Historian, a position Bill created to utilize my expertise. I am grateful for his trust and friendship.

Reinvigorated, I placed years of pentup energy to use. I renewed my interest in writing and began cranking out articles for *The Gettysburg Magazine, Civil War Times Illustrated, Blue & Gray Magazine, The Journal of Confederate History,* and *Civil War Regiments,* to name a few. My writing was guided and greatly aided by Edwin Cole Bearss who was then serving as Chief Historian of the National Park Service. Ed and his wife Marge painstakingly reviewed and edited my writing, and their efforts have greatly enhanced my abilities. Ed also helped to promote me as a speaker on the Civil War Round Table circuit. He and Marge have become dear friends, and I cherish them both.

Years ago there wasn't much of an interest in The Vicksburg Campaign, and thus many of my articles dealt with Gettysburg. Besides, Ed had just published in 1985-86 his three-volume work *The Vicksburg Campaign,* which did not leave much to write about. (These volumes are never far from my reach.) Consequently, I produced self-guiding tour brochures for the various battlefields associated with the campaign, and wrote papers on various aspects of its military operations for presentation to CWRTs or at symposia.

I have been honored to have two such papers appear in the pages of *Civil War Regiments: A Journal of the American Civil War,* a truly outstanding publication founded and originally produced by Theodore P. Savas and David A. Woodbury. Ted and David published a special Vicksburg edition (their first thematic issue) which featured my article on the 1st Battalion, 13th United States Infantry entitled, "The First Honor at Vicksburg." A second article, "To Rescue Gibraltar: Efforts of the Trans-Mississippi Confederates to Relieve Fortress Vicksburg," appeared in *Civil War Regiments* the following year.

Ted and I were featured speakers at the Midwest Civil War Symposium in Chicago a few years ago. We arrived at O'Hare minutes apart and had made arrangements independently with the same company for shuttle service to the hotel. The van broke down en route to pick us up, and a stretch limo was dispatched in its place. The idea for this collection of essays came to life in the back of that limo when Ted expressed an interest in producing a new Vicksburg study. By the time we reached the hotel, we had decided to publish an entire collection of my essays on the Vicksburg Campaign.

Triumph & Defeat: The Vicksburg Campaign, is the result of our collaborative efforts. I can but hope that you will enjoy reading them, and that this publication contributes to the fine reputation of Savas Publishing Company.

ACKNOWLEDGEMENTS

Few individuals in this world can claim that they are self-made. This author is nestled deep in the larger grouping of people who owe their position and stature in life to the selfless efforts of others who have provided guidance and direction, encouragement and support, and, above all, have harbored unfailing belief in me--far beyond my worth. To those of you who have worked diligently and waited patiently for such an occasion as the publication of this collection of essays, the author is truly grateful and extends his heartfelt thanks. My fervent wish is that the Lord bless you and keep you all the days of your lives.

To single out individuals to whom special recognition is due is not a simple task and is one that this author does not take lightly. My beloved parents come first to mind for their constant love. They instilled in me a love for God and country and a passion for the history that is unique to this nation and her people. Although they are gone, their love is ever-present and continues to inspire me. To my brothers and sisters who indulged me the opportunity to pursue my passion for history, thank you for the world of happiness you provide. To my precious wife Therese and children Jennifer, Bert, and Evan—who make my world complete—my love is ever yours.

The author is indebted to my mentors Edwin Cole Bearss and his wife Margie for the many acts of kindness extended toward me over the years, for taking an impressionable and inexperienced young man under their wings and making a professional historian of me; and to Albert P. Scheller along whose side the author worked for many years in awe of his vast knowledge—all are proudly called friends. To Stacy D. Allen, Ken Parks, Hank Hanisee, Parker Hills, Michael Ballard, Warren Grabau, Gordon Cotton, and Blanche Terry who have aided my study of the Vicksburg Campaign; to William O. Nichols, Sam Weddle, Mary Cox Davis, Greg Zeman, and the staff at Vicksburg National Military Park past and present who share in the stewardship of our national heritage, a public trust that we hold sacred.

Above all these, the author extends undying gratitude to William Titus Rigby, former captain of Company B, 24th Iowa Infantry and resident commissioner of Vicksburg National Military Park from 1899-1929, to you dear friend may my work be a source of pride for your example of duty is the very soul of my work. I await the honor of meeting you as a member of the "Church Triumphant."

CHAPTER ONE

UNVEXED TO THE SEA

An Overview of the Vicksburg Campaign

Biographer and newspaperman Lloyd Lewis accurately portrays the Mississippi River in the mid-nineteenth century as being "The spinal column of America"—"the symbol of geographic unity." He refers to the great river as "the trunk of the American tree, with limbs and branches reaching to the Alleghenies, the Canadian border, the Rocky Mountains." For more than two thousand miles the river flows silently on its course to the sea providing a natural artery of commerce. Gliding along the Mississippi's muddy water were steamers and flatboats of all descriptions heavily laden with the rich agricultural produce of the land en route to world markets. Indeed, the silent water of the mighty river was the single most-important economic feature of the continent, the very lifeblood of America. One contemporary wrote emphatically that "The Valley of the Mississippi is America."[1]

Upon the secession of the Southern states, and in particular Louisiana and Mississippi, the river was closed to unfettered navigation which threatened to strangle Northern commercial interests. With the advent of civil war, President Abraham Lincoln gathered his ranking civil and military leaders to discuss strategy for opening the Mississippi River and ending what he termed a "rebellion" in the southern states. Seated around a large table examining a map of the nation, Lincoln made a wide sweeping gesture with his hand then placed his finger on the map and said, "See what a lot of land these fellows hold, of which Vicksburg is the key. The war can never be brought to a close until that key is in our pocket." It was the President's contention that "We can take all the northern ports of the Confederacy, and they can defy us from Vicksburg. It means hog and hominy without limit, fresh troops from all the states of the far South, and a cotton country where they can raise the staple without interference." Lincoln assured his listeners that "I am acquainted with that region and know what I am talking about, and, as valuable as New Orleans will be to us, Vicksburg will be more so."[2]

These powerful statements coming from the Sixteenth President were no exaggeration. Confederate cannon mounted along the bluffs commanding the Mississippi River at Vicksburg were not only trained on the river, but denied that important avenue of commerce to Northern shipping. It is important to further note that Vicksburg was also the connecting link between the eastern and western parts of the Confederacy, what Jefferson Davis referred to as "the nailhead that held the South's two halves together." In addition, the city sat astride a major Confederate supply route over which the armies of Braxton Bragg and Robert E. Lee received much needed food, clothing, medicine, and ammunition, as well as fresh troops.[3]

It was imperative for the administration in Washington to regain control of the lower Mississippi River, thereby reopening that important avenue of commerce enabling the rich agricultural produce of the Northwest to reach world markets. It would also split the Confederacy in two, sever that vital supply route, achieve a major objective of the Anaconda Plan, and effectively seal the doom of Richmond.

The following statements underscore the significance of the Mississippi River, and Vicksburg in particular:

—William T. Sherman, a man destined to play a prominent role in the military operations which centered on Vicksburg, wrote, "The Mississippi, source and mouth, must be controlled by one government." So firm was his belief that Sherman stated, "To secure the safety of the navigation of the Mississippi River I would slay millions. On that point I am not only insane, but mad."

—General-in-Chief Henry W. Halleck wrote in similar, direct, albeit less eloquent terms, "In my opinion, the opening of the Mississippi River will be to us of more advantage than the capture of forty Richmonds."

—And finally, Confederate President Jefferson Davis in writing to Lt. Gen. John C. Pemberton after the fall of Vicksburg stated his view, "I thought and still think you did right to risk an army for the purpose of keeping command of even a section of the Mississippi River. Had you succeeded, none would have blamed, had you not made the attempt few would have defended your course."[4]

In order to protect the Mississippi Valley, Confederate authorities established a line of defense which ran from Columbus, Kentucky, on the left overlooking the Mississippi River, through Bowling Green, to Cumberland Gap where the right flank was anchored on the mountains. On the great river south of Columbus, fortifications were also placed at Island No. 10, and on the Chickasaw Bluffs north of Memphis. Seventy miles below New Orleans, two powerful masonry forts, Forts Jackson and St. Philip, stood guard near the mouths of the Mississippi River.

Eager to confront the difficult task before them, Union land and naval forces moved with a vengeance from two directions in a massive converging attack to wrestle control of the river from Confederate troops. Driving south from Cairo, Illinois, Federal forces seized Forts Henry and

Adm. David Glasgow Farragut

Donelson on the Tennessee and Cumberland rivers respectively

and opened the pathway of invasion to the Deep South. Continuing the drive, Union forces gained victory at Shiloh in April, Corinth in May, and having forced the surrender of Island No. 10, seized Memphis in June.

Moving upriver from the Gulf of Mexico were the ships of the West Gulf Blockading Squadron commanded by then Flag Officer David Glasgow Farragut. His ships bombarded and passed Forts Jackson and St. Philip on April 24 and compelled the surrender of New Orleans thirty-six hours later. With initial success behind him, Farragut sent an advance flotilla up river. Baton Rouge fell to the Federals on May 8, Natchez four days later, and the flotilla steamed on toward Vicksburg.

After the fall of New Orleans, as the Union pincer slowly closed along the river, the Confederates began to fortify Vicksburg. The city's geographical location made it ideal for defense. Equally important, existing rail lines which connected Vicksburg with Jackson and, via Jackson, points elsewhere in the Confederacy, enabled the shipment of big guns to the "Hill City." It was not long before Vicksburg became known as the "Gibraltar of the Confederacy," and it would prove a tough nut to crack. The strategic significance of Vicksburg greatly increased after the fall of Memphis as it then became the northern most point below Memphis where the bluffs met the river. It was only a matter of time before war in all its horror centered on Vicksburg.

Initial efforts by Union land and naval forces to capture Vicksburg and open the great waterway to navigation ended in failure. The first threat developed on May 18, 1862, when the ships of the West Gulf Blockading Squadron arrived below Vicksburg and demand was made for the city's surrender. In terse words the demand was refused. Lt. Col. James L. Autry, the post commander, replied, "Mississippians don't know, and refuse to learn, how to surrender to an enemy." Incensed, Federal authorities opened fire upon the city and maintained an intermittent bombardment from late May, all through June, and into late July, but to no avail. The bombardment was ineffective and Farragut's fleet, wracked with sickness and plagued by rapidly falling waters, withdrew to New Orleans and deeper waters.[5]

It was then and there realized by both Union and Confederate high commands that if Vicksburg were going to fall it would be at the hands of a combined land and naval effort. The batteries which overlooked the Mississippi River at Vicksburg were powerful, indeed formidable. But all the land accesses were open. The decision was made to construct a line of defense to guard the city's landward approaches and control the roads and railroad access to Vicksburg. The responsibility for design and construction of these

Maj. Gen. Ulysses S. Grant
Generals in Blue

works was assigned to Maj. Samuel Lockett, Chief Engineer of the Department of Mississippi and East Louisiana. Lockett, a graduate of West Point, Class of 1859 in which he stood second, was a skilled and trained engineer who set about his task with vigor.

Reconnoitering through the hills and hollows around Vicksburg, Lockett quickly realized that the city was naturally defensible. Because of the series of sharp narrow ridges, fronted by deep steep ravines, Vicksburg was a natural fortress which he planned to make even stronger by the construction of field fortifications. The line as constructed consisted of nine major forts connected by a continuous line of trenches and rifle pits. The line formed a huge semicircle around Vicksburg the flanks of which rested on the river above and below the city. It would be manned by a garrison of 30,000 troops, mount 172 big guns, and pose the major challenge to Union domination of the river.

Late that same year, a two prong Federal advance on Vicksburg met with disaster. Maj. Gen. Ulysses S. Grant, commander of the Union Army of the Tennessee, had divided his force in two for an advance on Vicksburg. One column, under Grant's personal command, marched overland from Grand Junction, Tennessee, into north Mississippi. The object was to draw Confederate forces responsible for the defense of Vicksburg into the northern portion of the state and there keep them pinned while the other column, under Maj. Gen. William T. Sherman, made a rapid push down the Mississippi River and seized Vicksburg.

As Grant's column pushed south through Holly Springs and Oxford toward Grenada, his ever lengthening supply and communications line became dangerously exposed. The Mobile & Ohio Railroad, on which Grant depended for supplies, fell prey to raiding Confederate cavalry under Nathan Bedford Forrest. His advance base at Holly Springs also fell victim to raiding Confederate cavalry under Earl Van Dorn. Destruction of the vital rail line and his advance base at Holly Springs compelled Grant to begin a pull back to Memphis. This retrograde enabled Confederate forces, utilizing interior rail lines, to rush to Vicksburg arriving in time to thwart Sherman's strike just northeast of the city along the banks of Chickasaw Bayou. In reporting the action, Sherman simply wrote, "I reached Vicksburg at the time appointed, landed, assaulted and failed."[6]

Checked on the overland route, Grant seized upon Federal naval supremacy on the inland waters to transfer his army to Milliken's Bend and Young's Point, Louisiana, on the Mississippi River just north of and opposite Vicksburg. He also stationed troops farther to the north at Lake Providence, Louisiana. During the winter months, Federal forces stockpiled tremendous quantities of rations, clothing, medicine, ammunition, and countless other items for the spring campaign aimed at Vicksburg. Grant also orchestrated a series of ill-fated bayou expeditions the object of which was to reach the rear of Vicksburg.

After months of frustration and failure, Grant was at a crossroads in his military career. There was tremendous clamor in the Northern press to remove him from command. Even members of the Cabinet urged Lincoln to replace Grant as commander of the western army. But the President responded to those critical of Grant by saying, "I can't spare this man, he fights. I'll try him a little longer." Aware of the clamor against him, Grant examined his options.[7]

Three options were discussed at army headquarters. The first was to launch a direct amphibious assault across the Mississippi

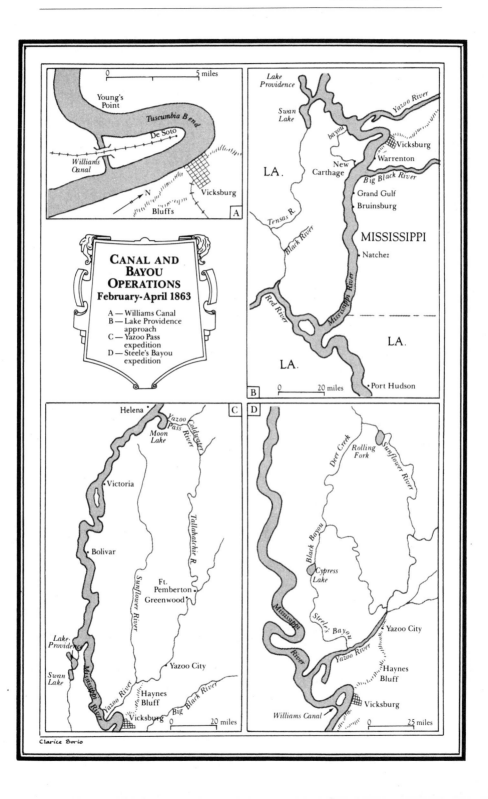

CANAL AND
BAYOU
OPERATIONS
February-April 1863

A — Williams Canal
B — Lake Providence
    approach
C — Yazoo Pass
    expedition
D — Steele's Bayou
    expedition

Clarice Borio

River and storm the Vicksburg stronghold. The second was to pull back to Memphis and try the overland route once again. And, the third, was to march the army down the west side of the river, search for a favorable crossing point, and transfer the field of operations to the area south and east of Vicksburg. In characteristic fashion and with grim determination, Grant boldly opted for the march south. On March 29, 1863, Grant ordered Maj. Gen. John A. McClernand of the XIII Corps to open a road from Milliken's Bend to New Carthage on the Mississippi River below Vicksburg. The movement began on March 31, and thus the Vicksburg campaign began in earnest.

As Grant's infantrymen slogged their way south through Louisiana corduroying roads and building bridges each step of the way, the Union fleet commanded by R. Adm. David Dixon Porter prepared to run by the batteries at Vicksburg. On the dark, moonless night of April 16, Porter's vessels raised anchor and moved downriver toward the citadel of Vicksburg. With engines muffled and running lights extinguished, Porter hoped to slip pass the batteries undetected. Suddenly the night sky was ablaze from bales of cotton soaked in turpentine which lined the river on both banks and barrels of tar set afire by the Confederates to illuminate the river and silhouette the fleet as it passed the batteries.

For several hours the fleet withstood the punishing fire which was poured from Confederate batteries. Admiral Porter paid close attention to where the shot and shell were landing and noticed they were hitting his smokestacks, the pilothouses and hurricane decks, some were even hitting the gundecks, but few were hitting any lower where the vital parts of his boats—the engines, boilers, steam-drums, and mud drums were located. He reasoned that the Confederates were either poor gunners, or else there was a fatal flaw in the placement of their batteries which prevented them from depressing the guns to direct an effective fire against the gunboats and transports. After two years of war, he knew the Confederates to be skilled artillerists. Porter quickly directed his vessels to move across the channel and hug the Mississippi shore. As they did so, the shot and shell began to fly harmlessly overhead. So close did the fleet approach Vicksburg, that sailors reported hearing Confederate gun captains giving commands. They also heard bricks tumbling into the city streets, the effect of their own gunfire. When the shelling stopped, Porter tallied the damage to his fleet and recorded the loss of only one transport vessel. What was deemed impossible by many was achieved. With Porter's fleet now below Vicksburg, Grant had the wherewithal to cross the mighty river.

It was Grant's intention to force a crossing of the river at Grand Gulf where there was a good all weather landing and from which point roads radiated deep into the interior of Mississippi. Two forts guarded Grand Gulf and posed an obstacle to Federal plans. On April 29, Porter's gunboats bombarded the Grand Gulf defenses in preparation for a landing by Grant's troops. The fleet silenced the guns of Fort Wade, but could not quiet those of Fort Cobun.

Ever adaptive, Grant disembarked his men from the transports and marched them five miles farther down the levee. That evening, Porter's fleet ran passed the Confederate batteries and rendezvoused with Grant at Disharoon's plantation. On April 30—May 1 Grant hurled his army across the mighty river and onto Mississippi soil at Bruinsburg. A band aboard the flagship *Benton* struck up "The Red, White, and Blue" as Grant's infantrymen came ashore. In one of the largest amphibious operations in American history up to that time, Grant landed 22,000 men and began the inland campaign to capture Vicksburg.

Once ashore, Grant's forces pushed rapidly inland and marched through the night. In the early morning hours of May 1, Confederate resistance was encountered west of Port Gibson. In a furious battle which raged throughout the day, Union soldiers fought with grim determination to secure their beachhead on Mississippi soil while Confederate soldiers fought with equal determination to drive the invaders into the river. By day's end, Confederate forces, outnumbered and hard-pressed, retired from the field.

Rather than march north on Vicksburg, Grant directed his army in a northeasterly direction. It was his intention to cut the rail line which connected Vicksburg with Jackson and sever that vital line of communications and supply, cutting the Confederate garrison off from supplies and reinforcements. In a seventeen-day

period, which is often referred to as the blitzkrieg of the
Vicksburg campaign, Grant's army marched more than 200 miles,
fought five battles, and drove the Confederates into the city's defenses.

The campaign thus far had been a stunning success for the
Union army. Grant's force had met and overcome Confederate
resistance at Port Gibson on May 1, Raymond on May 12, and
two days later captured the capital of Mississippi. Not wishing to
waste combat troops on occupation, Grant neutralized Jackson
with the torch then turned west toward his objective—
Vicksburg. En route from Jackson to Vicksburg, his force inflicted
devastating casualties on the Confederate army commanded by
Lt. Gen. John C. Pemberton at the battle of Champion Hill on
May 16. The following day, May 17, Grant soundly defeated
Confederate forces at the Big Black River Bridge and hurled
Pemberton's army into the defenses of Vicksburg.

Having witnessed the debacle at the Big Black River and the
wild flight of his troops, Pemberton dejectedly stated, "Just thirty
years ago I began my military career by receiving my appointment to a cadetship at the U.S. Military Academy, and to-day—
that same date—that career is ended in disaster and disgrace." For
all practical purpose it was, but it was a disaster which would effect an entire nation.[8]

The citizens of Vicksburg watched in fear as the shattered
remnants of Pemberton's army poured into the city on that fateful day. Emma Balfour, wife of a prominent Vicksburg physician,
stood in her doorway as the demoralized mass of humanity filled
the streets. She later wrote with trepidation, "I hope never to witness again such a scene as the return of our routed army!" With
pen in hand she recorded the scene which enveloped her, "From
twelve o'clock until late in the night the streets and roads were
jammed with wagons, cannons, horses, men, mules, stock, sheep,
everything you can imagine that appertains to an army being
brought hurriedly within the intrenchment." She confided to her
diary the fears of many in Vicksburg as she wrote, "What is to become of all the living things in this place. . .shut up as in a trap. . .God
only knows."[9]

On through the long day and into the evening marched the weary soldiers clad in butternut, gray, and undyed wool. Singly or in small groups, with no sense of order or discipline, the men filed into the rifle-pits and turned to meet Grant's rapidly approaching army. A medley of sounds filled the night air as the Confederates readied their defenses: officers shouted orders, teamsters whipped their animals and dragged artillery into position, and, as the soldiers worked with picks and shovels, some men cursed while others prayed. Throughout the night, the ringing of axes was constant as additional trees were felled to strengthen fortifications, clear fields of fire, and form abatis. Work continued at a feverish pace and, by sunrise, the city was in a good state of defense.

Late in the afternoon, Confederate soldiers peering over their parapets spotted long columns of Union infantrymen moving slowly toward the city. It was a terrifying spectacle, and yet magnificent in the extreme as battleflags snapped in the breeze above the columns and bayonets glistened in the sunlight. Union skirmishers were quickly deployed and artillery roared into action, but the day wore away with nothing more than a long range artillery duel. That night, as darkness enveloped the fields, the soldiers of both armies rested on their arms. Each knew that the bloody work at hand would commence with the rising sun and prepared for battle in his own way.

Grant was anxious for a quick victory and, after making a hasty reconnaissance, ordered an attack. On the morning of May 19, Union cannon opened fire and bombarded the Confederate works with solid shot and shell. The thick smoke from the guns shrouded the fields and made it virtually impossible to see. At 2:00 p.m., when the guns fell silent, Union soldiers deployed into line of battle astride Graveyard Road, northeast of Vicksburg, and stormed toward the city's defenses. They succeeded in planting several stands of colors near the parapets of Vicksburg, but were driven back with the loss of 942 men.

At the height of the attack, several regiments were pinned to the ground less than 125 yards from the Confederate works. Under a sweltering sun the men on the firing line began to run low on ammunition. One unit in desperate need of cartridges was the Fifty-fifth Illinois Infantry led by Col. Oscar Malmborg.

Faced with the decision to either re-supply his men or pull his regiment back, Malmborg asked for volunteers to run to the rear and call up a fresh supply of cartridges.

Four men volunteered for the hazardous assignment including a young musician named Orion P. Howe. Braving a murderous fire of musketry, they ran to the rear along Graveyard Road just as fast as their legs would carry them. Three of the four men were killed en route. The sole survivor, Orion Howe, was badly wounded—taking a bullet in the leg—and was toppled hard to the ground. Despite his wound, the lad picked himself up, dusted himself off, and continued down the road.

Howe hobbled up to a familiar figure on horseback and cried: "General Sherman, send some cartridges to Colonel Malmborg, our men are all out." Although he could tell by the ashen complexion on his face and the blood streaming down his leg that the boy was wounded, Sherman listened intently to his story then sent Howe to the rear and medical treatment. As he limped along, the young soldier wheeled about and shouted "Calibre 54." The requested cartridges were carried to the front and distributed to the men on the firing line, but to no avail as they were the wrong calibre and the attack was checked and driven back.[10]

Recalling the bravery demonstrated by Howe, Sherman wrote Secretary of War Edwin M. Stanton recommending that the young musician be given a medal. In time he was—no less an award than the Medal of Honor. Although the medal was not issued until 1896, on May 19, 1863, the day he performed the action for which he was a recipient of the medal, Orion Howe was 14 years of age.

Undaunted by his failure on the 19th, Grant decided to make a more thorough reconnaissance then hurl his entire force against Vicksburg on May 22. Early that morning Union artillery roared into action and for four hours bombarded the works with solid shot and shell tearing large holes in the earthen fortifications. At 10:00 a.m., the prearranged time for the assault to begin, the artillery fell silent. Union soldiers moved forward over a three-mile front toward the defenses of Vicksburg. They succeeded in planting their colors on the parapets of Vicksburg in several areas and made a short-lived penetration at Railroad Redoubt, but were driven back a second time with severe loss. In the assault on May 22, Grant lost more than 3,000 officers and men killed, wounded, or missing.

Although his nose was bloodied a second time, Grant was not yet willing to toss in the towel and lay siege to the city. As he contemplated his next move, Grant left behind his dead and wounded, many of whom had been lying exposed since May 19. Exposed to the sun and heat the bodies of the dead began to bloat and turn black—the stench was sickening. One Confederate soldier complained that, "the Yanks are trying to stink us out of Vicksburg." On May 25, white flags appeared along the Confederate line. Union soldiers were hopeful that the city would soon be surrendered. Their hopes were dashed as word quickly spread that a note was passed from Pemberton to Grant "imploring in the name of humanity" that Grant bury his dead as the odor had become quite offensive.[11]

A truce was granted for two and one-half hours during which time men in blue and gray mingled between the lines. "Here a group of four played cards," recalled one soldiers, "two Yanks and two Rebs," while others swapped tobacco for coffee. While the gruesome task of the burial details was completed, it was almost as if there were no war in progress. At the appointed time, however-er, the flags were taken down and everyone ran for cover. The siege of Vicksburg began in earnest that day.[12]

Throughout the month of May and into June Union soldiers slowly extended their lines to the left and right until they invest-ed the beleaguered city. Once the investment was complete, Pemberton's garrison was effectively cut off from all supply and communications with the outside word. The Confederates had to subsist solely on what they had stockpiled in Vicksburg prior to the siege. With each passing day those supplies dwindled until they were nearly exhausted. In order to conserve what food sup-plies were on hand, Pemberton ordered the daily ration cut to three-quarters, then to half, then to quarter, then they were cut again, and yet again, and yet again. By the end of June the garri-son was issued only a handful of peas and rice per man per day. Even their water was rationed.

Disease began to spread rapid through the ranks. Dysentery, diarrhea, malaria, and various fevers all took a heavy toll of human life and were more certain of death that were Union sharpshooters. At first, scores then hundreds of men could be seen laying their weapons aside and walk or crawl as best they could to the hospitals in Vicksburg. Public buildings were filled to capacity, many handsome private residences were converted to hospitals. But even there, there was no succor as medicines were in short supply. Each day the "dead wagons" made the rounds of the hospitals and the dead were brought out in ever increasing number and carried to their long rest northeast of town in the city cemetery.

As May slowly faded into June, Union soldiers began to dig approaches toward the Confederate line. Forming zig-zags and then parallels, Grant moved up his infantry and artillery first to within 300 yards, then 200 yards, then 100 yards. The digging then continued as Union soldiers worked their way up to the parapets of Vicksburg. The object was to get as close as possible wherefore if an attack was ordered all they need do is pour out of their trench, over the parapet, and among the enemy. This would minimize their casualties and maximize the troop strength with which they hit the enemy. Hopefully it would be with enough strength of numbers to seize the forts and gain access to Vicksburg. An option was to tunnel underneath the enemy works, hollow out chambers, fill them with black powder, and destroy the fortifications of Vicksburg.

Thirteen approaches were excavated by Union soldiers at different points along the siege line with the object of mining the Confederate works. Of these thirteen approaches, the most successful was known as "Logan's Approach." Situated along the Jackson road, Logan's Approach inched forward toward the Third Louisiana Redan. Excavating a sap, or trench if you will, that was seven feet deep and eight feet wide, Union fatigue parties reached the Third Louisiana Redan on June 23. A gallery was then carved under the fort and preparations made for mining.

On June 25, 2,200 pounds of black powder were placed in the mine. At 3:00 p.m. the fuse was lit. Tense moments passed as the

Federals waited to storm into the breach and seize Vicksburg. Suddenly there was a muffled thud, then a loud explosion as the ground began to heave and a column of flame and dirt reached to the sky. Inside the column of flame one could see men, mules, and accouterments blown skyward. Before the dust could even settle, Union soldiers poured into the crater and attempted to secure the breach. In the wild melee which ensued clubbed muskets and bayonets were freely used and hand grenades were tossed back and forth. The battle raged in unabated fury for twenty-six hours as Grant threw in one fresh regiment after another, all to no avail. The breach was sealed by the Confederates at the point of bayonet. The great gamble had failed.

Undaunted, a second mine was planted and detonated on July 1, but was not followed by an infantry assault. That day, Grant was notified by his subordinates that given just a few more days of digging, thirteen mines could be planted and detonated simultaneously. This was the moment Grant and his army had been working toward all these many weeks of siege. It is not likely that the Confederates could have withstood such an attack.

On the hot afternoon of July 3, Grant was in the process of planning an attack (which he scheduled for July 6), when white flags of truce again appeared along the lines. Riding out from the city came a trio of officers in gray led by Lt. Gen. John C. Pemberton. Grant rode to meet with him between the lines. Pemberton asked Grant on what terms would he receive the surrender of the garrison and city of Vicksburg. Grant replied that he had no terms other than immediate and unconditional surrender. These terms were unacceptable to Pemberton who assured Grant that he would bury many more of his men before he gained entrance to Vicksburg. The generals agreed only upon a cessation of hostilities, then rode their separate ways. Grant assured Pemberton that he would have his final terms by 10:00 that night.

True to his word, Grant sent in his final, amended terms. Instead of an unconditional surrender of Vicksburg, Grant offered parole to the garrison. Pemberton received the note in the quiet of his headquarters. In the company of his generals, Pemberton read the note then passed it around for his subordinates to read and comment upon. Almost to a man, they agreed they were the best terms to be had.

On the morning of July 4, 1863, white flags fluttered in the breeze above the fortifications of Vicksburg. Marching out from their works, Confederate soldiers furled their flags, stacked their arms, and turned over their accouterments at which time a victorious Union army marched in and took possession of Vicksburg—the fortress city on the Mississippi River which had eluded them for so long.

Grant rode in along the Jackson Road and down to the Warren County Court House where he watched the Stars and Stripes placed atop the building. He then rode down to the waterfront where he personally thanked and congratulated Admiral Porter for the assistance rendered by the United States Navy during the operations against Vicksburg. Almost as an afterthought, he sent a message to Washington informing President Lincoln of the city's surrender. It took several days for the message to reach the capital and within less than two days thereafter the only remaining Confederate bastion on the Mississippi River—Port Hudson, Louisiana, fell into Union hands. Upon receipt of Grant's message, Lincoln sighed, "Thank God," and declared that "The Father of Waters again goes unvexed to the sea."[13]

CHAPTER TWO

THE ONLY VIABLE OPTION

Grant's March Through Louisiana

Frustration and death plagued Maj. Gen. Ulysses S. Grant and his Army of the Tennessee throughout the winter of 1862-1863 as he maneuvered to seize the fortress city of Vicksburg. The Confederate citadel on the Mississippi River remained defiant, seemingly impervious to capture by Union land and naval forces. From Yazoo Pass and Holly Springs in north Mississippi; to Lake Providence in Louisiana, along the banks of Chickasaw Bayou north of the city, and the abortive canal across De Soto Point opposite Vicksburg, Grant's efforts had ended in failure. The only result of his operations thus far was an ever lengthening casualty list. The Northern press ridiculed Grant and clamored for his removal. Even members of the Cabinet urged President Lincoln to find a new commander for his Western army. The President, however, answered those critical of Grant by saying, "I can't spare this man, he fights. I'll try him a little longer."[1]

At forty-one years of age, "Sam" Grant was at a crossroads in his military career. An 1843 graduate of the United States Military Academy at West Point and a veteran of the Mexican War, he was no stranger to adversity. Having battled his way to national prominence at Belmont, Fort Donelson, and Shiloh, he struggled with rumor and innuendo to establish a reputation of respectability. Cognizant of the criticism which swirled around him in both military and political circles, Grant appeared stoic, but confided the torment he felt to his wife Julia. Determined to persevere, he ignored the critics and remained focused on his objective--Vicksburg. After months of frustration and failure, Grant examined his options.

Three options were discussed at army headquarters. The first option was to launch an amphibious assault across the Mississippi River and storm the Vicksburg stronghold. The second was to pull back to Memphis and try the overland route once again. And the third option was to march the army southward down the Louisiana side of the river, search for a favorable crossing point, and transfer the field of operations to the area south and east of Vicksburg. In characteristic fashion and with grim determination, Grant boldly opted for the march south. Historian Edwin C. Bearss writes of Grant's decision: "The third alternative was full of dangers and risks. Failure in this venture would entail little less than total destruction. If it succeeded, however, the gains would be complete and decisive."[2]

On March 29, 1863, Grant directed Maj. Gen. John A. McClernand of the XIII Corps to open a road from Milliken's Bend to New Carthage on the Mississippi River below Vicksburg. Energetic, aggressive, and ambitious, John Alexander McClernand was also bombastic, egotistical, and extremely irritating to those around him. Born in Kentucky, he was raised in southern Illinois and had a strong dislike for abolitionists. He was short, spare of frame, heavily bearded with a rather large nose and scraggly hair. He had piercing eyes, a hearty laugh, and an engaging smile, yet at all times McClernand was calculating and deceitful. A lawyer by training and a politician by profession, McClernand had risen to the pinnacle of power in the House of Representatives only to be defeated for the speakership in

Maj. Gen. John A. McClernand
Generals in Blue

1860. He looked to the field of battle to win victories and headlines in his quest for the White House.

The selection of McClernand to lead the march through Louisiana is a source of controversy still today. Although an experienced fighter in the halls of Congress, his only military experience prior to the Civil War was in the Black Hawk War. As a political appointee in the military, he was inexperienced and at times inept in the handling of troops. The former congressman disdained administrative details and was contemptuous of military protocol. He did not work well with superiors or those subordinates that had graduated from the U.S. Military Academy and his dislike and well grounded suspicions for West Pointers did not endear him to his fellow corps commanders--William T. Sherman and James B. McPherson.

McClernand, however, had demonstrated his willingness to fight at Fort Donelson and Shiloh and had developed into an able combat officer. Although Grant knew of widespread distrust of McClernand among West Pointers and his staff and later wrote that he "doubted McClernand's fitness," in the spring of 1863 Grant was confident that the former congressman could and, if necessary, would fight.[3]

On March 31, a task force commanded by Col. Thomas W. Bennett of the 69th Indiana left its encampment at Milliken's Bend with instructions from McClernand to reconnoiter the road south to New Carthage. Accompanied by two companies of the 2d Illinois Cavalry, a detachment of the 6th Missouri Cavalry, and two mountain howitzers, the Hoosiers moved out at 8:00 a.m. and headed south over muddy roads. Extending the length of the column and slowing the rate of march considerably was Capt. William F. Patterson's Kentucky Company of Engineers and Mechanics with pontoons and yawls to bridge flooded bayous.

Bennett's task force neared Richmond, on Roundaway Bayou, at 2:00 p.m. where the men encountered slight resistance from Maj. Isaac F. Harrison's 15th Louisiana Cavalry Battalion. Two companies were quickly ferried across the bayou and, after a brief skirmish, the troopers from Louisiana were driven back. (The skirmish was the first of many that would take place over the next few days between Union forces and Harrison's men.) Rather than cross the bayou in force and occupy Richmond, the Federals bivouacked on the north bank.

That same day, March 31, as Bennett's task force headed south toward Richmond, ground was broken on the ill-fated Duckport Canal. Designed to connect the Mississippi River with Walnut Bayou, the canal would establish a water route for supply of the army as it headed south through Louisiana. Union fatigue parties made rapid progress with pick and shovel and water was let in on April 13. Although several barges successfully passed through the canal and into Walnut Bayou, only the tug *Victor* managed to reach New Carthage. By May 4 even the engineers had to admit defeat and the canal was abandoned.

The success of Grant's move would depend in large part on the United States Navy and, in particular, the Mississippi Squadron commanded by Rear Adm. David Dixon Porter. To support the projected amphibious assault, Grant requested Porter to run one or two of his powerful ironclads below the batteries at Vicksburg. Although agreeable to the idea, the admiral cautioned Grant that once his vessels were below the batteries they could not fight their way upstream. A man who always kept his options open, Grant, accompanied by Sherman and Porter, examined the Confederates' Yazoo River defenses on April 1. Convinced that Vicksburg could not be turned on the north without, in Grant's terms, "immense sacrifice of life, if not with defeat," the Union commander fully committed himself to the march on New Carthage.[4]

The following day, on April 2, additional troops were ordered south from Milliken's Bend. With lofty spirits and in anticipation of *Victory*, men of the XIII Corps shouldered their rifle-muskets and took up the line of march. Meanwhile at Richmond (then the seat of government for Madison Parish, as counties are called in Louisiana), Federal engineers bridged Roundaway Bayou and Colonel Bennett's task force reached the plantation of Josiah Stansbrough, three and one-half miles below town. There, the ever-cautious Bennett halted his infantry and cavalry patrols were thrown forward to reconnoiter the road to New Carthage. After a ten-mile ride, however, the Federal horsemen encountered Major Harrison's troopers near T. C. Holmes' plantation and returned to Bennett's camp at Stansbrough's.

Dissatisfied with Bennett's progress, Brig. Gen. Peter Osterhaus, commander of the Ninth Division, XIII Corps, or-

Brig. Gen. John S. Bowen
Generals in Gray

ganized a strike force of his own on the morning of April 4. Consisting of the 49th and 69th Indiana Infantry, detachments of the 2d and 3rd Illinois and 6th Missouri Cavalry, Osterhaus' force, accompanied by General McClernand, pushed beyond Holmes' plantation. Around noon, the Federals reached Pliney Smith's plantation--Pointe Clear, where an advanced staging area was established two miles north of New Carthage.

As the area between Pointe Clear and New Carthage was inundated by flood water from the Mississippi River, Osterhaus led a cavalry patrol westward with the dual purpose to investigate the road skirting Bayou Vidal and to break up Major Harrison's encampment which informants placed on Judge John Perkins' Somerset plantation. Unable to reach Perkins' plantation due to the high water in Bayou Vidal, Osterhaus left an advance contingent of the 2d Illinois Cavalry at Dunbar's plantation and returned to Pointe Clear.

Such a movement by large numbers of troops was difficult to conceal from the eyes of roving Confederate cavalry. Rumors of the Federal advance reached the ears of Brig. Gen. John S. Bowen, Confederate commander at Grand Gulf, twenty-five miles below Vicksburg. A native of Bowen's Creek, Georgia, Bowen graduated from West Point in 1853, standing thirteen in a class of fifty-one cadets. Resigning from the army three years later, he moved to St. Louis where he worked as an architect. Active in the Missouri militia, Bowen established a reputation for efficiency and military bearing. As Missouri teetered on the brink of secession, he served as chief of staff to Brig. Gen. Daniel M. Frost of the pro-secession state militia and was captured by Federal troops at Camp Jackson. Upon his release, Bowen organized the 1st Missouri Infantry at Memphis and was appointed colonel of the regiment. He served in Kentucky then Tennessee and was wounded at Shiloh. Bowen inspired men by his personal bravery and gallant conduct; fiery, aggressive, hard-hitting, he would prove the perfect choice for command at Grand Gulf.

Bowen acted instinctively when rumors of a Federal movement were confirmed and, on April 4, sent Col. Francis M. Cockrell across the river to reinforce Harrison's troopers and make contact with the enemy. Ordered to keep his superior appraised of enemy movements, Cockrell crossed the river with the 1st and 2d Missouri Infantry regiments and a section of artillery. Landing at Hard Times, the Missourians moved quickly to locate McClernand's Federal vanguard.

The Federals were busy attempting to reach New Carthage. Securing a scow, Captain Patterson's engineers quickly converted the craft into a landing barge equipped with a mountain howitzer. "She was boarded up with 3-inch planks almost as high as a man's head, with oars on each side like a war galley of yore," is how one Union soldier described the strange looking vessel. Christened *Opossum*, Osterhaus' gunboat (if we may dignify it as such) led a small convoy of yawls and skiffs through the murky water toward New Carthage. Landing on the levee which bounded the Mississippi River, the Federals pushed south to Ione plantation where they encountered a handful of Harrison's

Col. Francis M. Cockrell
Generals in Gray

Confederate cavalrymen. After a few well-aimed rounds from *Opossum*, the troopers fled.

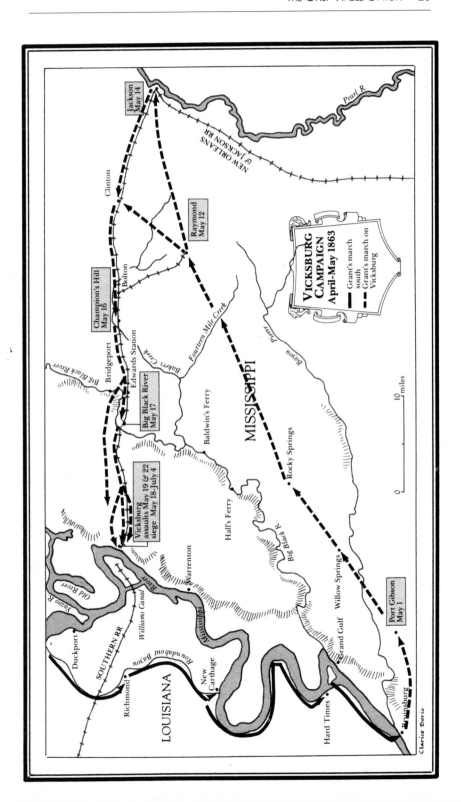

Garrisoned by the 69th Indiana, Colonel Bennett's command was instructed to hold Ione "at all hazards."[5]

On April 8, the aggressive Cockrell made contact with the Federals at Ione plantation and, for the next several days, sent Bowen frequent and fairly accurate reports of the Federal movements. Bowen, in turn, notified departmental headquarters in Jackson, Mississippi, of the developing threats and braced himself to meet the Union onslaught should it be aimed at Grand Gulf. The ominous messages from Bowen, however, were all but ignored in Jackson.

Anxious for a fight, Cockrell determined to overwhelm the Union cavalry outpost at Dunbar's plantation with a portion of his command, while his other units attacked the Federals at Ione. In the pre-dawn darkness of April 15, the 1st Missouri of Cockrell's brigade began the advance. "Most of the route lay through a vast sheet of water," recalled one Confederate, "covering the surface of both woods and fields, from knee to waist-deep, through which the men had to wade, and, at the same time, carefully protect their guns and ammunition."[6]

At 4:00 a.m. the rugged soldiers from Missouri waded Mill Bayou and attacked the 2d Illinois Cavalry at Dunbar's plantation. Driving in the Federal pickets, the Southerners captured several men and a large number of blacks. Ephraim McD. Anderson of the Missouri brigade recalled that upon entering the main house, "several of us rushed up the steps, and, upon entering one of the rooms, a very ludicrous and amusing scene was presented." Ushering the occupants out of the room, Anderson noted "The result was, a tall, spare, grave-looking personage, accompanied by a young, full-grown, athletic and very black negress, was marched down." Much to the amusement of the Missourians, "this live and interesting sybarite," as Anderson called him, "turned out to be the chaplain of the 2d Illinois Cavalry."[7]

Confederate success at Dunbar's, however, was short-lived as the Federals quickly recovered. When Union reinforcements arrived and formed line of battle, the Missourians had no recourse but to withdraw across Mill Bayou. In light of the failure at Dunbar's, Cockrell called off the projected attack on Ione plantation and waited for another opportune moment to strike. Events at Vicksburg, however, soon destined an end to Cockrell's service in Louisiana.

On April 16, as the vanguard of Grant's army concentrated at Pointe Clear, part of Admiral Porter's Union fleet, north of Vicksburg, prepared to run by the city's powerful batteries. At 9:15 p.m., lines were cast-off and the vessels moved away from their anchorage with engines muffled and all lights extinguished. As the boats rounded De Soto Point, above Vicksburg, they were spotted by Confederate lookouts who spread the alarm. Bales of cotton soaked in turpentine and barrels of tar lining the shore were set on fire to illuminate the river and the boats. Although each vessel was hit repeatedly, Porter's fleet successfully fought its way past the Confederate batteries with the loss of only one transport and headed toward a rendezvous with Grant on the Louisiana shore south of Vicksburg.

(Passage of the Vicksburg batteries compelled Bowen to recall Cockrell's Missourians from the west side of the river, lest their avenue of retreat be cut, and virtually all contact with the Union army was broken.)

With Confederate presence in their front and the threat from enemy vessels on the Mississippi River virtually eliminated, the pace of the Federal movement quickened. By April 17, all four of McClernand's divisions were at Pointe Clear, with outposts at Dunbar's and Ione plantations. Grant arrived at Pointe Clear the following afternoon and approved of McClernand's disposition. The two generals discussed the next phase of the operation then Grant returned to Milliken's Bend to expedite the movement of James B. McPherson's XVII Corps.

To make way for McPherson's corps at Pointe Clear, McClernand pushed his men forward. On April 19, Osterhaus' division was transferred by boat to New Carthage with instructions to march south along the levee to Judge John Perkins' Somerset plantation. Two days later, Brig. Gen. Alvin P. Hovey's division was directed to march to Dunbar's and open the road paralleling Bayou Vidal. Hovey's men had the more difficult task as they had to build bridges and corduroy roads each step of the way. It took the Federal engineers and fatigue parties five days to build three bridges across Bayou Vidal but, by nightfall on April

26, the road was open to Somerset plantation. The following day, Hovey's soldiers reached Mrs. Perkins' where they bivouacked on a patch of dry ground.

Due to the flooded nature of the countryside between Bayou Vidal and the Mississippi River, McClernand recognized the need to find an area below Somerset plantation that was large enough and dry enough in which the army could stage preparatory to the invasion of Mississippi. He directed Col. James Keigwin of the 49th Indiana to take a combat patrol and reconnoiter the road flanking Lake St. Joseph to Hard Times landing on the Mississippi River. Accompanied by the 114th Ohio, a detachment of the 2d Illinois Cavalry, and a section of guns from the 7th Michigan Battery, Keigwin moved out on April 25 and by nightfall had bridged both Holt's Bayou and Bayou Du Rossett.

The march resumed on April 26 as Keigwin led his patrol past the many beautiful plantation homes that graced the west bank of Lake St. Joseph. The march was without incident until his troops were brought to a halt midway along the lake as they neared Phelps Bayou. Not only was the bridge across the stream a smoldering ruin, but Confederates were sighted on the opposite bank. More formidable an obstacle, however, was the main body of Major Harrison's 400-man Confederate force formed in line of battle, just beyond Clark Bayou in the distance, supported by four guns. Keigwin wasted no time as he ordered up his own artillery and drove away the horsemen in gray.

It took Union engineers two days to bridge the two bayous with spans of 120 and 130 feet respectively. Eager to resume the advance, Keigwin crossed the bridges at an early hour on April 28. Fearful lest the Confederates destroy the bridges behind him, the wary Union officer sent a patrol to ascertain the position of Harrison's cavalrymen. The enemy horse soldiers were located south of Choctaw Bayou below where that stream empties into Lake Bruin. It was a formidable position as the Confederate right flank was anchored on the lake and had an unfordable stream in front. Alerted by the ominous sound of artillery, Keigwin rushed forward with his main force and deployed both his cannon and skirmishers. The Union artillery pounded the Confederate position and forced Harrison's troopers to withdraw to St. Joseph.

Less concerned now for the safety of his bridges, Keigwin withdrew his command to Winter Quarters, the plantation home of Dr. Haller Nutt on Lake St. Joseph, where the troops bivouacked that night.

On April 25, meanwhile, as McClernand's men labored to open the road, the XVII Corps, commanded by Maj. Gen. James B. McPherson, took up the line of march south from Milliken's Bend. An 1853 graduate of the United States Military Academy, McPherson stood first in his class and was assigned to the prestigious engineer corps. Performing engineering duties until the outbreak of the Civil War, the Ohioan gained little experience that would serve him as a line officer. McPherson, however, rose rapidly in rank once hostilities began and, in a 14-month period, went from first lieutenant of engineers to major general of volunteers. His meteoric rise was based largely on his winning personality, by which he became a favorite with Grant, on whose staff he served as chief engineer in the campaign for Forts Henry and Donelson and at Shiloh. Due to McPherson's inexperience, Grant sought to shield him throughout this campaign by placing the XVII Corps in a supporting role.

The hard-marching soldiers of the XVII Corps camped between Dawson's and Pointe Clear plantations on April 26. Ordered to resume the march the next morning to Somerset, the infantrymen found the road in wretched condition. McPherson reported of the march that "Heavy rains had rendered the roads across the alluvial bottoms on the Louisiana side almost impassable, and it was only by the most strenuous exertions on the part of the men, and by doubling teams, that the artillery and trains could be got along." In spite of the road conditions, McPherson's men arrived at Perkins' plantation late at night on April 28.[8]

Anxious for a quick strike against Grand Gulf, Grant now rapidly began to concentrate his forces at Hard Times, upstream and opposite the Confederate batteries. On April 28, three divisions of the XIII Corps, commanded by Brig. Gens. Peter Osterhaus, Eugene Carr, and Alvin Hovey, were shuttled by boat from Mrs. Perkins' to Hard Times, while units of A. J. Smith's division (XIII Corps) were moved to Hard Times from Pointe Clear by boat or marched along the marge of Lake St. Joseph to the staging area from Somerset plantation. At midnight, McPherson took up the line of march from Perkins' with the divisions of Maj. Gen. John A. Logan and Col. John Sanborn and reached Hard Times on the 29th.

By the end of April the XIII Corps and two divisions of the XVII Corps, along with Porter's gunboats, were poised at Hard Times for a strike across the Mississippi. To prevent Confederate reinforcements from being sent to Grand Gulf and thus improve his chances for a successful crossing, Grant ordered the XV Corps to make a demonstration toward Snyder's Bluff, northeast of Vicksburg. The XV Corps, which was still encamped at Milliken's Bend and Young's Point, was commanded by Maj. Gen. William T. Sherman, Grant's most trusted and, next to McClernand, his most combat experienced subordinate. The demonstration, made April 29-May 1 in conjunction with naval forces on the Yazoo River, was a feeble effort which made little impression on the Confederates.

Pemberton and many of his subordinates, however, continued in the belief that the Federal movement against Vicksburg would be launched north of the city. Even though most of Porter's fleet was below Vicksburg, Sherman's demonstration served to strengthen that belief. So firm were Pemberton's expectations that the reports emanating from Grand Gulf, which detailed the Federal movements in Louisiana, were not taken seriously until after the situation became critical.

By April 28, Bowen considered the situation at Grand Gulf to be just that--critical. That day, from his lookout atop Point of Rocks, above Grand Gulf, Bowen watched in awe as the invasion armada prepared for action. He informed Pemberton of these dramatic developments and requested "that every man and gun that can be spared from other points be sent here." His plea was largely ignored and Bowen was left to his own devices for the defense of Grand Gulf. (Two brigades and a battery of artillery were finally sent from Vicksburg late on April 29, but these troops would not arrive in time to assist Bowen at Grand Gulf.)[9]

Fortunately for Bowen, the fortifications were strong. Situated forty feet above the river, dug into the side of Point of Rocks, was Fort Cobun. Protected by a parapet nearly forty feet thick, the

fort contained four guns manned by Company A, 1st Louisiana
Heavy Artillery. A double line of rifle-pits and a covered way led
south from Cobun three-quarters of a mile to Fort Wade. The
lower fort, erected behind the fire-gutted town, was on a shelf
twenty feet above the muddy Mississippi. Fort Wade contained
four large guns and several light field pieces manned by the
skilled artillerists of Capt. Henry Guibor's and Col. William
Wade's Missouri batteries. With or without assistance, Bowen was
determined to check the powerful force gathered at Hard Times,
Louisiana, opposite his batteries, and prepared the Grand Gulf
garrison for battle.

Preparations were also underway at Hard Times where Union
soldiers and sailors worked feverishly throughout the night. By
sunrise all was in readiness. The troops were in high spirits. Sgt.
Charles E. Wilcox of the 33rd Illinois wrote on April 29:

> The sun rose throwing an impressive splendor upon the exciting scenes of the
> early morn. Every boat--transport and barge--lies at the landing, about five
> miles above Grand Gulf, covered till they are black with troops. Every heart
> here is full of anxiety and emotion; wondering eyes and eyes not altogether
> tearless, gaze ever and anon upon the Father of Waters where lie the formida-
> ble fleet of gunboats and rams, transports and barges, the latter heavily loaded
> with troops whose courage and valor are sufficient, when combined with that
> of the rest of this mighty army to redeem this lovely valley of the Mississippi
> from fiends and traitors who are desecrating it.[10]

At 7:00 a.m., the Union fleet pulled away from Hard Times
Landing and steamed into action. The gunboats, which included
"City Series" ironclads--*Carondelet, Louisville, Mound City*, and
Pittsburg, each mounting thirteen big guns, bombarded the Grand
Gulf defenses for five hours in an attempt to silence the
Confederate cannon and clear the way for a landing by Grant's
infantry. From the deck of a small tug, Grant watched as the battle
opened. Thick clouds of white-blue smoke soon obscured his vision, yet the sheets of flame which pierced the smoke evidenced
the magnitude of resistance. The hours slowly passed and the
chances of success dimmed. Yet Grant maintained his composure
and with the ever-present stub of a cigar clenched in his teeth
and field glasses in hand, he kept his eyes fixed on the bluffs tow-
ering over the opposite shore.

The bombardment raged in unabated fury throughout the morning hours. The powerful ironclads hammered away at the earthen forts sending solid shot and shell crashing among the Confederate defenders. Although his guns silenced Fort Wade, Porter's fleet failed to quiet the guns of Fort Cobun. In the exchange of fire with Bowen's batteries, the gunboats were hit repeatedly and the fleet sustained heavy damage. Aboard the flagship *Benton*, 7 men were killed and 19 wounded; *Pittsburg* reported the loss of 6 killed and 13 wounded; and *Tuscumbia*, hit 81 times, suffered the loss of 5 killed and 24 wounded. Total casualties were 18 killed and 57 wounded. (Confederate casualties were light by comparison with 3 killed and 19 wounded.) Bitterly disappointed, Porter was forced to disengage his vessels and declared, "Grand Gulf is the strongest place on the Mississippi."[11]

Not wishing to send his transports loaded to the gunwales with troops to attempt a landing in the face of enemy fire, Grant disembarked his command and continued the march south along the levee at the base of Coffee Point. That evening, as the infantrymen and wagons headed toward Disharoon's plantation, Porter's fleet again cast-off from Hard Times and moved downriver at forced draft. Screened by the gunboats, which bombarded the forts with solid shot and shell, the transports and barges slipped past the Confederate batteries unscathed. Looking now to cross his army at Rodney, Grant was informed that there was a good road ascending the bluffs east of Bruinsburg, midway between Grand Gulf and Rodney. Elated by this intelligence, Grant seized the opportunity and decided to hurl his army across the mighty river at Bruinsburg.

By daybreak on April 30 the fleet rounded to at the levee at Disharoon's plantation, where the army had spent the night, and infantrymen were quickly loaded. At 8:00 a.m. the fleet cast-off with steam whistles blowing and signal flags snapping in the breeze. As the mighty armada moved downstream, one soldier noted, "The decks were covered with anxious soldiers, the guns were cleared for action, and the crews were at quarters." All eyes watched the shore for signs of enemy presence, and the soldiers and sailors were relieved to find only a lone citizen at the landing to greet them. The landing was made unopposed and a band aboard *Benton* struck up "The Red, White, and Blue" as soldiers of the 24th and 46th Indiana came ashore.[12]

In one of the largest amphibious operations in American military history up to that time, Grant hurled 22,000 men across the river onto Mississippi soil and began the inland campaign toward Vicksburg. On May 1, in a furious battle which raged throughout the day, his forces overcame stiff resistance from Confederate troops under Bowen's command 4 miles west of Port Gibson. Union victory at Port Gibson not only secured the beachhead at Bruinsburg, but forced the Confederate evacuation of Grand Gulf. The former Confederate bastion was then used by Grant as an advance supply base to support the army as it pushed deep into the interior of Mississippi.

Anxious to unite his command for the drive on Vicksburg, Grant ordered Sherman to join him in Mississippi. Over the next few days, the XV Corps hastened through Louisiana from camps at Milliken's Bend, Young's Point, and Duckport to Hard Times. One Union soldier described the route of march through Madison and Tensas parishes by writing: "Sometimes for miles the road was shaded by beautiful live oaks, and catalpas in full bloom, or bordered by a tangled hedge of red and white roses, forming a barricade of beauty eight feet high and more in breadth."[13]

Although impressed by the beauty of the land, the men in blue marveled at the stately homes which dotted the bank of Lake St. Joseph. One soldier observed that, "These residences, mostly of modern construction and by far the most costly and elegant we had seen in the South, were filled with every appliance of taste and domestic utility." A soldier in the 55th Illinois recorded of the treatment these homes received at the hands of the Federals:

> The lords of these manors had deserted them in haste, and a few slaves only remained in charge. The troops that had passed before us left proofs of their customary lack of respect for the deserted property of rebels, and at our noon halts groups of tired, dust-covered "mud-sills" were to be seen seated on satin-upholstered chairs amid roses or in the shade of fig-trees, and eating their bacon and hard-tack from marble-topped tables and rosewood pianos.

In the wake of the Union army these elegant homes were destroyed by fire. The torch was liberally applied and, with the exception of Winter Quarters, the destruction of these stately residences was complete.[14]

The XV Corps' vanguard reached Hard Times on May 6 and was ferried across the river to Grand Gulf (May 6-7) from where Sherman's men marched to join Grant deep in Mississippi. The opening scene of the Vicksburg drama thus closed as the rugged veterans of Sherman's corps scrambled ashore on Mississippi soil. Although the march through Louisiana had ended, it was only the prelude to victory as the fighting was still ahead.

The movement from Milliken's Bend to Hard Times was boldly conceived and executed by a daring commander who was willing to take risks. The sheer audacity of the movement demonstrated Grant's firmness of purpose and reveals his many strengths as an army commander. The bold and decisive manner in which he directed the movement set the tone for the campaign in Mississippi and inspired confidence in the ranks of his army. Although the opening phase of the Vicksburg campaign went virtually unnoticed by contemporaries and has been largely ignored by historians, it set the stage for the ultimate victory of Union arms. The march through Louisiana was one of which Maj. Gen. John McClernand, whose XIII Corps led the march, could boast that "The achievement is one of the most remarkable occurring in the annals of war, and justly ranks among the highest examples of military energy and perseverance."[15]

CHAPTER THREE

PLAYING SMASH WITH THE RAILROADS

The Story of Grierson's Raid

As the spring of 1863 burst forth in all its beauty upon the land, Union armies were in motion across the broad spectrum of war. In this a decisive year of combat during the Civil War, Union commanders in the western theater of operations sought ways to cripple their opponents in preparation for the campaigns soon to be launched in Tennessee and along the Mississippi River. The most effective method would be destruction of the vital railroads that served their enemies as lines of communications and supply. For Maj. Gen. William S. Rosecrans, in command of the Union Army of the Cumberland, then positioned around Murfreesboro, Tennessee, destruction of the Western & Atlantic Railroad was deemed essential. The iron rails which connected Atlanta with Chattanooga served as the lifeline which enabled Braxton Bragg and the Army of Tennessee to remain in the field. Farther west, from his headquarters at Milliken's Bend, Louisiana, Maj. Gen. Ulysses S. Grant eyed the Southern Railroad of Mississippi which connected Vicksburg with Jackson and via Jackson points elsewhere in the Confederacy, as a key component in his efforts to secure defeat of Lt. Gen. John C. Pemberton and capture Vicksburg, the stronghold on the Mississippi River.

To accomplish these missions, both commanders turned loose their cavalry on daring raids deep behind enemy lines. In a remarkable display of interdepartmental cooperation, the raids were coordinated to give each a better chance for success. Although many Civil War historians, in writing of these raids, fail to establish their relationship, Edwin C. Bearss observes that they "were part of a well-orchestrated combined operation." Although this writer concurs with the validity of Ed's observation, this essay will focus on the most successful and well-known of these raids, that conducted by Col. Benjamin Grierson against the Southern Railroad of Mississippi.[1]

By 1863, Grant had developed into a master strategist. His operations focused on Vicksburg reveal the basic characteristics of the modern AirLand Battle: "surprise, concentration, speed, flexibility, and audacity." Stating, "It exemplifies the qualities of a well-conceived, violently executed offensive plan," FM 100-5, the manual on operations used by the present-day Army of the United States, features a case study of the Vicksburg Campaign in the chapter on offensive operations, and emphasizes that "the same speed, surprise, maneuver,

Colonel Benjamin Henry Grierson. General Sherman called his raid "the most brilliant expedition of the war." *Generals in Blue*

and decisive action will be required in the campaigns of the future."[2]

Unlike most of his contemporaries, Grant understood the essence of offensive operations and recognized, as does FM 100-5, that "Any operational plan must seek to achieve surprise." According to the manual, "Commanders achieve surprise by striking the enemy at a time or place, or in a manner, for which he is unprepared." The advantages to be gained by such an action are decisive. "Surprise," cites FM 100-5, "delays enemy reactions, overloads and confuses his command and control, reduces the effectiveness of his weapons, and induces psychological shock in soldiers and leaders." By transferring the field of operations to the area south and east of Vicksburg, the area in which the Confederates least expected him, Grant would achieve the element of surprise. Although achieving outright surprise has never been easy, the manual suggests that "Surprise can. . .be created. . .by

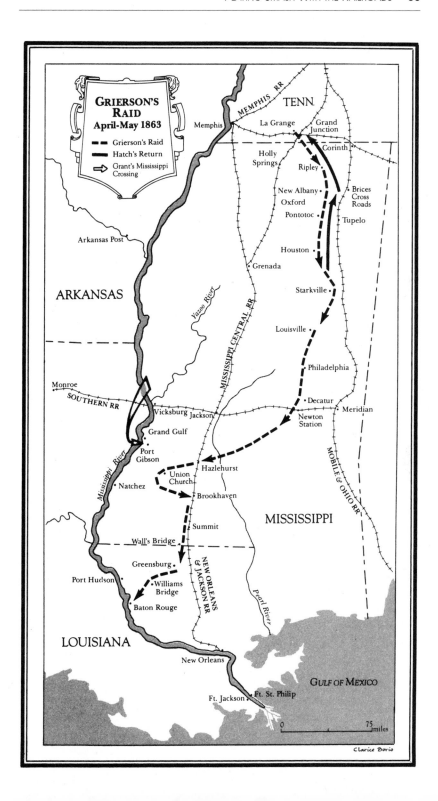

GRIERSON'S
RAID
April-May 1863

- - - Grierson's Raid
—— Hatch's Return
⇒ Grant's Mississippi
Crossing

Memphis

MEMPHIS RR

TENN.

La Grange Grand Junction

Corinth

Holly Springs

Ripley

New Albany
Oxford
Pontotoc

Brices Cross Roads

Tupelo

Arkansas Post

Houston

Grenada

ARKANSAS

Yazoo River

MISSISSIPPI CENTRAL RR

Starkville

Louisville

Philadelphia

Monroe

SOUTHERN RR

Vicksburg Jackson

Grand Gulf

Port Gibson

Natchez

Decatur Meridian

Newton Station

MOBILE & OHIO RR

Hazlehurst

Union Church

Brookhaven

Mississippi River

MISSISSIPPI

Summit

Wall's Bridge

Greensburg

NEW ORLEANS & JACKSON RR

Port Hudson

Williams Bridge

Baton Rouge

Pearl River

LOUISIANA

New Orleans

GULF OF MEXICO

Ft. Jackson Ft. St. Philip

0   75
         miles

Clarice Borio

the insertion of. . .special operating forces deep in the enemy's rear [which] can sharply and suddenly increase the enemy's sense of threat, sowing fear and confusion, and in the extreme case, inducing outright paralysis."

Grant determined to do just that, insert a special operating force in the form of Grierson's cavalry deep in the enemy's rear. The raid thus had a two-fold mission, to sever the vital railroad into Vicksburg and improve the chances of success for Grant's planned amphibious landing south of Vicksburg.[3]

Grant was not the only one with an eye toward the Southern Railroad. Following the removal of Maj. Gen. Earl Van Dorn's Confederate cavalry from north Mississippi late in January 1863, that part of the Magnolia state was left comparatively unprotected, a situation not lost on Union officers at various levels of command whose troops were stationed in West Tennessee. On February 12, from his headquarters in Memphis, Maj. Gen. Charles Hamilton informed Maj. Gen. Stephen Hurlbut, commander of Grant's Sixteenth Corps, that "This movement of Van Dorn's clears our front of all cavalry." Eager to seize the opportunity thus presented, Hamilton stated, "It is the time to strike the Vicksburg and Jackson road." He recommended that a brigade of cavalry push south from La Grange, Tennessee, along the headwaters of the Tallahatchie and Yalobusha rivers, and while the main body made a demonstration around Pontotoc, Mississippi, a single regiment drive night and day for Jackson. "The bridge over the Pearl River [at Jackson] could be destroyed," he advised Hurlbut, "as well as all the railroad shops and rolling stock, and a dash made at the Big Black River Bridge, which, if destroyed, will completely isolate Vicksburg from the interior." Confident of success, he wrote of the expedition, "I deem [it] feasible almost to a certainty."[4]

Harboring little hope for the success of the Bayou Expeditions then being conducted by his forces around Vicksburg, Grant began to formulate the plan which led to ultimate success with surrender of the city on July 4, 1863. Seeking to destroy Pemberton's line of communications and supply, he wrote to Hurlbut on February 13: "It seems to me that Grierson, with about 500 picked men, might succeed in making his way south and cut the railroad east of Jackson." Although he recognized that the "under-taking would be a hazardous one," he predicted that "it would pay well if carried out." Not yet sure as to his own timetable for oper-ations, however, Grant did not specify a date for or even order that the expedition be carried out. Rather, he left it to Hurlbut's discretion stating, "I do not direct that this shall be done, but leave it for a volunteer enterprise."[5]

Prior to receiving Grant's message, Hurlbut had evaluated the merits of Hamilton's proposal and liked the idea. On February 16, he wrote to Lt. Col. John Rawlins, Grant's A.A.G., concerning the proposed raid. In summary he admitted, "It appears perilous, but I think it can be done with safety, and may relieve you some-what at Vicksburg." Acting on his own authority, Hurlbut directed that the raid commence. The commander of the Sixteenth Corps informed Grant that Grierson's brigade had been ordered into north Mississippi and that the Second Iowa under Col. Edward Hatch would push on to the Southern Railroad. The movement, however, was suspended because of intelligence reports indicating sizeable numbers of enemy troops in central Mississippi.[6]

Anxious for the raid to be launched, Grant expressed his disap-pointment in a letter to Hurlbut written on March 9. "I regret that the expedition you had fitted out was not permitted to go," he wrote, but added, "The weather, however, has been so intolera-bly bad ever since that it might have failed." Upon reflection, the Federal commander realized that had the expedition been launched at that time, even if successful, it would have benefitted him little as his army was still mired in the swamps of Louisiana and unable to exploit the effects of the raid.[7]

Perhaps it was providential that the raid was postponed, for it gave Grant the opportunity to thoroughly evaluate the timing and potential effects of the proposed raid. For maximum effect, the raid had to be led by a daring, aggressive officer, one who would push himself and the command to the limits of human en-durance and beyond. Although he respected the abilities of the men who were being considered by Hurlbut to lead the raid--Brig. Gen. Albert Lee or Cols. Edward Hatch and John Mizner--Grant advanced his own choice and stressed, "I look upon Grierson as being much better qualified to command this expedition." Backing up Grant's assessment of the colonel was that of William T. Sherman who stated emphatically of Grierson, "He is the best cavalry officer I have yet had." In closing, Grant informed Hurlbut, "The date when the expedition should start will depend on movements here. You will be informed of the exact time for them to start."[8]

Independent of the correspondence among the army's high command, Brig. Gen. William Sooy Smith, in command of the First Division, Sixteenth Corps, and Grierson discussed a similar plan for destruction of the Southern Railroad. Headquartered in La Grange, the two men were familiar with the geography of north Mississippi and condition of affairs in that portion of the Magnolia state. They recognized a situation ripe for action. Although striking deep in enemy territory, both were confident that a raiding party could reach and destroy the railroad. Thinking the raid through to a successful conclusion, they turned their attention to routes of escape. Returning to La Grange would be difficult, if not impossible, regardless of the route through Mississippi or Alabama. Believing it to "be much the less hazardous" and thus avoid Confederate forces certain to concentrate against its return to La Grange, Smith and Grierson were of the opinion, after destroying the railroad, the raiding column was to ride south and secure safety behind Federal lines at Baton Rouge, Louisiana.[9]

Late in March, Smith and Grierson traveled to Memphis to confer at length with Hurlbut concerning the details of the proposed raid. The corps commander listened to their plan but disapproved of the movement through to Baton Rouge as being "too rash and hazardous." Smith later wrote, "I urged it strenuously on the ground that it was far less dangerous to go on through than to attempt to return; which would bring him [Grierson] right into the hands of Forrest's and Chalmer's [sic] combined forces pursuing him." [Smith refers to Brig. Gens. Nathan Bedford Forrest and James R. Chalmers whose Confederate cavalrymen were stationed in Middle Tennessee and North Mississippi respectively.] Grierson agreed and expressed confidence in his ability to go through to Baton Rouge. In spite of their argument however, Smith lamented that, "Hurlbut could not be convinced."[10]

By mid-April the vanguard of Grant's army had reached New Carthage, below Vicksburg, and R.Adm. David Dixon Porter prepared the vessels of the Mississippi Squadron for a daring attempt to pass the batteries of the Confederate fortress. The night of April 16 was selected for Porter's fleet to run by the batteries. After the fleet was below Vicksburg, Grant would have the wherewithal to hurl his army across the mighty river and onto Mississippi soil to begin the inland campaign. If the proposed raid under discussion now for months was to be of any benefit to Grant, it had to be launched immediately. Hurlbut was instructed to order the cavalry into action.

Anticipating the order, Hurlbut wired Smith on April 10 that "The time for our projected cavalry movement is rapidly approaching." To prepare properly for the raid, he advised that the horses "be got into the best order possible, both by grooming and care and by rest and feed." He emphasized, "Let no exertion be spared in this matter."[11]

There was one problem, however, Grierson was home on leave in Jacksonville, Illinois, where he was enjoying what he termed "an oasis of love" in the arms of his wife and children. On April 13, the colonel's enjoyment of hearth and family came to an end when he was instructed by Hurlbut to "Return immediately." Should Grierson not arrive in time, Col. Edward Hatch of the Second Iowa Cavalry was to take charge of the expedition. Regardless of who was in command, the raid was to "start sharply at or before daylight on Friday morning," April 17.[12]

Grierson kissed his wife and children goodbye. With knowledge of what Hurlbut's message held in store for him, he cautioned his wife "not [to] be alarmed should you not hear from me inside a month." The steamboat on which he booked passage tied up at the Memphis wharf on the morning of April 16 and Grierson went to Hurlbut's headquarters where the two men conferred for hours. After a hasty meal, he penned a quick letter to his wife then boarded the train to La Grange where he arrived at midnight.[13]

Although tired from his long journey from Jacksonville and pressed for time, Grierson met with Sooy Smith to review his orders and receive last minute instructions. Hurlbut's orders were specific and called for the command to proceed by way of Pontotoc, where he was to throw one regiment to the right, another to the left, cutting the Mississippi Central at or near Oxford, the Mobile & Ohio near Tupelo, while Grierson with his own regiment raced to the Southern Railroad. After cutting the road, his troopers were to return to La Grange by way of Alabama.[14]

In writing of this midnight conference, Smith states that he and Grierson "were sorely puzzled" by Hurlbut's instructions as they felt that "any attempt to return by way of north Alabama would almost certainly end in disastrous failure." With the safety of Grierson's command a paramount concern, Smith turned to the colonel and said, "that Hurlbut's order was directed to me and that he was not supposed to know what it was, that he would go in obedience to the orders I should give him, and that I would take the responsibility and order him to go straight through to our army at Baton Rouge." In light of the consequences of his action, Smith assured Grierson, "If he succeeded, no questions would be asked; and if he failed, I would take the consequences and should probably be cashiered for disobedience of orders."[15]

The stage thus set for what would be the most remarkable adventure of his long military career, Benjamin Grierson stepped into the night and prepared his command for the long ride to Baton Rouge and into history.

Termed an "unlikely warrior" by biographers, Ben was the youngest of six children born to Robert and Mary Grierson. Natives of Ireland, his parents had immigrated to the United States in 1818 and settled in Pittsburgh, Pennsylvania, where Ben was born on July 8, 1826. When only three years of age, Ben moved with his family to Youngstown, Ohio, where he grew into maturity. As a child he demonstrated only a "casual attitude toward school" preferring games and outdoor recreation. He had a passion for excitement and adventure which almost resulted in his death when he was eight years old. Tagging along with his brothers Robert and John, who were clearing a wooded area, Ben asked to be hoisted onto a horse. No sooner was he in the saddle when the horse bolted. Ben grabbed the horse around its neck and hung on for dear life to no avail. Thrown hard to the ground and badly bruised, the young boy staggered to his feet when the recalcitrant animal suddenly reared and kicked him in the head, opening a deep gash in his face. Ben was in a comma for two weeks. When he regained consciousness, he was blind in one eye. In time, however, his vision returned, but he carried the facial scars for life and attempted to cover them by growing a beard. Due to this incident, the "unlikely warrior" was certainly an unlikely cavalryman.[16]

Grierson developed a lifelong love for music and played an array of instruments with ease which included the piano, guitar, violin, flute, trumpet, clarinet, and drums. He also composed music. His musical talents resulted in him being voted leader of the Youngstown Band when he was only thirteen. In addition, Ben enjoyed literature and poetry and even wrote plays, acting in many of them.

His mother helped to cultivate Ben's love for music and literature and it was she who convinced him to pursue a career in music rather than seek an appointment to the United States Military Academy at West Point.[17]

"In disposition, Grierson was affectionate, kind, humane, humorous, and generous to a fault," wrote his biographers. "He had a temper but rarely lost it and avoided whenever possible a quarrel or petty controversy, often at the sacrifice of his own interests." Such character traits endeared him to those he met and were of immense benefit in his marriage to Alice Kirk whom he wed in 1854. His biographers assert that in disposition "He was remarkably consistent. The public figure was simply a reflection of the private man."[18]

Having moved to Illinois, Ben entered into partnership in the mercantile business in which he struggled for several years, finally ending in failure. Mired in debt, Ben and Alice moved back in with his parents and he scrapped out a living playing music until the outbreak of the Civil War. After hostilities erupted, Grierson was quick to offer his services as a volunteer aide and was assigned to the staff of Brig. Gen. Benjamin Prentiss. Without an income, however, Ben was unable to support his wife and family, and sought a position with both rank and salary. Almost in desperation, he appealed to his Jacksonville friend Governor Richard

Yates who appointed him major in the Sixth Illinois Cavalry on October 24, 1861. Although grateful for the position, Grierson appealed to Maj. Gen. Henry W. Halleck in command of the Department of the Missouri for commensurate rank and salary in service other than the cavalry. He later wrote, "General Halleck jocularly remarked that I looked active and wiry enough to make a good cavalryman." For good or ill, Ben Grierson was in the cavalry.[19]

The unit to which Ben was assigned had been organized earlier that month at Camp Butler, near Springfield, and then sent to Shawneetown on the banks of the Ohio River. Major Grierson joined the regiment at Shawneetown in November only to discover that no arrangements had been made for food, clothing, or shelter, and that the colonel was absent. The regiment was commanded by Col. Thomas Cavanaugh, a man more interested in political gain than in service to his country. (The colonel was at that moment in Springfield attempting to secure promotion to brigadier general.) Fortunately, Cavanaugh resigned under pressure on March 28, 1862, at which time Ben was elevated to colonel and given command of the regiment.[20]

Grierson quickly demonstrated that Halleck's estimation of him was correct for he soon transformed the regiment into one of the best in Federal service. The unlikely warrior came to be recognized by his superiors "as an ideal cavalry officer--brave and dashing, cunning and resourceful." More important, to his men, the colonel was "tough as a ten penny nail."[21]

In the spring of 1862, the Sixth Illinois Cavalry moved to Kentucky and then Tennessee were it operated against guerrillas. The horsemen from Illinois saw action in several engagements and had sharp encounters with the enemy at Dyersburg, Tennessee, and at Olive Branch and along the Coldwater River in Mississippi. Under Grierson's command they had matured as soldiers and, by the spring of 1863, were seasoned troopers anxious for the type of action promised by the raid.

Leading the unit out of La Grange on April 17 was Lt. Col. Reuben Loomis of DuQuoin, Illinois, former captain of Company I. Promoted to lieutenant colonel six months earlier, Loomis had been a loyal second in command and was praised by

Grierson for his "coolness, bravery,. . .and untiring perseverance." The raid was destined to be his moment of glory for Loomis would be killed in action later that year.[22]

Also swinging into their saddles for the ride south were the veterans of the Second Iowa Cavalry commanded by Col. Edward Hatch. Considered by all to be an "intrepid commander," his conduct in the handling of his troops "was worthy of praise." One trooper observed that Hatch "was possessed of the true military spirit in such large degree that he was from the first conspicuous for his superior ability, and was held in the highest esteem by. . .all the officers and men of the regiment."[23]

Organized at Davenport in July 1861, the Second Iowa initially served in Missouri against M. Jeff Thompson, and saw action at New Madrid and Island No. 10. Riding into Tennessee and Mississippi, the troopers participated in the Siege of Corinth, and were engaged at Iuka, Corinth, and in Grant's north Mississippi campaign. On this cool, damp April morning the Iowans were also eager for action and took up the line of march with their customary zeal.

Completing the complement of regiments in Grierson's brigade was the hard-riding Seventh Illinois Cavalry commanded by Col. Edward Prince. A native of Ontario County, New York, he was raised in Payson, Illinois. After graduation from college in 1852 he studied law and opened a practice in Quincy. Regarded as a man of "active mind" and "great genius," he was quick to enlist at the outbreak of war. From the start he demonstrated a taste for military life and studied cavalry tactics with a passion. One trooper wrote that, "As a military man he has few superiors, and is perfectly conversant with the tactics."[24]

Prince, however, was egotistical and harbored contempt for those above him. Believing himself superior to Grierson, he found it difficult to veil his resentment of Ben's authority. Due to the friction that was always present between the two men (which would erupt after the raid), Grierson preferred to confer with the regiment's lieutenant colonel William Blackburn. Grierson considered Blackburn "a brave and efficient field-officer" whose conduct during the raid would be exemplary.[25]

The Seventh had been organized in October 1861, at Camp Butler. Serving first in Missouri, then in Tennessee and Mississippi, the unit saw action during the Siege of Corinth and in the Battles of Iuka and Corinth. Following a winter of light activity, the men were "spoiling for a fight."[26]

On the raid into Mississippi, the brigade was accompanied by the six 2-pounder Woodruff guns of Company K, First Illinois Light Artillery, commanded by Capt. Jason Smith.

As the expedition prepared to mount up, Grierson's brigade was a veteran unit made up of seasoned troopers who at all levels of command were led by men of experience and merit. On this raid, however, their mettle would be tested as never before.

At 3:00 a.m. on Friday, April 17, the shrill notes of "Reveille" echoed through the camps and faded in the distance. Instantly, the fields and scattered forests around La Grange were full of the sounds of an army coming to life: the tooting of bugles, voices of sergeants calling company roll, and the clanking of cooking utensils. Equipped with five days "light rations, consisting of hard bread, coffee, sugar and salt only," the troopers rode out armed with Sharp's carbines and 40 rounds of ammunition each. Grierson also traveled light carrying only a compass, a map of Mississippi, and a jew's harp.[27]

"Just as the sun rose full and fine over a charming expanse of small pine-clad hills," wrote 18-year-old Sgt. Stephen Forbes of Company B, Seventh Illinois Cavalry, "the first brigade, stretching itself slowly out from the little village, slid like a huge serpent into the cover of the Mississippi woods." The first day of the raid was an uneventful one in the saddle and, after a 30-mile ride, the horse soldiers bivouacked just north of Ripley. Around the fires that night the men conjectured as to their destination, but the seasoned troopers knew instinctively that regardless of their destination they were off to "play smash with the railroads."[28]

On April 18, the column started at an early hour. Throwing one regiment to the east as a decoy toward the Mobile & Ohio Railroad, Grierson's command pushed south and in a driving rain bivouacked five miles below New Albany on Sloan's plantation. As was the custom that would be followed throughout the raid whenever the command stopped, demand was made for the keys to the smokehouses and barns. When the demand was refused, the locks were broken. Grierson recalled of Sloan's reaction, "When he saw his stores issued out, he was completely beside himself; alternately was going to cut my throat, and desirous of having his own throat cut." Later when Mr. Sloan saw his horses and mules being rounded up, "He fairly foamed," wrote the colonel, "and for the fiftieth time demanded that we take him out and cut his throat and be done with it."

Grierson, who loved acting, captured the moment for amusement at Sloan's expense. Brigade Adjutant Sandy Woodward recorded, "worn out by his whining, Colonel Grierson called his personal orderly, a man of large stature, dark complexion and sinister expression, [whose appearance was] enhanced by a fierce mustache. . . ." With the wink of an eye, the colonel instructed, "Mr. Sloan is very desirous of having his throat cut. Take him out in the field and cut his throat, and be done with it." The aide quickly seized the old man by the collar and brandishing a large hunting knife, dragged Sloan down the long hall toward the door. All the while Mrs. Sloan screamed "in chorus with the servants" to the delight of Grierson and his staff. According to the adjutant, "Mr. Sloan immediately discovered new attractions in life and begged that the order be countermanded." Amidst the pleas and screams, the charade was brought to an end as Grierson ordered his release. The much subdued planter was later pleased to learn that the troopers had exchanged their broken down mounts for his horses as a favorable rate.[29]

To screen the character of the raid, the Federal commander launched the first of his many diversion as several detachments were thrown out on April 19 to break up enemy camps reported nearby. Once the command reassembled, the column moved south and rode through Pontotoc, bivouacking for the night at Daggett's plantation on Chiwapa Creek.

Having reached Pontotoc, it was time for Grierson to swing into action against the railroads as ordered. To prepare his command for the hard work ahead, the colonel personally inspected the men and horses in the pre-dawn darkness on Monday, April 20. Identifying those who were sick or had broken down mounts, Grierson culled out 175 men whom he termed "the least effective portion of the command." Placing Maj. Hiram Love of the Second Iowa Cavalry in charge of this detachment, known as the "Quinine Brigade," he ordered the men to return to La Grange. By riding in column of fours back through Pontotoc, it was hoped that Love's detachment "would leave the impression that the whole command had returned." At 5:00 a.m., as the "Quinine Brigade" rode north, the main column saddled up and continued south. Riding at a faster pace, the troopers skirted Houston and bedded down on Dr. Benjamin Kilgore's plantation, eleven miles southeast of town.[30]

Fearful lest the "Quinine Brigade" fail to divert Confederate attention from the main column, Grierson on April 21 detached Colonel Hatch and the Second Iowa Cavalry to cut the Mobile & Ohio Railroad in the vicinity of West Point. With luck, Hatch's command would rivet enemy attention on defense of that vital rail line and serve to draw pursuers away from Grierson. After trailing the main column for several miles, the Iowans doubled back obliterating Grierson's tracks, then headed east toward the railroad.

The ruse worked for, as Grierson suspected, Confederate cavalry from Chesterville was on his trail. The Second Tennessee Cavalry led by Lt. Col. Clark Barteau trailed the Northerners by only a few hours when it reached the intersection of the Starkville-Columbus roads near the village of Montpelier. After studying the maze of tracks, Barteau was satisfied that the enemy was heading toward the railroad and rode east in pursuit. Tall, thin, more wiry than Grierson, with short dark hair and sandy colored mustache, Barteau's physical appearance belied the tenacity with which he would hound the Iowans.

Hatch halted his command to rest at Palo Alto, a village which no longer exists. The troopers were enjoying their brief respite when suddenly the crack of a carbine announced the arrival of Barteau's Tennesseans and a regiment of Mississippi State Troops. Charging headlong toward the Federals, the Southerners were greeted by a rapid fire which emptied a number of saddles. When the inexperienced state troops began to falter, Hatch ordered his men to mount and charged through the Mississippians. A running fight ensued in which the Iowans opened the road in their front then raced for the safety of La Grange. Although Barteau had saved the Mobile & Ohio Railroad and forced Hatch northward, the more important prey eluded him.

While battle raged at Palo Alto, Grierson's column approached Starkville. The command was now deep in enemy territory. Cautious lest the column be ambushed, the colonel had that morning acted on the recommendation of one of his officers and clothed several volunteers in Confederate garb. Led by Sgt. Richard Surby, these men known as the Butternut Guerrillas, rode ahead of the column and acted as scouts gathering information on roads, bridges, supplies, and enemy troop locations. The Butternut Guerrillas rendered invaluable service during the raid and, according to Surby, "enjoyed ourselves very much at the expense of the deluded citizens."[31]

Freed of Barteau by Hatch's diversion and led by the Butternut Guerrillas, Grierson could now move unimpeded toward his objective. A member of the raiding party recognized that "His only chance of failure was in a correct interpretation of his movement by Pemberton, and the concentration of troops by rail across his line of march--a danger which induced still further feints against the Mobile and Ohio road, intended to keep Confederate attention focused on the protection of that line."[32]

In keeping with that rationale, on April 22, the sixth day of the raid, Capt. Henry Forbes and the 35 men of Company B, Seventh Illinois Cavalry, were detached and ordered southeast to Macon to destroy the railroad and telegraph lines. The captain was considered "a brave, intrepid, and confident officer," who relished the assignment. Knowing of the dangers which lay ahead, Forbes realized as his company turned from the main column, that he was leading the men on what would be the most exciting and terrifying ordeal of their lives. (The captain's younger brother, Stephen, later boasted that Company B was "absent from the column five days and four nights, during which time it marched about three hundred miles in ten different counties and kept the attention of the enemy fixed on the defense of the Mobile and Ohio road.")[33]

On April 22, with Forbes en route to Macon, the main column pushed south through Louisville where the troopers were cheered by townspeople who mistook the mud spattered horsemen for

Confederate cavalry. The following day, Grierson's column crossed Pearl River and entered Philadelphia where a number of armed citizens were captured. Evidently, the colonel was not impressed with Philadelphia for as the column departed one citizen asked in surprise, "Aren't you going to burn the town?" Grierson replied with a smile that his orders were not to improve the country.

At 10:00 p.m., while the weary troopers rested south of Philadelphia, two battalions of the Seventh Illinois under Colonel Blackburn and some Butternut Guerrillas swung into their saddles and rode for Newton Station, only twenty-five miles away. Grierson followed with the main column an hour later. Arriving near the station at sunrise on April 24, Blackburn halted his command to water the horses and directed Sergeant Surby and his Butternut Guerillas to reconnoiter.

Surby boldly rode into town and scouted about the depot when suddenly, the shrill whistle of a train approaching from the east was heard. Blackburn also heard the whistle and within minutes his troopers came charging into Newton Station. Concealing themselves behind buildings and in the tall grass which lined the tracks, the Federals waited for the train to stop. The train, loaded with ordnance and commissary supplies for Vicksburg, eased onto a siding where the troopers sprang aboard. Taking the startled crew captive, the Northerners again concealed themselves and waited to seize a second train scheduled to arrive momentarily from the west.

"On she came rounding the curve," wrote Surby, "her passengers unconscious of the surprise that awaited them." As the engine pulled opposite the depot, the sergeant jump aboard and pointed his revolver at the engineer who brought the train to a stop. "The train is ours," shouted the Federals as they swarmed out of hiding. The passengers and much of their baggage were removed from the cars and both trains were soon ablaze.[34]

Hearing the sound of exploding shells, Grierson raced into town with the main column and was relieved to discover the cause. Knowing that time was short, the colonel sent strong detachments east and west along the road with instructions to proceed eight to ten miles and destroy bridges, trestles, and water tanks, as well as the telegraph lines. Adjutant Woodward details,

"This latter was rendered useless by cutting the wires in places where the foliage was dense, bending the ends into a loop and connecting them with a piece of leather; this destroyed the connection, and it was exceedingly hard to find the break."[35]

At 2:00 p.m., after four hours of destruction, the raiders moved out and rode southeast toward Garlandville--the only direction in which Grierson believed his command would find safety. The damage inflicted on the enemy's supply line, however, was not as extensive as was hoped and within days the line was repaired. The Jackson *Appeal* reported: "The damage to the Southern railroad extends over a distance of four and a half miles, commencing a mile west of Newton, and running east. Two bridges, each about 150 feet long, seven culverts and one cattle gap, constitute the injury done."[36]

With his vital line of supply and communications cut, Pemberton now knew the location of the raiders and ordered troops in pursuit. Soldiers from Jackson, Meridian, and a dozen other points were set in motion to track down the Federals or intercept the raiders should they try to return to Tennessee. Pemberton also warned Confederate units to the south and west to be on watch should Grierson head in their direction.

The net was beginning to close, but the sly colonel had no intention of getting caught. With luck, thought Grierson, he might be able to link up with Grant on the Mississippi River near Grand Gulf. After spending the night near Montrose, the raiders turned southwest and for the next two days rode over muddy roads through the dense forest of the Piney Woods country eluding pursuers and burning bridges behind them. At Raleigh, on April 26, the Butternut Guerrillas captured the sheriff of Smith County in whose saddlebags they found $3,000 of county funds. The unfortunate sheriff later escaped and the following day came back to haunt the raiders.

After crossing Strong River late that night, two battalions of the Seventh Illinois under Colonel Prince were ordered forward ten miles to Pearl River to seize the ferry, the only means by which to cross the stream. Reaching the riverbank early on the morning of Monday, April 27, the Federals saw the ferryboat on the far side of the stream. Unable to cross, Prince woke the ferryman by shouting, "First Regiment, Alabama Cavalry from Mobile!" and added, "It's harder to wake up you ferrymen than it is to catch the damned conscripts."[37]

The deception had the desired result. As soon as the boat was brought across the time consuming task of ferrying the command, twenty-four horses and men at a time, began. The crossing would take eight hours to complete, during which time three hard-riding and exhausted troopers of Company B reached Strong River just as the rear of the Grierson's column crossed the span. Reining in his horse a relieved horse soldier reported to the colonel, "Captain Forbes presents his compliments, and begs to be allowed to burn his bridges for himself." The remarkable saga of Company B came to an end as Forbes and the rest of his men soon arrived.[38]

The command, now reunited by the arrival of Company B, pushed toward Hazelhurst led by the Butternut Guerrillas. Upon entering the town Sergeant Surby rode to the depot where a false telegram was sent to Pemberton in Jackson, which read "The Yankees have advanced to Pearl River, but finding the ferry destroyed they could not cross, and have left, taking a northeasterly direction."[39]

The ruse might have worked had it not been for the untimely arrival of the escaped sheriff. Riding into town on a horse stolen from the Federals, the sheriff yelled "Help! Stop the Yankees!" Near the depot he spotted Surby. Recognizing the guerrilla as one of the raiders, he pointed and shouted all the louder, "Stop the Yankees." The guerrilla opened fire then quickly mounted and rode out of town. Within moments the head of Grierson's column raced through the streets and secured Hazelhurst.[40]

Before the troopers could begin their systematic destruction of military goods, a train approached from the north. Seeing the depot surrounded by bluecoats, the engineer reversed the train and sped away managing to escape his Federal pursuers. Grierson would have been disappointed had he then known that the lost train carried "seventeen commissioned officers and eight millions in Confederate money, which was en route to pay off troops in Louisiana and Texas"[41]

At 7:00 p.m. the long column left Hazelhurst and rode west toward the Mississippi River. Grierson's departure was not a moment too soon for, alerted by the engineer of his location, Confederate units were hot on his trail. The colonel realized that time was running out. Where was Grant? and when would he cross the river? were questions for which he needed answers. Desperate to learn information concerning Grant and the landing of his troops, Grierson interrogated citizens and blacks along the way, but received only blank stares.

The following day, April 28, the ride west continued. While halted for a brief rest two miles east of Union Church, the men were startled by the sound of carbines as their pickets were fired upon by a "considerable force" of horsemen in gray. A battalion of Col. W. Wirt Adams' Mississippi Cavalry had stumbled upon the Federals and threw the Northerners into momentary panic. Order was quickly restored and the Illinois troopers drove the Mississippians off. Bivouacking for the night at Union Church, Grierson's heart must have sunk as he realized the road to Grand Gulf was probably blocked and still no word of Grant. Unable to wait for Grant to effect a crossing of the Mississippi River, Grierson decided to push south for Baton Rouge.

Boots and saddles sounded at an early hour on April 29, and the weary troopers mounted up. During the night a trap had been set for them to the west by Wirt Adams, but the Federals gave him the slip and rode southeast instead toward Brookhaven. Throughout the morning, the bombardment of Grand Gulf by Porter's fleet in preparation for a landing by Grant's troops could be distinctly heard. Yet, as Adjutant Woodward relates, "the little command could not dally to await developments. The enemy were concentrating from every direction to envelop it, and its only salvation was rapid movements to deceive them, and long marches."[42]

The raiders reached Brookhaven that afternoon and seized a Confederate training camp along with 216 men. After destroying everything of military value, the column turned south and for the next 24 hours followed along the New Orleans, Jackson & Great Northern Railroad destroying bridges, trestles, water tanks, and tearing up tracks. So effective was their destruction that this section of the line was not reopened until after the war.

On April 30, at Summit, Grierson learned of a large troop concentration farther south along the railroad at Osyka. Rather than risk his command in combat with a possibly superior force, he turned the column southwest. The only hope now to save his weary band of cavalrymen was to reach the safety of Union lines in Louisiana. He told his officers, "A straight line for Baton Rouge, and let speed be our safety!" Pushing ahead till late in the night, the troopers dropped to the ground on Dr. Alten Spurlark's plantation for a few hours sleep--their last sleep during the raid.[43]

The men were up and mounted at an early hour on the first day of May 1863. The column moved rapidly until it reached the road between Centreville and Osyka (near present-day Gillsburg) where the men spotted newly-made tracks and fresh manure indicating that a column of horsemen had recently passed across their front. The tracks had been made by Maj. James De Baun and 115 men of the Ninth Louisiana Partisan Rangers and Ninth Tennessee Cavalry Battalion as they rode from Woodville toward Osyka. The Southern horsemen had unknowingly crossed Grierson's path less than an hour before.[44]

Sergeant Surby and two of his Butternut Guerillas cautiously rode forward with revolvers in hand to investigate. They soon came across three dismounted Confederates, pickets of De Baun's command, at the driveway to Oak Grove, the plantation home of Charles Wall. The veteran troopers instinctively knew that the main enemy force was not far ahead, probably stopped for its noon bivouac. Surby slid from his horse and while studying his surroundings engaged the pickets in conversation attempting to learn the whereabouts and strength of their command. Suddenly, two shots rang out from the nearby plantation home followed by a scattered volley of carbine fire. (Some of Grierson's men had ridden up to the house and stumbled across four Confederates in the yard who opened fire on the Union horsemen.) Both sides were now aware of the other's presence.

Colonel Blackburn came galloping up to investigate and, without stopping, called for Surby to follow him. Although the sergeant considered it "a rash movement," he rode forward toward

Wall's Bridge over the Tickfaw River where moments before De Baun's men had been watering their horses. As the Federals approached the span, carbine fire spat out from the trees which lined the stream. Unharmed, Blackburn and Surby continued at a gallop onto the bridge when a second volley toppled the colonel and his mount, both mortally wounded. Surby too, was hit but managed to keep his saddle and rode to safety.[45]

The wounded sergeant pulled off the road just in time to avoid the horsemen of Company G, Seventh Illinois, charging in column toward the bridge with sabers drawn. Led by Lt. William Styles, the lead platoon thundered onto the wooden span and raced across the bridge. A deadly volley ripped into their ranks emptying a number of saddles. Seven horses and three men went down and five bluecoats were taken prisoner. De Baun's luck, however, had run out.

Hearing the sounds of battle, Grierson arrived with the main column and directed Companies A and D of the Seventh Illinois to dismount and advance as skirmishers. Capt. Jason Smith also brought up two of his Woodruff guns, dropped trail, and began landing shells among the enemy. With the shrill notes of bugles echoing along the stream, Colonel Loomis charged over the bridge with his regiment while other units forded the stream down- and upriver of the span. The terrifying sight of overwhelming numbers bearing down upon them was more than the Confederates could bear. De Baun's men saddled up and fled in the direction of Osyka with cavalrymen from the Sixth Illinois in pursuit. One of the Federals noted that "The road over which the enemy had fled was found, as far as the pursuing party followed them, strewn with saddles, blankets, hats, coats and firearms, indicating that after firing their one murderous volley they had been seized by an uncontrollable panic."[46]

The largest engagement of the raid, the fight at Wall's Bridge cost Grierson one killed, five wounded, and five captured. The Union commander lamented most the loss of Blackburn and Surby who had to be left behind at Newman's plantation. (Blackburn died on May 17 whereas Surby, who recovered from his wound, was later exchanged and returned to duty.) Colonel Prince was shaken by the loss of Blackburn and recommended that the column go into bivouac. But the need to push on was apparent to Grierson who considered it vital for the safety of his command. His only chance of reaching Baton Rouge was to cross the unfordable Amite River before the Confederates could destroy the bridge or block his path.

At 4:00 p.m. the column reached Greensburg where the horsemen turned southwestward and continued on toward the Amite, sixteen miles distant. For the weary horsemen it was a seemingly endless ride. There was no halting for the men to rest or eat or even for watering the horses which collapsed along the route with alarming frequency. As the ride to the river continued, darkness enveloped the column and officers continually urged their men to "keep moving, close up."

The captain of the rear guard captured the essence of the ordeal that night as he wrote:

> Men by the score, and I think by fifties, were riding sound asleep in their saddles. The horses excessively tired and hungry, would stray out of the road and thrust their noses to the earth in hopes of finding something to eat. The men, when addressed, would remain silent and motionless until a blow across the thigh or the shoulder should awaken them, when it would be found that each supposed himself still riding with his company, which might perhaps be a mile ahead. We found several men who had either fallen from their horses, or dismounted and dropped on the ground, dead with sleep. Nothing short of a beating with the flat of a saber would awaken some of them. In several instances they begged to be allowed to sleep, saying that they would run all risk of capture on the morrow. Two or three did escape our vigilance, and were captured the next afternoon.[47]

The head of the column approached Williams' Bridge across the Amite near midnight. Sam Nelson, who had replaced Surby as leader of the Butternut Guerillas, went forward on foot to determine the size of the guard. Two men stood the lonely vigil. Only two men stood between the horse soldiers and safety. The Confederates were quickly taken prisoner by the scouts. "They had not even suspected our approach," recalled Stephen Forbes, "and in a few minutes, just as the moon rose to light us on our way, the muffled thunder of our horses' feet resounded from its [the bridge] entire length."[48]

Having successfully crossed Amite River, the raiders for all intent and purpose had made it, they were safe. (Unbeknownst to

Grierson, Grant's army was now across the Mississippi River and had that day defeated Confederate forces at Port Gibson. In response to these developments, Pemberton called off pursuit of Grierson.) The raiders, however, continued to ride through the night surprising and capturing from the rear Confederate detachments at Sandy Creek and the Comite River. With the last obstacle behind him, Grierson halted his exhausted command within six miles of Baton Rouge where his troopers dropped to the ground numb with sleep. It was May 2.

One of Grierson's men who had fallen asleep in the saddle continued on until awakened by the stern challenge of a Federal soldier on the picket line outside of Baton Rouge. "Halt! Who goes there?" Identifying himself as a member of the Sixth Illinois Cavalry, the horseman explained that there were two regiments of Union horsemen coming down the road behind him who had ridden all the way from LaGrange, Tennessee. Such an amazing story was difficult for the sentry to believe and the cavalryman was soon ushered into the presence of Maj. Gen. Christopher C. Auger in command of Federal forces in Baton Rouge. Auger, likewise, was skeptical and sent out two companies of cavalry to "ascertain the truth." The incredible story was soon confirmed as Grierson reported to Auger in person.[49]

The news of Grierson's arrival spread throughout the city on May 2 and a jubilant crowd lined the streets to greet the cavalrymen. The column of dust-covered horsemen, many of whom were on lame and jaded mounts, formed what one historian described as "the most tatter-demalion procession ever officially sponsored by the United States Army." Amidst the cheers and applause offered by citizens and soldiers alike, the long column wound its way through the streets of Baton Rouge to the banks of the Mississippi River. After watering their horses, the men of Grierson's command rode to Magnolia Hall two miles south of town and bivouacked for an extended and well-deserved rest. The great raid had come to a successful end.[50]

"A cavalry raid at its best is essentially a game of strategy and speed, with personal violence as an incidental complication," wrote Stephen Forbes. "It is played according to more or less definite rules, not inconsistent, indeed, with the players' killing each other if the game cannot be won in any other way; but it is commonly a strenuous game, rather than a bloody one, intensely exciting, but not necessarily very dangerous." Grierson's raid from Tennessee through Mississippi to Louisiana had been just that, and infinitely more.[51]

The raids that were launched in the spring of 1863, of which Grierson's was the most successful, were designed not only to sever Vicksburg's vital supply and communications lines, but to confuse Pemberton and keep him off balance. Destruction of the Southern Railroad, although only for a limited time, prevented the Confederate commander from stockpiling additional supplies of food and munitions in Vicksburg for which the garrison of that city would later have a desperate need. Destruction of the New Orleans, Jackson & Great Northern Railroad also severed Confederate supply lines into Port Hudson and contributed materially to the fall of that bastion which surrendered on July 9, five days after Vicksburg capitulated. Bombarded with reports of enemy movements throughout his department and pleas for reinforcements as a result of these raids, Pemberton acted in characteristic fashion—indecisively. In a futile effort to capture Grierson, he weakened his strategic river defenses and scattered his available manpower. In the crucial opening stages of the Vicksburg campaign the Southern commander acted defensively and yielded the initiative to a dangerous opponent—Grant.

The raid was hailed throughout the country and in light of its bold success was praised by friend and foe alike. In writing of the raid, General Grant, the man who benefitted most by the daring operation, exclaimed that it "has been the most successful thing of the kind since the breaking out of the Rebellion," and lauded, "Grierson has knocked the heart out of the state [Mississippi]." No praise, however, was more eloquent than that which came from William T. Sherman who emphatically termed the feat "The most brilliant expedition of the Civil War."[52]

Chapter Four

The Inland Campaign Begins

The Battle of Port Gibson

Despite having missed linking with the Army of the Tennessee by less than thirty hours, the hard-riding cavalrymen led by Col. Benjamin Grierson materially aided the landing of Union troops at Bruinsburg. For Confederate horsemen, ordered in pursuit of the elusive raiders, were unavailable to guard potential crossing points along the Mississippi River and could not be recalled in time to contest the invasion. As a result, not a shot was fired as Federal soldiers under Maj. Gen. Ulysses S. Grant came ashore at Bruinsburg Landing on April 30, 1863. Throughout the day, Union troops were shuttled across the river in what was the greatest amphibious operation in American history up to that time. Grant later wrote:

> When this was effected I felt a degree of relief scarcely ever equalled since. Vicksburg was not yet taken it is true, nor were its defenders demoralized by any of our previous moves. I was now in the enemy's country, with a vast river and the stronghold of Vicksburg between me and my base of supplies. But I was on dry ground on the same side of the river with the enemy. All the campaigns, labors, hardships and exposures from the month of December previous to this time that had been made and endured, were for the accomplishment of this one object.[1]

Elements of the Union army pushed inland and took possession of the bluffs which loom over Bruinsburg, thereby securing the landing area. By noon, most of Maj. Gen. John A. McClernand's XIII Corps—17,000-strong—was ashore. McClernand's disdain for administrative details, however, soon jeopardized the operations for rations had not been issued to his men prior to embarkation. Precious time elapsed before the necessary three days' rations were brought ashore and distributed to the troops, after which the column was formed and placed in motion. By late afternoon of April 30, 22,000 soldiers were ashore and the inland campaign began.

The long blue columns were formed and under a merciless sun pushed out from the landing area and up the steep bluffs. Charles B. Johnson of the 130th Illinois, a hospital steward from Greenville, observed "For two miles the road ran through the river bottom, then up a long hill of red clay [loess soil], next by quiet farmhouses and cultivated fields, through pretty wooded groves and up quiet lanes, all bearing the marks of peace, and resting in supposed security from the inroads of invading armies."[2]

The march was a difficult one for the Federal soldiers who were ladened with 60 rounds of ammunition and more rations than could be carried in their haversacks. First Lt. Samuel C. Jones of Company A, Twenty-second Iowa, recorded the method by which extra rations were carried: "The bayonets were placed on their guns and run through the meat, so each man had his extra ration of meat fixed on his bayonet. Then at a right shoulder shift, we proceeded on our march." Men of other units did the same and, as Lieutenant Jones observed, "the whole army could be seen for miles, worming its way over that vast flat country with the bayonets gleaming in the sunshine, and the ration of meat in its place. It was picturesque and beautiful to behold."[3]

The soldiers reached the top of the bluffs where a panorama beautiful in the extreme opened before their eyes. Off to their left, amidst vast fields of corn, was one of the largest, most ornate mansions in the ante-bellum South—Windsor. Built between 1859-1861 by Smith Coffee Daniell, II, Windsor epitomized the opulence associated with the Southern aristocracy. General McClernand established his headquarters at Windsor while many Union soldiers availed themselves of the stately oaks and rested in the shade. At Windsor, McClernand made the decision to "push on by a forced march that night" in hopes of securing the bridges across Bayou Pierre at Port Gibson.[4]

The march was resumed at 5:30 p.m. with Col. Samuel Merrill's Twenty-first Iowa in the lead. Instead of taking the Bruinsburg Road, which was the direct road from the landing area to Port Gibson, Merrill's Hawkeyes led the column south to

Bethel Church where they turned left onto the Rodney–Port Gibson road. Darkness soon settled over the fields and scattered forest and the pace of the march slowed to a crawl. First Sgt. Charles A. Hobbs of the Ninety-ninth Illinois recorded of his experience that night:

> As we pass along an old darkey gives us his blessings, but fears there will be few of us ever to return. The moon is shining above us and the road is romantic in the extreme. The artillery wagons rattle forward and the heavy tramp of many men gives a dull but impressive sound.
>
> In many places the road seems to end abruptly, but we come to the place we find it turning at right angles, passing through narrow valleys, sometimes through hills, and presenting the best opportunity to the Rebels for defense if they had but known our purpose.[5]

To provide greater security for the column as it advanced through the night, Merrill recalled his skirmishers and replaced them with a 16-man patrol led by Lt. Col. Cornelius W. Dunlap. Ordered to "go forward until fired on by the enemy," the men of the advance guard knew they would eventually find the Confederates, but where and when? As they pushed through the darkness, the tension was unbearable. Shortly after midnight, the vanguard moved down a steep hill, crossed Widows Creek, and started up a long grade toward the A. K. Shaifer house having marched 13 miles from the landing site.[6]

Back at Grand Gulf, Bowen had watched helplessly as the fleet passed his batteries on the evening of April 29. It was imperative that he redeploy his force to counter the Federal threat to his downstream flank. But without heavy reinforcements he was almost powerless to contest a crossing of the river. Fortunately, the sounds of heavy firing at Grand Gulf convinced the post commander at Vicksburg to send the troops which Pemberton had ordered held in readiness to assist Bowen. Marching orders were finally issued to the brigades led by Brig. Gens. Edward D. Tracy and William E. Baldwin.[7]

The twenty-nine-year-old Tracy was a native of Georgia, and a lawyer by profession who established a reputable practice in Huntsville, Alabama. An ardent states' rightists who campaigned in support of John Breckinridge for president in 1860, he welcomed

secession and was quick to orga-
nize a company in Madison
County. Elected captain of
Company I, Fourth Alabama

Brig. Gen. Edward Tracy
Generals in Gray

Infantry, he first saw action at
First Manassas. Elevated to lieutenant colonel of the Nineteenth
Alabama (Joe Wheeler's regi-
ment), he also fought at Shiloh and in East Tennessee. Promoted
to brigadier general to rank from August 16, 1862, Tracy assumed
command of a brigade composed of five Alabama regiments.
Although personally brave, he was also cautious—a solid and reliable brigade commander. Ordered to Mississippi in December,
General Tracy spent the winter months drilling his men in anticipation of the spring campaign.

Tracy's brigade of Alabamians, 1,500-strong, left their camps
near Warrenton, just below Vicksburg, and headed toward
Hankinson's Ferry on the Big Black River. Moving out at sunset
on April 29, Tracy's men soon found the night march a grueling
one as the roads were wet and both man and beast mired in mud.
Yet, the Alabamians managed to reach the river shortly after midnight where they rested for several hours before pushing on toward Grand Gulf.

Along with Tracy's men marched the Virginians of the
Botetourt Artillery (6 guns)—the only unit from Virginia to par-
ticipate in the Vicksburg campaign. Sgt. James L. Burks of the
Virginia battery suffered through the march and recalled:

> We reached Big Black about 12 o'clock at night and were engaged from that
> time until daylight marching about one mile. We had to pass through mud in
> which the guns would sink up to the axel-trees and the horses mired so deep
> that they couldn't pull out at all and had to be taken out.
> The guns and caissons had to be pulled out by hand, having to take the am-

munition chest off before they could be moved at all. We finished ferrying our battery over about daylight on the morning of the 30th and then moved on towards Grand Gulf without stopping to feed the horses.[8]

Also hastening to Bowen's assistance was the brigade commanded by William Baldwin. Although a South Carolina native, he was raised in Mississippi and served as an officer in the state militia for twelve years prior to the Civil War. Elected colonel of the Fourteenth Mississippi Infantry, Baldwin was destined to experience repeated misfortune during his service to the Confederacy. Captured at Fort Donelson, he spent six months in the Federal prison at Fort Warren, Massachusetts, prior to being exchanged in August 1862. The following month he was promoted to brigadier general and given command of a split brigade which consisted of regiments from Mississippi and Louisiana. Baldwin and his brigade saw little fighting during the winter months, and so were anxious for action as the spring campaign opened.

Positioned north of Vicksburg when the marching orders arrived, Baldwin's men quickly broke camp and took up the line of march. Although they had a long and difficult road ahead of them, the men moved out in high spirits with the anticipation of battle. At 2:00 a.m., the men halted and rested until sunrise at which time the march was resumed and the brigade pushed across the Big Black River at Hankinson's Ferry. Once south of the river, William Pitt Chambers of the Forty-sixth Mississippi Infantry noted of the march:

> The roads were now more level, the air seemed purer and the spirits of the men were wonderfully elated. Again and again we made the echoes ring with our shouts. Jest and repartee were heard on every side and altogether "Baldwin's Cavalry". . .enjoyed themselves better than in any march they had ever made. But physical fatigue will dampen the ardor of the most elastic spirit, and as the long hours dragged by with no orders save "close up!" the enthusiasm seemed to die away and a great weariness of limb overtook us.[9]

These capable brigadiers and their combat-ready veterans would provide Bowen with desperately needed manpower, but would they prove enough? Regardless of the answer, the combative Bowen moved to do battle with Grant's Union Army of the Tennessee.

Bowen did not wait for the arrival of reinforcements to redeploy his command in an effort to meet the Federal threat. On the evening of April 29, he ordered Brig. Gen. Martin E. Green with a small strike force of 450 men from Grand Gulf to picket the roads leading from Port Gibson south to Natchez and west to Rodney.

Green was the obvious choice for such an assignment. A native of Fauquier County, Virginia, he later moved to Lewis County, Missouri, where he operated a sawmill until the outbreak of the Civil War. He immediately organized a cavalry command as part of the Missouri State Guard and served with Sterling Price at Pea Ridge. Promoted to brigadier in the Confederate army, Green assumed command of an infantry brigade and fought at Iuka, Corinth, and at Hatchie Bridge in which engagements he earned the reputation as a daring and aggressive officer. Upon receipt of orders, Green moved quickly to carry out his assignment by sending the strike force beyond Port Gibson.

Green arrived in person at Port Gibson at daybreak on April 30 and immediately began reconnoitering along the Rodney road. He found the terrain near Magnolia Church (approximately 3 1/2 miles from Port Gibson) suitable for a delaying action. Bowen also examined the area and approved of Green's selection of ground. At dusk, Green advanced his small brigade (approximately 1,000 men) and posted his regiments athwart the Rodney road with the Sixth Mississippi (Col. Robert Lowry) on the right, followed to the left by the Twelfth Arkansas Sharpshooter Battalion (Capt. Griff Bayne) astride the road, the Fifteenth Arkansas (Lt. Col. W. W. Reynolds), and the Twenty-first Arkansas on the left extending the line into the Widows Creek bottom. The four guns of the Pettus Flying Artillery were posted just north of the road near the Foster house. Lt. William D. Tisdale and four men of the Twelfth Arkansas Sharpshooter Battalion were ordered forward by Green to establish an outpost near the A. K. Shaifer house, 600 yards farther west. There his men settled down for the night in full expectation of meeting the enemy on the morrow.

The terrain selected by Green was ideal for defense. A maze of ridges, flattopped and of equal height, ran in all directions. Although the ridge tops were cultivated, they were separated by steep-sided and extremely deep ravines that were filled with a tangled, almost impenetrable mass of cane, vines, and trees. Visibility from the ridge tops was excellent, but, as Historian Edwin C. Bearss so vividly describes, "upon descending into the ravines the jungle closed tightly about, so that each man's world became a tiny green-walled room only a few yards across." Such terrain features would prevent the Federals from bringing their overwhelming superiority of numbers into full play and would help to neutralize the powerful Union artillery. (The Federals would have a clear advantage with 58 pieces of artillery compared to Bowen's 16 guns.)[10]

Green's brigade was strengthened by the addition of Tracy's Alabama brigade which arrived at 10:00 p.m., having marched 40 miles in 27 hours. Posted on the Confederate right, astride the Bruinsburg road, Tracy placed the Twenty-third Alabama (Col. F. K. Beck) on the left, followed to the right by the Thirty-first Alabama (Col. D. R. Hundley), Thirtieth Alabama (Col. C. M. Shelley), and the Twentieth Alabama (Col. Isham W. Garrott) on the right with his flank anchored on a prominent knoll overlooking Bayou Pierre. (The Forty-sixth Alabama commanded by Col. M. L. Woods would not arrive on the field until the morning of May 1.) Supporting Tracy's line were two sections (4 guns) of the Botetourt Artillery positioned in center of the line.

The hours passed slowly and tension mounted as rumors of the Federal advance spread like wildfire. At 12:30 a.m., on May 1, the ever vigilant Martin Green rode forward to see that Lieutenant Tisdale and his men were alert. Riding into the yard at the A. K. Shaifer house, Green was amused to see Mrs. Shaifer and the women of the house frantically loading a wagon with all their household items. The general tried to calm their fears by telling them that the enemy could not possibly arrive before daylight. Just then, the crash of musketry shattered the stillness and several bullets buried themselves in the wagon-load of furniture. Contrary to Green's assurances the enemy had arrived. The women were terrified and, screaming with fright, leaped into the wagon and whipped the animals toward Port Gibson. Green quickly mounted and, after ordering Lieutenant Tisdale to contest the enemy advance, rode hard to Magnolia Church to alert his brigade. Just east of the church, where Green's main line of resistance was posted behind a worm fence, Lt. John S. Bell of the Twelfth Arkansas Sharpshooter Battalion waited nervously for the Federals. He later recalled:

> We could hear the enemy forming, and it was so still we could hear every command given. Our men had orders not to fire until word was given. Soon we could see their line of skirmishers coming down the road and could hear them say there was no one here, it was only a cavalry scout. When they were within 50 yards the word "fire" was given.[11]

Several Federal soldiers crumpled to the ground as Green's line opened fire and Colonel Dunlap's Hawkeyes recoiled under the murderous volley. The other companies of the Twenty-first Iowa were quickly brought forward and the guns of the First Iowa Battery thundered into position, dropped trail, and opened fire. Col. William M. Stone, commander of the Second Brigade, Fourteenth Division, of McClernand's XIII Corps, ordered up his three remaining regiments. Stone deployed the Twenty-third Iowa to the left of and in line with the Twenty-first Iowa, and formed the Twenty-second Iowa and Eleventh Wisconsin in a second line behind the guns. Adding strength to the Federal deployment were three cannon of the First Indiana Battery which soon arrived and dropped trail abreast of the Iowa battery, but south of the road. In a matter of moments the Hoosiers added their deadly rounds of canister to the fray.

A spirited skirmish ensued which lasted until 3:00 a.m. The night, however, was so dark that the only targets either army had were the muzzle flashes of the enemy guns. Fearful lest their men fall into a trap, Union officers decided to wait until dawn before deploying additional troops. The Confederates held their ground, and for the next several hours an uneasy calm settled over the woods and scattered fields. Soldiers of both armies rested on their arms, but few slept. Throughout the night the Federals gathered their forces in hand and both sides prepared for the battle which they knew would come with the rising sun.

Grant was anxious to complete the river crossing and hurry James B. McPherson's troops to McClernand's support. With the sound of battle audible in the distance, the crossing continued. Huge fires were built to illuminate the landing area and guide vessels ferrying troops across the river. Nonetheless, at 3:00 a.m., the transports *Horizon* and *Moderator* collided. *Horizon* sank taking with her the guns, horses, and equipment of Company G, Second Illinois Light Artillery. Reluctantly, Grant suspended the crossing for the night, but, with first light, the crossing resumed and the troops rushed to the field where battle had been joined.

At dawn, May 1, Union troops began to move in force along the Rodney road from the Shaifer house toward Magnolia Church. At the same time, Maj. Gen. John A. McClernand, commander of the XIII Corps and senior officer present on the field, ordered the division of Brig. Gen. Peter Osterhaus to advance along a connecting plantation road to the left toward the Bruinsburg road along which Tracy's Confederates could be seen in force. With skirmishers well in advance the Federals began a very slow and deliberate advance around 5:30 a.m. The skirmishers posted by both Tracy and Green contested the advance and the bloodshed began in earnest.

McClernand directed most of his force along the Rodney road against Green's position on the Confederate left. His lead division, which had opened the battle at midnight, was led by Brig. Gen. Eugene Asa Carr. Already partially deployed with Stone's brigade north of the road, Carr called up his remaining brigade led by Brig. Gen. William P. Benton which moved into position on the right, south of the road. It was Carr's intention to swing his right brigade forward and seize Magnolia Church ridge 450 yards to his front. Supported by the 12 guns of the First Iowa and First Indiana batteries, Carr ordered his men forward at 6:30.

Green watched in dismay as the Federals surged through the ravines and canebrakes south of the road and, in spite of a "galling fire of shell and musketry," probed for his left flank. The skirmishers clad in butternut and gray were forced to fall back to the main line 200 yards east of Magnolia Church. As Union soldiers solidified their newly won position near the church, sharpshooters peppered the Confederate line with a heavy and accurate fire.

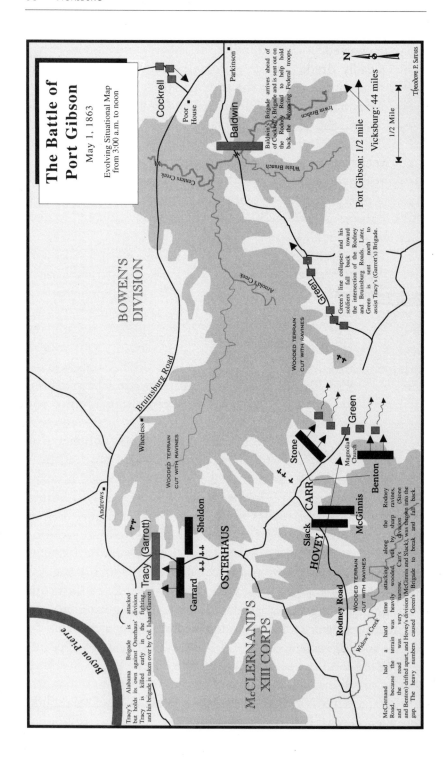

The Battle of
Port Gibson

May 1, 1863

Evolving Situational Map
from 3:00 a.m. to noon

Theodore P. Savas

N

Port Gibson: 1/2 mile

Vicksburg: 44 miles

1/2 Mile

Cockrell

Parkinson

Poor
House

Baldwin

Baldwin's Brigade arrives ahead of
of Cockrell's Brigade and is sent out on
the Rodney Road to help hold
back the advancing Federal troops.

Irwin Branch

White Branch

Centers Creek

BOWEN'S
DIVISION

Bruinsburg Road

Wheeless

Andrews

WOODED TERRAIN
CUT WITH RAVINES

Arnold's Creek

Green

Green's line collapses and his
soldiers fall back toward
the intersection of the Rodney
and Bruinsburg Roads. Later,
Green is sent north to
assist Tracy's (Garrott) Brigade.

WOODED TERRAIN
CUT WITH RAVINES

Stone

Green

Magnolia
Church

CARR

Benton

McGinnis

Slack

HOVEY

Rodney Road

WOODED TERRAIN
CUT WITH RAVINES

Widow's Creek

Tracy (Garrott)

Garrard

Sheldon

OSTERHAUS

McCLERNAND'S
XIII CORPS

Bayou Pierre

Tracy's Alabama Brigade is attacked
but holds its own against Osterhaus' division,
Tracy is killed early in the fighting,
and his brigade is taken over by Col. Isham Garrott

McClernand had a hard time attacking along the Rodney
Road, because the terrain was heavily wooded, cut by sharp ravines.
and the road was very narrow. Carr's division (Stone
and Benton) drifted apart, and Hovey's division (McGinnis and Slack), was thrown into the
gap. The heavy numbers caused Green's Brigade to break and fall back.

Benton reported, "Now came the `tug of war' in good earnest." In the deadly firefight which erupted, soldiers of both armies went down with horrifying frequency and the once peaceful setting of Magnolia Church became a killing ground.[12]

It was not long before Green's line became hard pressed and the artillery unit supporting him out of ammunition. At 7:00 a.m., Green sent a courier to Tracy requesting that he send an infantry regiment and a section of the Virginia battery. It was Green's opinion that "he could not sustain his position on the left fifteen minutes unless re-enforced," and added, "if the left was not sustained the right would be cut off from all chance of retreat." Although his main line was not yet engaged, Tracy reluctantly acquiesced. Lt. William Norgrove of the Botetourt Artillery limbered up his section of 12-pounder howitzers and went rumbling down the road behind the Twenty-third Alabama Infantry.[13]

Shortly after Norgrove's section was sent to the left, the six 10-pounder rifled Rodmans of the Seventh Michigan Battery supporting Osterhaus' advance moved into position on a ridge 1,500 yards from Tracy's line. The artillerymen clad in blue unlimbered and opened fire. The Virginians of the Botetourt Artillery, however, responded quickly—and on target—with their two 12-pounder Napoleons, disabling one of the Rodmans and inflicting casualties of two killed and two wounded. Despite the "galling fire" of Confederate artillery, Capt. Charles H. Lanphere held his Wolverines grimly to their task and in short order hurled a destructive fire of their own at the Virginians. The artillery duel raged in unabated fury for 45 minutes, but the powerful Michigan battery soon gained the upper hand. Lanphere would later boast in his report that the shells from his battery landed among the enemy with "great effect."[14]

As the Michiganders methodically began pounding the Virginians' position, Osterhaus deployed his troops into line of battle astride the plantation road with Brig. Gen. Theophilus T. Garrard's brigade in the lead followed by the one commanded by Col. Lionel A. Sheldon. Regiments from Illinois, Indiana, Kentucky, and Ohio quickly formed their lines with man touching man and rank pressing rank. Regimental and national colors were uncased and fixed bayonets glistened in the morning light as the troops dressed their lines and prepared to advance. These veteran units went forward with a rush and, raising a mighty cheer, surged into the ravines before them. Order was difficult to maintain in such rugged terrain and gaps opened in the Federal lines. Regiments soon became separated from one another in the dense vegetation and the advance ground to a halt as it came up against Tracy's line of Alabamians.

With the advance temporarily checked, Union sharpshooters were ordered forward in an effort to develop Tracy's line and silence the Confederate artillery. Inching their way forward through the tangled jungle, the sharpshooters soon found their prey. Exposed on the forward slope of a ridge, near several slave cabins, men and horses of the Botetourt Artillery began to go down at an alarming rate. Fearing for the safety of the battery, Lt. Phillip Peters sent Sgt. Francis G. Obenchain to General Tracy requesting that the caissons be sent to the rear and that the infantry open fire. Tracy, not wishing to develop his line and, therefore, its weakness, denied the request. The Virginians stood to their post and fired their cannon with determination and skill. The odds, however, were against them. A second time Obenchain was sent to Tracy with the same request, and a second time denied.

The skirmishers from Alabama began falling back in the face of enemy pressure and Tracy's main line opened fire. The scattered fields and forest were soon ablaze from massed volleys and quickly obscured by the thick smoke of battle. Sergeant Obenchain was yet again sent to Tracy requesting that the caissons be run to the rear for safety. The sergeant recalled that while speaking to

Brig. Gen. Peter Osterhaus
Generals in Blue

Tracy, "a ball struck him on back of the neck passing through. He fell with great force on his face and in falling cried 'O Lord!' He was dead when I stooped to him." Edward Tracy was the first of several Confederate generals to die in defense of Vicksburg. Col. Isham W. Garrott of the Twentieth Alabama as senior officer present assumed command of the brigade and was determined to hold firm the Confederate right at all hazards.[15]

Federal pressure continued to mount all along the line as McClernand threw in additional brigades upon their arrival from Bruinsburg. Determined to drive the Confederates before him, McClernand directed the greater part of his corps forward on the Rodney road. As the blue lines slowly felt their way forward, Bowen arrived from Grand Gulf to survey the situation and take personal command. At a glance, he realized the enemy was present in overwhelming numbers. Yet, his keen eye for terrain features convinced him that if reinforcements would arrive in time he could possibly check the Federal advance. The question remained, would reinforcements arrive in time and in sufficient number to drive Grant back toward the river?

Green's line was on the verge of collapsing when, at 8:30 a.m., the Twenty-third Alabama arrived and was quickly sent to extend Green's right as it was in danger of being turned. Lieutenant Norgrove and his section of howitzers also arrived on Green's front, wheeled his guns into position on a ridge near the Foster house, east of Magnolia Church, and there entered the fray. The Virginians were joined by Lt. John R. Sweaney's section of the Pettus Flying Artillery which had found enough ammunition to return to the field. The Southern guns, however, were exposed to a hail of iron and Union artillery hammered their position with telling effect.   One member of Norgrove's section, Pvt. John Smith, volunteered to climb to the roof of a nearby building to get a better view of the Federal batteries. While doing so he was shot in the hip and fell hard to the ground. Smith, unlike many of his comrades that day, recovered from his wound.

Both Bowen and Green realized that the key to their position was Magnolia Church ridge from which the Federals now raked their line with a murderous fire. If not retaken, it would only be a matter of time before the Confederate line was forced back. Reacting instinctively, Bowen directed the Twenty-third Alabama and Sixth Mississippi forward to drive back the Union artillery and enable the Twelfth Arkansas Sharpshooters Battalion to seize the ridge.

Shouting, "Follow me! Let's take that battery!" General Bowen spurred his horse forward and was followed by his men who raised the "Rebel yell." Sweeping through the open fields near the Foster house and into the tangled ravines before them, his men were exposed to a most destructive fire from Federal batteries the guns of which were doubled charged with canister. Although the regiments advanced bravely with grim determination, they were hurled back by the deadly canister and withering volleys of musketry from Stone's brigade. Their ranks thinned and badly bleeding, the Confederates fell back to the main line. Capt.

Brig. Gen. Alvin P. Hovey
Generals in Blue

William C. Thompson of the Sixth Mississippi wrote, "As we went back we were amazed and shocked to see how many of our men were lying dead or wounded in the path of our advance."16

The battle increased in fury as more Northern soldiers entered the fight against Green. Brig. Gen. Alvin P. Hovey's division arrived and was quickly deployed into line of battle near the Shaifer house. Forming line with the brigades of Brig. Gen. George McGinnis on the right and Col. James L. Slack on the left, Hovey advanced his division along the Rodney road and into the gap between Benton and Stone. Presenting now a solid front from near Widows Creek on the right to near Centers Creek on the left, the Federal line extended well beyond Green's flanks. The Confederate line was threatened with envelopment and Green pleaded for additional men to help hold his tenuous position.

Bowen, however, had none to provide and sent couriers dashing off toward Port Gibson and Grand Gulf in search of desperately needed reinforcements.

Racing through town, the courier came upon Baldwin's brigade which was just entering the outskirts of Port Gibson. Reigning in his horse, the courier greeted Baldwin with news of impending disaster. The brigadier immediately ordered his men forward at the double-quick and guided his troops through the streets of town. William Pitt Chambers of the Forty-sixth Mississippi observed the panic in Port Gibson and later wrote:

> It was an exciting time! The loud peals of artillery rent the sky and reverberated along the hills till their echoes blended with the sharp din of musketry. . . In the streets all was confusion. Men with pale faces were running hither and thither, some with arms and seeking a command, women sobbing on every side, children in opened eyed wonder clinging to their weeping mothers not understanding the meaning of it all, and negroes with eyes protruding like open cotton bolls were jostling each other and every body else and continuously asking about "dem Yankees."

> The ladies cheered us through their tears, and besought us to drive the invaders from their homes. One lady while she prayed Heaven to protect us, said we felt as near to her as though we were her own sons going forth to battle. The wounded, too, were meeting us, some in vehicles and some on litters, and many a poor fellow with a shattered limb or a gaping wound would wildly hurrah for the "brave Mississippians."

West of town, the men were greeted by General Bowen who had ridden from the field to personally urge them forward. Baldwin reported: "The brigade passed through the town at a rapid pace, and thence marched in double-quick about 2 miles southwest, on the Rodney Road, when we found our troops falling back from all points, pressed by greatly superior numbers."[17]

As Baldwin's men rushed toward the field of battle, Green's position astride the Rodney road on the Confederate left eroded. Sharpshooters of the Eighteenth Indiana crept close to the Confederate line and began firing on the artillerymen with deadly accuracy. Lieutenant Norgrove went down, shot twice through the body. George Obenchain of the Virginia battery also fell "riddled with balls." So many of the battery horses were downed

Maj. Gen. A. J. Smith
Generals in Blue

that it was impossible for the Virginians to withdraw the guns, if necessary, except by hand. The intrepid Virginians, however, con-

tinued to coolly work their cannon with lethal effect.[18]

By 10:00 a.m., McClernand had massed three divisions astride the Rodney road—the divisions of Hovey and Carr in the front line and that of Brig. Gen. Andrew Jackson Smith held in reserve near the Shaifer house. In places, Union regiments were stacked two, three, and four deep. Referred to as an "exponent of brute force," the pugnacious McClernand sought to overwhelm the enemy by a direct frontal attack. Before the deployment was complete, however, the impatient Hovey ordered two regiments forward in an effort to take the Southern artillery. In an instant, the men of the Thirty-fourth Indiana and Fifty-sixth Ohio leaped over a fence and advanced "with loud shouts and fixed bayonets, toward the battery."[19]

The cannoneers of the Botetourt Artillery were ready for them. The gunners had by this time switched to canister and trained their cannon on the advancing lines. Firing their howitzers with alacrity and at pointblank range, the Virginians raked the ground before them and broke the charge. In the face of this "intense and concentrated" fire, the blue line fell back to the shelter of the ravines, but only for a short time.[20]

"At this juncture," wrote General Hovey," I gave the command `forward' as loud as I could." The entire Federal line advanced as regiments from Illinois, Indiana, Iowa, and Ohio surged forward in overpowering numbers. One soldier boasted, the movement was "executed with the wildest enthusiasm." Rushing through the dense forest amidst a hail of lead, the men of the XIII Corps plunged into the ravines, through the canebrakes and scampered up the opposite slope. Bursting into the open fields near the Foster house, they surged toward the Confederate guns which stood only a few yards away. The advance was so rapid that the Mississippians of the Pettus Flying Artillery barely had enough time to limber up and retire. The Virginians were not as fortunate. With only two horses left, they double shotted their weapons with canister for a final volley. Before the lanyards were pulled, however, the cannoneers where shot down or captured and the section swept away. The captors, Company K, Eleventh Indiana, quickly turned the guns on the fleeing Confederates and "delivered a few effective shots."[21]

The Confederate left collapsed. As Green's men scrambled to the rear without semblance of order, Baldwin's brigade arrived and began setting up a new line between White and Irwin branches of Willow Creek, a mile and a half east of Magnolia Church. As the men scurried into position, William Chambers observed, "Louder roared the cannon and din of the musketry grew more deafening. We met our flying squadrons, regiments cut to pieces till a remnant only were driven from their position by a force fivefold greater than their own." With the knowledge that additional troops were en route from Grand Gulf, Bowen was confident he could hold on the left long enough with Baldwin's brigade and ordered Green's weary soldiers to regroup on the march and move out the Bruinsburg road to assist Garrott. Bowen was determined to prevent Grant from cementing his grip on Mississippi soil—he would fight for every inch of ground.[22]

At Magnolia Church Generals Grant and McClernand inspected the field and surveyed their spoils of war. Two 12-pounder howitzers, three caissons, three ammunition wagons complete with teams, and more than 200 prisoners had been seized in the opening clash. The colors of the Fifteenth Arkansas were also captured. Amidst cheers of victory, John McClernand and Illinois Gov. Richard Yates took a few moments to congratulate the troops and do some campaigning of a different nature. Grant was not amused by the stump speeches and with quiet authority suggested that the advance be resumed. McClernand directed his divisions forward in pursuit of the enemy and, once reformed, the lines moved forward at noon.

As the morning hours witnessed Green being driven from his position by the principal Federal attack, the Alabamians under Garrott's command held their tenuous line on the Confederate right against steadily mounting pressure. At 8:15, the Northern soldiers of Osterhaus' division came on in splendid array, their lines neatly dressed with skirmishers well in advance, their battle flags blowing in the breeze above them, and their bayonets glistening in the sunlight. It was a sight the Alabamians had seen before on several hard fought fields, a sight they had come to respect, and a sight which would live long in the memories of men who survived the conflict.

The sight was also a familiar one to the Virginians of the Botetourt Artillery who stood in the middle of the brigade's line coolly working their guns. The section commander, Lieutenant Peters, was a veteran of the Mexican War. "[He] was not only a brave man, but the coolest man I ever saw," recalled one member of the battery. "Not for a moment did he ever lose his measure of mind." Peters kept his men posted at their guns even after "a wheel of a Napoleon was shot down. The rim and fellie shot in two and another one put on. Afterwards, axle of same gun was cut in two and gun fell. The flying splinters slightly wounded some of its detachment."[23]

The battle had been raging for hours when the battery commander, Capt. John Johnston (nephew of Confederate Gen. Joseph E. Johnston), arrived on the field. He had been sitting as a member of a court martial at Vicksburg when the battery went to Port Gibson. At the same time, the battery's remaining section, which consisted of two 6-pounders commanded by Lt. William Douthat, arrived and was sent to the aid of their struggling comrades.

With Federal fire increased by the addition of Lt. Charles B. Kimball's six 20-pounder Parrott rifles of the First Wisconsin Battery, the Virginians' position became untenable. Lieutenant Peters, with his hands behind his back, walked up to Sergeant Obenchain and said, "This is hot. And it was," wrote Obenchain years later. The sergeant continued, "William Couch #2 at right hand napoleon, was first to fall, cut almost in two at the waist. David Lieps was the second, shot just above the left eye while ramming down a charge. Frederick C. Noell shot in top of the head."[24]

Into this destructive fire went the section of 6-pounders under Lieutenant Douthat. "I tried to stop the section of 6 pound guns which had come upon me unexpectedly," wrote Obenchain. "Because of the already dead and wounded horses and the difficulty in turning, I was afraid the horses, just coming in, would become unmanageable, and just that thing did happen." "In a moment," recalled a member of the battery, "horses and gun carriage was one pile and we found it impossible to unlimber the gun. It was a horrible sight." Indeed, it was; yet the Virginians struggled frantically to free the guns and managed to get one 6-pounder into action.[25] By mid-morning, Osterhaus and his brigade commanders had untangled their regiments and resumed the advance. With Sheldon on the right and Garrard on the left, the Federals pushed forward astride the plantation road and into the valley of Centers Creek. Moving to the right oblique, Osterhaus' line swung like a huge door forcing the Confederates to slowly yield ground. On the extreme left, the 120th Ohio under Col. Marcus Spiegel surged across the Bruinsburg road and drove hard toward Garrott's flank overlooking Bayou Pierre. Spiegel reported, "I then charged upon them with the regiment, and quickly drove them from the bank to the knoll, where they rallied and made a stand, which only increased the determination of my brave boys. Rushing up the bank, we drove them pell-mell from behind the knoll."[26]

The Alabamians reluctantly fell back to the next ridge about 10:00 a.m. and reformed along a road near the Andrews house. Garrott constricted his line to present a strong front, but realized he could not hold for long unless heavily reinforced. Compounding his problems was the plight of the Virginia battery which had suffered terribly thus far at the hands of Union sharpshooters and artillery. As the Virginians withstood a galling fire from the enemy batteries, one member of the company observed that "Lieutenants Peters and Douthat [were] killed by the same shell. Lieut. Peters having upper front part of his head and

Douthat back part of his head carried away." Adding to the horrors of the day, Sergeant Obenchain heard an "agonizing shriek," which he took to be a woman's voice. Sgt. James P. Wright was ordered to investigate the voice. Obenchain wrote, "To my astonishment I found it came from a soldier at the bottom of the ravine just in front of second napoleon. For the first time I walked to edge and looked in. Two had been mortally hurt by a shell that had prematurely exploded."[27]

Although in desperate need of artillery support, Garrott mercifully ordered the Virginians to withdraw their guns. He later wrote of the situation, "Captain Johnston had exhibited distinguished gallantry, and his command had bravely stood by their guns; but by 10 o'clock the enemy's fire of artillery and sharpshooters had become so deadly that it seemed impossible for them to remain longer on the field without being sacrificed." The Virginians sadly left their dead and those who were seriously wounded on the porch of a building near which the guns had stood all morning. There was little time to mourn their loss as the two remaining guns were quickly limbered and withdrawn from the front line. As the guns were pulled to the rear, Captain Johnston, who was in ill health, turned command of the battery over to Sergeant Obenchain and rode to Port Gibson.[28]

Obenchain halted his guns and ordered a count made of the ammunition. The horses were also looked over at this time to see if any were too badly wounded for further service. This was quickly done, and the guns assumed a position one-half mile behind the Confederate line. Although the Virginians had suffered terribly, they would be called upon to render further service this day.

Without artillery support, Garrott's men found it impossible to stop the powerful Federal advance which now pushed east astride the Bruinsburg road. At this critical moment, the Alabamians were forced to slow their rate of fire and take more careful aim as ammunition was running low. "At 11 o'clock," observed Garrott, "heavy columns of the enemy could be distinctly seen, and it appeared evident that if they could be brought up to make a charge that our slender force would be overwhelmed by vastly superior numbers." Garrott dispatched Adj. John S. Smith of the Twentieth

Alabama to General Bowen with an urgent request for reinforcements and desperately needed ammunition. He then implored his men to hold on until succor arrived.[29]

Perhaps sensing the plight of his comrades on the firing line, Sergeant Obenchain of the Virginia battery returned to the field to ask for instructions. The sergeant reported to Colonel Garrott and pointed out to him where the guns were halted. Garrott asked the Virginian if he could once again assume his original position as the Confederate line was hard-pressed. Obenchain said that he could if so ordered, but Garrott slowly replied, "No that would not do you would all be murdered." The colonel then ordered Obenchain to use his judgment in selecting a position and beseeched him to "Help us all you can."[30]

The sergeant turned to return to his battery when his horse was wounded. Although the animal was badly hurt, Obenchain spurred his horse toward the battery and rode through a hail of enemy fire. Within minutes, the indomitable Virginian moved his guns forward and dropped trail on a knoll some 600 yards behind the main line. Garrott wrote with admiration in his report that, "Sergeant Obenchain, who had in the forenoon exhibited uniform coolness and unflinching nerve, promptly brought forward what was left of his command and took position as directed." The Virginians soon opened on the enemy and resumed their work.[31]

Early in the afternoon both armies regrouped for the fighting had been furious all morning and the casualties high. At 1:20 p.m., Bowen wired his superiors in Jackson:

> We have been engaged in a furious battle ever since daylight; losses very heavy. General Tracy is killed. The Virginia battery was captured by the enemy, but is retaken. We are out of ammunition for cannon and small-arms, the ordnance train of the re-enforcements not being here. They outnumber us trebly. There are three divisions against us. My whole force is engaged.

He emphasized, "The men act nobly, but the odds are overpowering."[32]

From his Jackson headquarters, Pemberton wired back, "[Maj.] General [William W.] Loring, with nearly two brigades, has started from Jackson to you," and added, "Endeavor to hold your own until they arrive, though it may be some time, as the distance is

great." He then advised Bowen, "You had better whip them before he reaches you."[33]

Fortunately for Bowen, additional reinforcements just then
came running up the road in a cloud of dust. The battle-hardened
soldiers of Col. Francis M. Cockrell's brigade, who had left Grand
Gulf at 10:00 a.m. that morning, arrived on the field full of fight
and were sent to the left to shore up Baldwin's position and help
reestablish the Confederate line. Along with Cockrell's troops
came the four guns (two 6-pounders and two 12-pounder howitzers) of Guibor's battery and the two 24-pounder howitzers of
Capt. John C. Landis' Missouri battery. The guns were quickly
moved into position and prepared to meet the Federal advance.

Francis Marion Cockrell was perhaps the best combat officer
in either army. Tenacious, daring, and bold, Cockrell was born in
Missouri in 1834 and exemplified the rugged independence of
the frontier. A lawyer by profession, he embraced the Southern
cause at the outbreak of war and became a captain in the
Missouri State Guard. He fought at Carthage, Wilson's Creek,
and Pea Ridge in which engagements he demonstrated excep-
tional combat abilities. Elevated through the grades to colonel,
Cockrell and his Missouri troops were the backbone of Bowen's
command, but, as fate would have it, the brigade was under-
strength when it reached the battlefield at Port Gibson.

Early afternoon found the Confederate right wing falling back
slowly in the face of Osterhaus' gradual, but steady advance.
Fearing for the safety of his right flank, Bowen directed the weary
soldiers of Green's brigade to reform on the march and hasten to
bolster the line astride the Bruinsburg road. The Sixth Missouri
(Col. Eugene Erwin) of Cockrell's Brigade was also rushed to the
right to steady Green's shaken troops. In reporting the movement
of his brigade, Green noted that the march was made "as speedily
as the wearied condition of my men would admit."[34]

Arriving on the right shortly after 2:00 p.m., Green moved
into position without first consulting Garrott. Rather than assume
position on the endangered right, commanding the drainages to
Bayou Pierre, his troops assumed position on Garrott's left—his
unengaged flank—near the Wheelees house overlooking Centers
Creek. As his troops settled into position, Green went to Sergeant

Obenchain of the Virginia battery. "He explained in detail our condition," wrote Obenchain, "and was afraid we could not hold the enemy back until night when we would have to retreat." The sergeant continued, "I was to be notified when the retreat was about to be begun and while the retreat was being made I was to do all in my power to hold the enemy in check until our regiments got far enough away when I would be notified to leave the field." Green added that the guns "might be captured, but it was the best that could be done."[35]

It is evident from the placement of his troops and the conversation with Obenchain that the morning engagement took a lot of the fight out of Martin Green which certainly attests to the bitter nature of the Battle of Port Gibson.

The same could not be said of John Bowen, however, whose fiery spirit was intensified as the fighting resumed early in the afternoon. The morning fight taught Bowen that the exposed ridge tops were not suited for a strong defense and directed Baldwin's men into position astride the Rodney road between White and Irwin branches of Willow Creek. In the tangled growth of the creek bottoms, the Confederates would make less conspicuous targets and minimize the effectiveness of both Federal superiority of numbers and the powerful Union artillery.

Baldwin's brigade was deployed with the Thirty-first Louisiana (Lt. Col. S. H. Griffin) on the right, north of the Rodney road, the Seventeenth Louisiana (Col. Robert Richardson) in the center, south of the road, and the Fourth Mississippi (Lt. Col. Thomas N. Adaire) on the left. The line formed a slight salient at the point of which were placed the two guns of Landis' battery. The Forty-sixth Mississippi (Col. Claudius W. Sears) was posted on a hill 600 yards in rear of the line in support of Guibor's battery. Cockrell's two regiments, the Third and Fifth Missouri commanded by Col. William R. Gause and Lt. Col. Robert S. Bevier respectively, were held in reserve and posted to protect Baldwin's left flank.

Shortly after noon, McClernand resumed the advance from Magnolia Church. The divisions of Hovey and Carr, deployed in double line of battle, led the way followed by A. J. Smith's division in column. Combing the area between the Rodney road and Centers Creek, the Federals gathered dozens of Confederate stragglers who attempted to hide in the brush. The advance was slow and meticulous as the troops clambered through the forest and crossed Arnolds Creek. Climbing out of the creek bottom and onto an open ridge, the Federals came under artillery fire from Guibor's and Landis' batteries and Confederate skirmishers added their sting.

The blue line came to a halt as McClernand and his subordinates reconnoitered the enemy position and straightened out their line. Puzzled by the enemy disposition, McClernand feared his men were advancing into a trap and brought up reserve units to extend his line. His also called on Grant for reinforcements. Responding to the situation as if by instinct, Captain Griffiths quickly moved the six guns of his First Iowa Battery into position on the ridge to provide fire support. The six 10-pounder Parrotts of Capt. Ambrose A. Blount's Seventeenth Ohio Battery were also wheeled into position and raked the woods in their front with shell. Under the protective fire of these batteries, McClernand completed his deployment by moving into position the two brigades of A. J. Smith's division, and Stevenson's brigade of Logan's division. Once completed, the former congressman had four brigades deployed along a 2,000-yard front with the left resting on Centers Creek, and three brigades were held in reserve near the center of the line in support of the artillery. Bowen watched in awe from his command post on the high ground east of Irwin Branch as the Federals deployed overwhelming numbers opposite his thin gray line. The Union line extended well beyond his flanks, yet he was determined to fight for every inch of ground in hope that the reinforcements promised earlier by Pemberton might arrive enabling him to conduct a successful defense of Port Gibson. At 3 o'clock, Bowen wired Pemberton, "I still hold my position. We have fought 20,000 men since dawn, besides skirmishing last night. They are pressing me hard on the right. My center is firm; the left is weak." He then asked in desperation, "When can Loring get here?"[36]

Around 3:00 p.m., McClernand's troops swept off the ridge and crossed White Branch. It was difficult for the soldiers to maintain alignment as they struggled through the dense canebrakes. Clawing their way up the opposite slope which separated the drainages of White and Irwin branches, the Federals were met by "a most terrific and jarring fire" as Baldwin's men let loose a well-aimed volley. Driven off the forward slope, the blue line instantly dissolved as men scrambled for cover. In "some confusion," recalled one Northern soldier, the men found shelter in the thickets along White Branch. Protected from the blistering fire of Guibor's and Landis' batteries, and a section of the Pettus Flying Artillery, the Federals clung to their position. For the next 90 minutes, a bitter firefight raged as McClernand determined his next course of action.[37]

As his favorite tactic, a frontal assault along the entire line, was being checked by determined resistance, the commander of the XIII Corps directed his subordinates to employ tactics similar to those that had won such sweeping success in the morning near Magnolia Church. Shuffling his units to provide adequate flank protection, McClernand massed 21 regiments on an 800-yard front with the intention of striking for the center of the Confederate line.

Reacting to the Federal buildup opposite his center and the slow extension of the enemy's line beyond his left flank, Bowen moved to strike the Federal right flank to prevent it from locating the Natchez road and roll it up. (Bowen was fearful that the Federals would locate the Natchez road, only 1,200 yards beyond his left, enabling them to push a strong force around his flank and seize Port Gibson.) Colonel Cockrell was directed to move his two regiments into position behind a knoll several hundred yards beyond the enemy flank. To conceal the movement, the Missourians pushed through the dense timber which lined Irwin Branch and reached their objective. Forming his men in column by battalions, Cockrell placed the Fifth Missouri in the lead followed by the Third Missouri. Once in position, Cockrell unsheathed his sword and yelled for his men to charge.

The Confederate movement, however, was not concealed as Bowen had hoped, but was spotted by General Hovey who moved quickly to counter this deployment. Hovey ordered the four batteries of his division (24 guns) into position on the right along the ridge overlooking White Branch. He also shifted several regiments to meet this threat to his flank and called up reserve

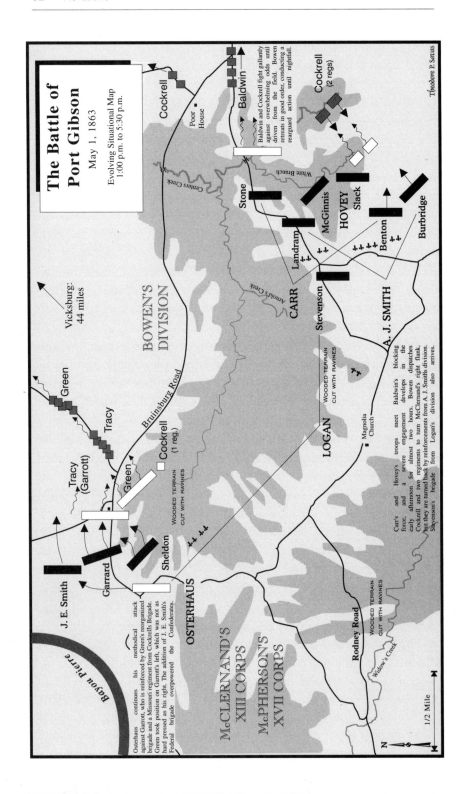

The Battle of Port Gibson

May 1, 1863

Evolving Situational Map
1:00 p.m. to 5:30 p.m.

Theodore P. Savas

Vicksburg:
44 miles

BOWEN'S DIVISION

Bayou Pierre

J. E. Smith

Tracy
(Garrott)

Tracy

Green

Green

Garrard

Cockrell
(1 reg.)

WOODED TERRAIN
CUT WITH RAVINES

Sheldon

Bruinsburg Road

Cockrell

Poor
House

Baldwin

Baldwin and Cockrell fight gallantly against overwhelming odds until driven from the field. Bowen retreats in good order, conducting a rearguard action until nightfall.

Cockrell
(2 regs)

Centers Creek

Stone

White Branch

McGinnis

HOVEY

Slack

Burbridge

Landram

Benton

Arnold's Creek

CARR

Stevenson

A. J. SMITH

LOGAN

WOODED TERRAIN
CUT WITH RAVINES

Magnolia
Church

OSTERHAUS

McCLERNAND'S
XIII CORPS

McPHERSON'S
XVII CORPS

Rodney Road

WOODED TERRAIN
CUT WITH RAVINES

Widow's Creek

Osterhaus continues his methodical attack against Garrott, who is reinforced by Green's reorganized brigade and a Missouri regiment from Cockrell's Brigade. Green took position on Garrott's left, which was not as hard pressed as his right. The addition of J. E. Smith's Federal brigade overpowered the Confederates.

Carr's and Hovey's troops meet Baldwin's blocking force, and a severe engagement develops in the early afternoon for almost two hours. Bowen dispatches Cockrell and two regiments to turn McClernand's right flank, but they are turned back by reinforcements from A. J. Smith's division. Stevenson's brigade from Logan's division also arrives.

1/2 Mile

N

units. Hurrying into position, the Federals formed their lines and fixed bayonets. "These lines had not more than been formed," reported Col. James R. Slack of the Forty-seventh Indiana, when the enemy charged "with terrific yells, and could not be seen, because of the very thick growth of cane, until they reached a point within 30 yards of my line."[38]

Pouring out of the creek bottom, Cockrell's Missourians raised the "Rebel yell" as they struck the flank of the Federal line and began rolling it up. The Fifty-sixth Ohio, on the extreme Union right, began to waver almost immediately and yield ground as did the next regiment in line, the Forty-seventh Indiana. Pushing onward, the Confederates slammed into the rugged veterans of the Twenty-ninth Wisconsin whose colonel reported them as "being hotly pressed with great slaughter." To stem the gray tide which swept irresistibly over the field, Union artillery poured canister into their ranks with devastating effect. Capt. George W. Covell of the Third Missouri recalled, "Their artillery opened on us with great rapidity, and as soon as we got within range the infantry poured the Minie balls into our ranks as thick and fast as hailstones from a thundercloud or rain drops in an April shower." Covell had never experienced such a heavy fire and later wrote, "The storm of leaden rain and iron hail which was flying through the air was almost sufficient to obscure the sunlight."[39]

Confederate momentum soon waned as the four battle-tested regiments of Brig. Gen. William P. Benton's brigade arrived to check their advance. Regiments from other Union brigades were also rushed to the area in a frantic effort to bolster the crumbling line. In the face of such concentrated fire power, the gallant charge ground to a halt and soldiers in blue and gray fired away at one another with "great spirit and pertinacity" at a distance of only 20 yards. One Union regimental commander enveloped by the fury of battle noted, "the pieces of our men became so heated from rapid, continuous firing as to make it impossible for them to continue firing longer with safety to themselves."[40]

From his command post on the high ground east of Irwin Branch, Bowen watched helplessly as the Federals sent large numbers of fresh troops to contain Cockrell's advance. His hopes for success were shattered as he saw the enemy deploy what he believed to be three brigades in front of their artillery to receive the charge. Bowen reported that of these brigades, "The first was routed, the second wavered, but the third stood firm, and, after a long and desperate contest, we had to give up the attempt." Their attack checked, Cockrell's men reluctantly fell back over the ridge to the east where they reformed alongside the Fourth Mississippi. Bowen rode among them offering words of encouragement and praised the valor of his Missourians saying, "I did not suspect that any of you would get away, but the charge had to be made, or my little army was lost."[41]

Bowen was somewhat relieved when the Federals did not press their advantage by a vigorous pursuit of Cockrell's battered regiments. Yet, he remained concerned about the security of his left flank where the Federals had massed sufficient strength to turn his line. Apprehensive that the enemy may have located the Natchez road and were marching on Port Gibson, Bowen boldly ordered Baldwin's weary soldiers to press forward to ascertain the enemy's strength.

The reliable Baldwin brought the Forty-sixth Mississippi up from its reserve position and placed the men in an open field north of the Rodney road. He endeavored to advance with a line of three regiments with the Forty-sixth Mississippi on the right, Seventeenth Louisiana in the center, south of the road, and the Fourth Mississippi on the left. "Before the dispositions could be entirely completed," he reported, "the enemy opened a sweeping fire of . . . shrapnel, completely enfilading the road and covering all approach from my center and right." Compelled by the heavy fire to fall back, Baldwin knew "that an attempt to move forward would result in the destruction of the entire command without accomplishing the object."[42]

Bowen also realized the futility of further action. At 5:15 p.m. he notified Pemberton, "I still hold my position. I will have to retire under cover of night to other side of Bayou Pierre and await reenforcements."[43]

The Confederates clung to their position in the creek bottom and desperately waited for the sun to set. Only grudgingly did they yield ground in the face of overwhelming numbers. Unable to shatter such determined resistance, Brig. Gen. John D.

Stevenson called on the Eighth Michigan Light Artillery to drive the enemy from his front. The battery was led by the redoubtable Capt. Samuel De Golyer, considered by many as the finest artillerist in the army. A man of tremendous courage and daring, De Golyer unlimbered his four 10-pounder James rifles and two 12-pounder howitzers just below the crest. Rounds of canister and case shot were rammed down the cannon which were then man-handled up the hill to a point where only the muzzles were exposed. On De Golyer's command the guns opened a "most unexpected and terrible fire" which dispersed the Confederates in "rapid flight." In reporting the action of the Michigan battery, Brig. Gen. John D. Stevenson wrote that De Golyer's guns "opened a destructive fire of shell and canister upon the enemy, compelling him to retire under cover of brush and timber."[44]

With Union artillery now in command of the Irwin Branch bottom, blueclad infantrymen poured over the ridge, crossed the creek, and drove Bowen's men slowly up the opposite slope. Within moments, Confederate resistance ceased and the soldiers clad in butternut and gray withdrew singly or in small groups from the field. At 5:30 p.m. Bowen reluctantly gave the order for his force to withdraw from the field via the Andrew's farm road toward Bayou Pierre. As Cockrell's troops took up the line of march, Bowen telegraphed his superiors in Jackson, "I am falling back across Bayou Pierre. I will endeavor to hold that position until reenforcements arrive. . . .Want of ammunition is one of the main causes of our retreat. The men did nobly, holding out the whole day against overwhelming odds."[45]

Along the Bruinsburg road, the battle still raged but with similar results. Throughout the afternoon, Osterhaus directed the Union force with uncharacteristic caution. Although he enjoyed numerical superiority over the thin brigades of Garrott and Green, the difficult terrain, dense vegetation, and stiff resistance offered by the Alabamians in particular, led Osterhaus to move with caution. Reinforced in mid-afternoon by the arrival of Brig. Gen. John E. Smith's brigade of Logan's division, the Union force renewed its efforts to flank the Confederates posted north of the road.

It was evident to Colonel Erwin (a grandson of Henry Clay) of the Sixth Missouri on the Confederate right that the Federals were making a concerted effort to turn Garrott's right flank. He also sensed that Garrott's left was about to falter under the steady pressure of enemy fire and knew "that unless some assistance was afforded them," the Alabamians "would be driven from their position." On his own initiative, Erwin ordered his men to fix bayonets. The 400 Missourians, led by their colonel, raised the Rebel yell and rushed over the astonished enemy skirmish line. Driving the Federals back, Erwin's men recaptured the two disabled guns of the Botetourt Artillery which had been abandoned earlier in the day. All this was to no avail, however, for the odds against them were too great. The attack was quickly contained and, after 90 minutes of fierce combat, the Missourians soon found themselves in danger of being enveloped. Erwin wrote of the situation, "I reluctantly determined to withdraw from a position which had been so gallantly won and perseveringly maintained." In their hasty withdrawal, the Missourians were compelled to abandon the disabled guns of the Virginia battery.[46]

Around 5:00 p.m., additional Union troops arrived to support Osterhaus on the Bruinsburg road as Brig. Gen. Elias Dennis' brigade of Logan's division reached the field. With such overwhelming numbers at hand, Osterhaus ordered a general advance along his entire line. Fortunately for the battle-weary Confederates, orders came from Bowen to withdraw from the field. Martin Green quickly pulled his regiments out of line and retreated in good order along the Andrew's farm road toward Bayou Pierre. Colonel Garrott was directed to withdraw by the left flank which movement he reported was "immediately executed as rapidly as possible." Capt. Samuel C. Kelly of the Thirtieth Alabama was more candid in his description of the withdrawal as he recorded in the pages of his diary, "We were gaunt and in fine condition for running." The Alabamians fell in behind Green and, after a march of 4 miles, crossed the suspension bridge over Bayou Pierre just as darkness fell.[47]

Near sunset, as the grayclad soldiers began their withdrawal from the bloody field, Sergeant Obenchain of the Botetourt Artillery was notified as "the information was necessary to prevent me from firing into our own troops." The Virginians did, however, kill some of their own troops in their efforts to keep Federal pursuit at a distance. When the troops had retired, Obenchain limbered up his two remaining guns and left the field. The sergeant wrote, "Overtaking the rear regiment [Thirty-first Alabama] it gave us the road to pass through and taking position again we marched in that order to the bridge over Bayou Pierre." Once over the suspension bridge, the weary soldiers of Garrott's, Green's, and Cockrell's brigades bivouacked for the night. Col. A. C. Riley with the First Missouri Infantry of Cockrell's brigade arrived from Coon Island Lake and was deployed to protect the crossing assisted by the guns of the Botetourt Artillery.[48]

Baldwin's men had been cut off from the Andrew's farm road by elements of John Smith's Federal brigade who seized the road before the Confederates could make good their escape. Forced to withdraw to the east through the town of Port Gibson, Baldwin reported, "The enemy pressed closely upon our rear until near the town, when they allowed us to continue our march undisturbed." His tired soldiers crossed Little Bayou Pierre at 9:00 p.m. and set fire to the suspension bridge behind them. On through the long night they marched, over roads crowded with fleeing citizens and crossed Big Bayou Pierre at Grindstone Ford at midnight. Taking no chances in case of Federal pursuit, Baldwin also had his men set fire to the bridge at that point. Finally, at 9:00 a.m. on May 2, Baldwin's footsore infantry staggered into Bowen's camp.[49]

There was no vigorous pursuit by the Federals as darkness enveloped the fields and forest west of Port Gibson on May 1, 1863. The troops were exhausted by the fierce combat and their strength drained by the heat and humidity. As the soldiers bivouacked for the night, details were sent to collect the wounded and bury the dead. Fred Grant, the general's eldest son who accompanied his father throughout the Vicksburg campaign, had arrived on the field in time to witness the closing action. Out of curiosity, the young boy joined one such detachment and later wrote of his experience:

> I joined a detachment which was collecting the dead for burial, but, sickening at the sights, I made my way with another detachment, which was gathering the wounded, to a log house which had been appropriated for a hospital. Here

the scenes were so terrible that I became faint and ill, and making my way to a tree, sat down, the most woe-begone twelve-year-old lad in America.

Young Fred was not alone in his anguish, but Union troops who had experienced battle for the first time and even those who had witnessed the horrors of battle many times, sickened at the sights on this bloody field. Dead and wounded soldiers could be seen everywhere as their bloody forms lie scattered in the fields, forests, and creek bottoms. Accouterments of all descriptions littered the field and, as darkness enveloped the scene of carnage, the cries of wounded soldiers pierced the night. Union losses totaled 131 killed, 719 wounded, and 25 missing.[50]

Confederate losses were reported at 68 killed, 380 wounded, and 384 missing. Although the returns are far from complete, Bowen's small force suffered proportionately far greater casualties than the Union Army of the Tennessee. The Confederate soldiers did indeed do "nobly," fighting for an entire day against an enemy superior in numbers and withdrawing from the field in good order. As Bowen's command was withdrawing from the field of battle, Pemberton relayed the news to Richmond, "A furious battle has been going on since daylight just below Port Gibson. . . .Large reenforcements should be sent me from other departments. Enemy's movement threatens Jackson, and, if successful, cuts off Vicksburg and Port Hudson from the east. . . ." The news was frightening to the most stout Southern heart which yearned to achieve independence. The consequences of Confederate reaction, both politically and militarily, to the deteriorating situation in Mississippi would determine the fate of a nation and her people.[51]

Grant ordered the attack renewed at dawn, but the Confederates had already evacuated the area. The battle was over, but for the rugged soldiers of the Union army, the inland campaign had just begun. For Grant, victory at Port Gibson not only secured his beachhead on Mississippi soil, but with the Confederate evacuation of Grand Gulf on May 3, he gained that strategic landing as a base to support the next phase of the campaign toward Vicksburg. From there the road led to Vicksburg, Chattanooga, and ultimately to Appomattox. The Battle of Port Gibson was but a prelude to victory.

CHAPTER FIVE

DISASTER AND DISGRACE

John C. Pemberton and the Battle of Champion Hill

On May 16, 1863, John A. Leavy, a surgeon with the Confederate Army of Vicksburg, took pen in hand to write in the pages of his diary critical observations of Lt. Gen. John C. Pemberton and the battle of Champion Hill. "To-day proved to the nation the value of a general," he began. "Pemberton is either a traitor, or the most incompetent officer in the confederacy. *Indecision, Indedecision* [sic], *Indecision.*" He lamented, "We have been badly defeated where we might have given the enemy a severe repulse. We have been defeated in detail, and have lost, O God! how many brave and gallant soldiers." Leavy's sentiments were echoed by hundreds of soldiers clad in butternut and gray who on that day and into the next streamed toward the fortress city on the river cursing their commanding general stating, "It's all Pem's fault."[1]

News of Confederate defeat spread as wildfire throughout the city. Mrs. Emma Balfour, a Vicksburg socialite, wrote with trembling hand, "My pen almost refuses to tell of our terrible disaster of yesterday. . . . *We are defeated*—our army in confusion and the carnage, awful! Whole batteries and brigades taken prisoners-awful! Awful!" Throughout the afternoon and well into the night of May 17 the flood of demoralized soldiers poured into Vicksburg. Mrs. Balfour recorded of the scene in which she was engulfed, "Nothing like order prevailed, of course, as divisions, brigades and regiments were broken and separated."[2]

Details of the engagement at Champion Hill were slowly pieced together by the shocked citizenry of Vicksburg. To those who listened to the woeful details of battle, one fact became apparent. The incisive Mrs. Balfour, sensitive of the discontentment with General Pemberton being freely expressed by soldiers and officers alike, recorded the essence of failure with these words: "I knew from all I saw and heard that it was want of confidence in the General commanding that was the cause of our disaster." Late that night, overcome by emotion, she confided her fears to the pages of her diary as she wrote, "What is to become of all the living things in this place . . .shut up as in a trap. . .God only knows." Mrs. Balfour's perception of affairs proved both accurate and ominous, for less than two months later, the Stars and Bars atop the courthouse in Vicksburg was replaced by the Stars and Stripes.[3]

A city of unparalleled significance, Vicksburg was known as the "Gibraltar of the Confederacy," and proved a tough nut to crack. Seemingly impervious to capture by Union land and naval forces, the city by 1863 had become the symbol of hope for Southern independence. President Jefferson Davis, himself a resident of Warren County, of which Vicksburg was the county seat, referred to the city as "the nailhead that held the South's two halves together." After the fall of Vicksburg he expressed his views more poignantly to General Pemberton: "I thought and still think you did right to risk an army for the purpose of keeping command of even a section of the Mississippi River. Had you succeeded, none would have blamed, had you not made the attempt few would have defended your course."[4]

The momentous events which transpired in Mississippi in the late spring and early summer of 1863 were largely ignored by the Northern press. Overshadowed by the bloody actions in the East at Chancellorsville and Gettysburg, the campaign for control of the Mississippi River failed to gain the national attention merited by such a large scale and significant operation. A century would pass before British military historian J.F.C. Fuller, in writing of the Vicksburg campaign, declared, "The drums of Champion's Hill sounded the doom of Richmond." (As General Fuller was among the first to recognize the significance of the Vicksburg campaign, we shall overlook the common mistake he makes in referring to the battle as "Champion's Hill" versus the correct name of Champion Hill.)[5]

Despite General Fuller's observation, only a few stalwart historians, most notable of whom is Edwin C. Bearss, have ventured to analyze the impact of Champion Hill on the Vicksburg campaign and the fate of the Confederate nation. Perhaps more significant than any larger or bloodier action of the Civil War, the Battle of Champion

Hill was the decisive action of the campaign for Vicksburg, led to the fall of the Confederate bastion on the Mississippi River, and truly, sealed the fate of Richmond. The battle which raged on the heights of Champion Hill on May 16, 1863, and the military leadership of John C. Pemberton in particular, thus warrant further investigation.

Lt. Gen. John C. Pemberton commanded the Department of Mississippi and East Louisiana from headquarters in the capital city of Jackson. A native of Philadelphia, Pennsylvania, born on August 10, 1814, he was the second of thirteen children born to John and Rebecca Clifford Pemberton. Although of Quaker stock, John grew quite active socially and enjoyed parties, dances, and the theater. Yet, he was a quiet young man who shied away from intimacy and counted few close friends. (Among his boyhood friends was George G. Meade who was destined to command Union forces at Gettysburg.) After entering the University of Pennsylvania, John sought an appointment to the United States Military Academy at West Point in order to study civil engineering. President Andrew Jackson, a close friend of Pemberton's father, gladly awarded the appointment on May 15, 1833, and John embarked on a military career.

At West Point, Pemberton was an average cadet who did not excel academically and accrued demerits by the score. At one point during his first class (senior) year, he was arrested for breaking academy regulations dealing with possession of liquor. Only after the entire class signed a pledge not to drink for the remaining days at the academy were the charges against him dropped. John went on to com-

Lt. Gen. John C. Pemberton
Generals in Gray

plete the rigorous curriculum of West Point and at graduation stood 27 out of 50 cadets in the class of 1837.

Pemberton was assigned to duty with the Fourth Artillery in which he served during the Second Seminole War and in the Mexican War. In Mexico, the young lieutenant saw action under Brig. Gen. Zachary Taylor in the early engagements of the war at Palo Alto, Resaca de la Palma, and Matamoras. He later served as an aide-de-camp on the staff of Maj. Gen. William J. Worth in the campaign for Monterrey and during the drive on Mexico City. John proved himself a brave and energetic officer of whom his superiors took notice. His actions on the fields of battle at Monterrey and Molino del Rey earned him two brevets for "gallant and meritorious conduct." The laurels won in Mexico would be the proudest achievement of his long military career.

Shortly after his return from Mexico, Pemberton married Martha Thompson of Norfolk, Virginia. Devoted to one another, their marriage was one of bliss and produced seven children. Pattie, the name by which Pemberton affectionately called his wife, was a beautiful, yet domineering woman who held tremendous sway over her husband. As the nation drifted to the brink of civil war, John was torn between love of country and love for his wife. Upon the secession of Virginia, Pemberton's adopted state, Pattie wrote John from Norfolk, "My darling husband why are you not with us? Why do you stay?" Pemberton biographer Michael Ballard asserts that "Pattie had made clear where her heart lay, and he would never have turned against her." On April 24, 1861, John Pemberton resigned his commission as captain in the United States Army and offered his sword to Virginia.[6]

Governor John Letcher of Virginia quickly nominated Pemberton to be a lieutenant colonel in the state force. Less than two months later, the northern-born Pemberton was made a brigadier general in the Confederate army. John's rapid rise was based more on the need for experienced officers than merited by his abilities. The trend continued as he was promoted major general to rank from January 14, 1862, and later that same year to the grade of lieutenant general. During this period Pemberton gained administrative experience as he served briefly in the Virginia tidewater, then as commander of the Department of South Carolina and Georgia. In the fall of 1862, with little useful field or combat experience, he was named commander of the Department of Mississippi and East Louisiana and left for a rendezvous with destiny at Vicksburg.

Responsible for the defense of the Mississippi River and the twin bastions of Vicksburg and Port Hudson, Pemberton had little time to acquaint himself with his new command as Federal forces were already active within the department. His administrative abilities were quickly taxed to the limit as the needs of his department were many and the resources few. Effective departmental operations were further plagued by a myriad of problems: poor staff work, mediocre subordinates, inadequate rail transportation, lack of troops, especially cavalry, and the necessities of food, clothing, medicine, and ammunition were in woefully short supply. Although Pemberton immersed himself in the administrative details of departmental command, it was combat abilities that were of greater need by the Confederacy. In that regard, however, events would soon demonstrate that John Pemberton had been promoted far beyond his capacities to command.

The Confederate commander was unbalanced by Grant's landing and the subsequent defeat of Southern forces at Port Gibson. Confused, uncertain, and with his confidence shattered, Pemberton stumbled through the crisis with predictable indecision. Biographer Ballard writes, "that when Grant crossed the Mississippi, he pushed Pemberton across his personal Rubicon." As the situation in Mississippi was rapidly deteriorating, Gen. Joseph E. Johnston advised Pemberton: "If Grant's army lands on this side of the river, the safety of Mississippi depends on beating it. For that object you should unite your whole force." Rather than move with determination to destroy Grant's invading army, however, Pemberton notified President Davis that he would "concentrate for defense of Vicksburg and Jackson." With only defense of the fortress city in mind, Pemberton moved to Vicksburg to assume field command of the army.[7]

Grant moved quickly to exploit his initial success. Rather than march due north toward Vicksburg, he advanced his army in a north-easterly direction with the intention of cutting Pemberton's line of supply, the Southern Railroad of Mississippi, which connected Vicksburg with Jackson and, via Jackson, points elsewhere in the Confederacy. Advancing over a broad front, Grant pushed deep into Mississippi with his left flank resting on the Big Black River forcing Pemberton to scatter his available force to guard all river crossings.

By May 7, Pemberton had divined Grant's intentions of cutting the railroad, probably at Big Black River Bridge, but it was not until

May 12, after a loss of five valuable days, that he began to move his army east toward that river. He informed both Davis and Johnston, "The enemy is apparently moving in heavy force toward Edwards Depot, Southern Railroad. With my limited force, I will do all I can to meet him." Boarding the cars, he then transferred his headquarters to Bovina, seven miles east of Vicksburg, near the Big Black River Bridge.[8]

On May 12, as Union forces approached the village of Raymond, Pemberton issued a circular to his army which read in part:

> The hour of trial has come! The enemy who has so long threatened Vicksburg in front, has, at last, effected a landing in this Department; and his march into the in-terior of Mississippi has been marked by the devastation of the fairest portions of the State!...The issue involves everything endeared to a free people! ...You fight for your country, homes, wives, children, and the birth-right of freemen!...God, who rules in the affairs of men and nations, loves justice and hates wickedness. He will not allow a cause so just, to be trampled in the dust. In the day of conflict, let each man appealing to Him for strength, strike home for victory, and our tri-umph is at once assured. A grateful country will hail us as deliverers, and cherish the memory of those who may fall as martyrs in her defense.

In closing, he urged his men, "Soldiers! be vigilant, brave and ac-tive; let there be no cowards, nor laggards, nor stragglers from the ranks—and the God of battle will certainly crown our efforts with success."[9]

In the fighting which raged along the banks of Fourteen Mile Creek, southwest of Raymond on May 12, elements of the Union army overwhelmed a lone Confederate brigade and forced it back toward Jackson. The fight at Raymond convinced Grant that Jackson must be neutralized before he pushed on to Vicksburg. It was Grant's intention to destroy Jackson as a rail and communications center and scatter any Confederate reinforcements which might be on the way to Vicksburg.

On May 13 as Pemberton advanced a portion of his army across the Big Black River to Edwards, Grant's army closed in on Jackson from two directions. In the capital city, as soldiers in butternut and gray worked feverishly to strengthen fortifications, clear fields of fire, and form obstructions of felled trees, Confederate reinforcements be-gan to arrive by train from the east. A train also brought Joseph E. Johnston with orders to save Mississippi. Informed that four Federal divisions were in Clinton, between Jackson and Edwards, Johnston dispatched three couriers to Pemberton urging him to, "If practicable, come up on his rear at once." He emphasized, "To beat such a detachment, would be of immense value. . . .Time is all-important." Although Johnston notified Pemberton that "The force here could cooperate," he had no intention of marching into battle. Realizing that the city's defenses were neither extensive nor properly placed, and believing that the enemy would soon advance on Jackson in force, he wired the authorities in Richmond, "I am too late." Rather than fight to save Jackson and arrest Grant's movements, Johnston ordered the city evacuated.[10]

The following morning, Union forces stormed Jackson, swept aside token resistance, and seized the capital of Mississippi. Not wishing to waste combat troops on occupation, Grant ordered Jackson neutralized militarily. The torch was applied to machine shops and factories, telegraph lines were cut and railroad tracks destroyed. With Jackson neutralized and Johnston's force scattered to the winds, Grant turned his army west with confidence toward his objective—Vicksburg.

As flames engulfed Jackson, Pemberton prepared to cross the Big Black River on May 14 and join his army at Edwards. Prior to leaving Bovina he received by one of the trio of couriers a copy of Johnston's dispatch of the 13th. Unaware that Jackson was now in Federal hands, Pemberton replied, "I move at once with whole available force about 16,000 [22,000]. . .The men have been marching several days, are much fatigued, and, I fear, will straggle very much." He cautioned Johnston, "In directing this move, I do not think you fully comprehend the position that Vicksburg will be left in, but I comply at once with your order."[11]

Doubt, however, soon overtook Pemberton on the road to Edwards. Believing that Johnston's plan was "extremely hazardous" and would have disastrous results for his army, upon his arrival in Edwards, Pemberton suspended the movement and called for a council of war. A Northerner by birth, Pemberton was well aware of the distrust which existed of him in the army and among his own subordinates. Consequently, he frequently called councils of war to determine what course of action his subordinates would support. More often than not, he would adopt the council's recommendations—even if they went against his own judgment. Reading out loud to his subordinates Johnston's orders, Pemberton expressed his doubts concerning the projected movement and reminded his generals that "the leading and great duty of . . .[the] army was to defend Vicksburg."[12]

Eager for battle, many of his subordinates favored Johnston's plan of attack and pressed their support on Pemberton. Maj. Gen. William W. Loring, Pemberton's senior and most troublesome division commander, then stood and offered an alternate plan of action. The irascible Loring recommended that the army advance against the Raymond-Port Gibson road to get astride Grant's supply and communications line at Dillon's plantation, and force the Federals to attack them in a position of their choosing.

Instructed by the president to hold Vicksburg at all cost, Pemberton was reluctant to move beyond the Big Black River, let alone farther east. He recommended that the army take up a strong position behind the Big Black River and await Grant's attack. Confident that the Federals would be checked, he could then seize the initiative, push the enemy into the interior of Mississippi, and defeat them in detail. In spite of Pemberton's rationale, the council favored Loring's proposal to which the commanding general reluctantly acquiesced. In informing Johnston of his decision, Pemberton noted his force was insufficient to attack the enemy or attempt to cut his way through to Jackson. Upon receipt of Pemberton's dispatch on May 15, Johnston was livid and reiterated his previous order stating "Our being compelled to leave Jackson makes your plan impracticable. The only mode by which we can unite is by your moving directly to Clinton." As the courier dashed off in a cloud of dust, Pemberton's army prepared to take up the line of march to the southeast.[13]

Reveille was sounded at an early hour on May 15, 1863. Before the shrill notes had faded in the distance the soldiers clad in butternut and gray were in motion rolling their blankets, kindling fires, and cooking their meager rations. The appearance of order within the ranks belied the situation among the army's high command. Through fault or neglect poor staff work led to a costly delay as insufficient rations and munitions had been stockpiled in Edwards. Before the troops could get underway, a train had to be sent to Vicksburg for the necessary supplies. Upon return to Edwards the cars were quickly unloaded and the supplies distributed. It was not until 1:00 p.m. that the

Maj. Gen. William W. Loring
Generals in Gray

column was formed and the men took up the line of march with a train of 400 wagons bringing up the rear.

The entire force moved over a single axis of advance, the Raymond—Edwards road. The soldiers marched at a slow yet steady pace for the road was narrow and muddy. After a march of only two miles the head of the column came to a halt as it reached rain-swollen Bakers Creek. Although the army had been in Edwards since the 13th, Pemberton was unaware that a key bridge only a few miles from his headquarters was out and the ford at that point impassable from the cloudburst that drenched the area at midday on the 14th. Unfamiliar with the area, Pemberton lost additional precious time as his troops waited for the water to subside.

Late that afternoon, however, the Confederate commander was informed that the bridge over Bakers Creek on the Jackson road was intact. Resuming the march, the long column moved up the right bank of the stream to the Jackson road and crossed the creek. Two miles beyond the bridge, the head of the column reached a plantation road where the men turned southwest and continued on until they reentered the Raymond-Edwards road. Turning east, the column continued the march until around 7:00 p.m. when the weary soldiers in the vanguard were instructed to bed down for the night near the home of Mrs. Sarah Ellison.

Loring's division, which led the march, bivouacked near the Ellison house at sundown. The rugged veterans of Brig. Gen. John S. Bowen's division stopped along the Ratliff plantation road at 10:00 p.m. Noticing the ominous glare of campfires to the east, Bowen

threw out pickets, placed his men in line of battle, and readied his artillery before letting his men get some much needed sleep. The divi-

Maj. Gen. Carter Stevenson
Generals in Gray

sion last in line, commanded by Maj. Gen. Carter Stevenson, did not leave Edwards until 5:00 p.m. After a grueling march, the weary soldiers finally halted along the plantation road at 3:00 a.m. No security measures were taken by Stevenson who permitted his men to fall by the side of the road to rest. The wagon train, which brought up the rear of the column, moved steadily throughout the night and reached the Crossroads at daybreak.

The soldiers of Pemberton's army were exhausted as they went into bivouac. Through a series of blunders, for which the commanding general must shoulder the blame, the men had been up since before daylight, waited throughout the morning for munitions and rations, then marched through the heat of the day until after sunset—in some cases well into the morning of May 16. In contrast, the Union Army of the Tennessee was well-rested after a day of leisurely marching during which Grant concentrated seven divisions (32,000 men), on a line from Bolton to Raymond facing east toward Edwards. The stage was thus set for the climatic battle which would decide the fate of Vicksburg, and on which rested the dreams of the Southern nation.

At 5:00 a.m., as the first streaks of dawn appeared in the eastern sky on May 16, a train heading east pulled into Clinton where it was stopped by Union soldiers. (As Pemberton was aware that Union troops had entered Clinton on May 13, it remains a mystery as to why he permitted the train to continue past Edwards.) Two men from the train were ushered into the presence of General Grant. Upon questioning, they informed Grant that Pemberton's army, which they estimated to number around 25,000-strong, was in Edwards and marching to attack his rear. The Union commander ordered his army to Edwards and cautioned his corps commanders to feel for the enemy. Advancing on three parallel roads, the Union army marched to battle, confident of victory.[14]

Early on the morning of May 16, as the Union army closed on Edwards, Pemberton gathered his officers for a morning briefing at Mrs. Ellison's house. Around 7:00 a.m., the distant boom of cannon gave warning that the enemy was near. Minutes later, Col. Wirt Adams rode up and announced that the enemy was moving in force on the Raymond road and driving in the pickets. As Pemberton questioned Adams concerning the enemy force, an exhausted courier arrived and handed the general a copy of Johnston's May 14 message. Scanning the note, he learned that Jackson had fallen. The message also reiterated Johnston's order to join him in Clinton. Now, in the presence of the enemy, Pemberton decided to comply with the order. After informing his superior by which route he would march to Clinton, Pemberton issued orders for his army to reverse the line of march.[15]

What had been in rear of the column was now in front—namely the 400 wagons filled with rations and munitions. It would take time to turn the wagons around on the narrow roads and move them sufficient distance to enable the infantry to take up the line of march. Pemberton, however, did not enjoy the advantage of time as the Federals were rapidly converging on Edwards. With the sounds of battle steadily intensifying, Loring recommended that the army form line of battle stressing, "the sooner. . .the better, as the enemy would very soon be upon us."[16]

Pemberton instructed Loring to deploy his lead brigade near Mrs. Ellison's house. Brig. Gen. Lloyd Tilghman quickly deployed his brigade of Mississippians astride the road, but Pemberton was not satisfied with the position as it was vulnerable to Federal artillery fire. Selecting a new line three-quarters of a mile west of Mrs. Ellison's, the Confederate commander directed Loring to deploy his division on a ridge overlooking Jackson Creek. As the Southerners pulled back to the designated position, they destroyed the bridge across the creek.

Although a commanding position, the ridge was open and provided no protection to the troops. Loring decided to pull his men back another 600 yards to the ridge on which still stands the Coker house. The frequent changes in position evidence the indecision which plagued Southern arms on May 16. One solider in Loring's division later wrote:

> A little after daylight we were startled by a cannonade directly in our front and close to us. As yet no preparations had been made to make or receive an attack; the artillery was parked, the horses unharnessed, the general staff officers galloped around furiously delivering orders, the soldiers sprang to arms, and after innumerable maneuvers, were finally formed.

Such confusion of movement did not inspire confidence throughout the ranks. Lt. William Drennan, a staff officer in Brig. Gen. Winfield S. Featherston's brigade of Loring's division, observed of Pemberton on the morning of battle, that he "gave orders in [an] uncertain manner that implied to me that he had no mature plans for the coming battle."[17]

Adding to Pemberton's woes was friction between him and his subordinates, most notable of whom was the acerbic William Loring. Drennan recalled a verbal exchange between the two generals that morning and wrote:

> Their manner was warm—and no good feeling was evinced by either party. There was ill-will and that too displayed in a manner that was a credit of neither party. That there was no harmony—no unity of action, no clear understanding of the aims and designs of our army was clearly apparent—and instead of there existing mutual confidence on the part of the Commanding General and his subordinates—there was just the opposite.[18]

In a letter to his wife, written shortly after the battle, Drennan expounded on the relationship between the two Confederate generals:

> There is quite a feud existing between Loring and Pemberton—so far as Loring is concerned. . .in fact it amounted to that degree of hatred on the part of Loring that Captain [William] Barksdale and myself agreed that Loring would be willing for Pemberton to lose a battle provided he would be displaced.
>
> I sat down under a tree and listened to Generals Loring, Tilghman and Featherston engaged in quite an animated conversation the principal topic being General Pemberton and the affairs of the country in general. They all said harsh,

ill-natured things, made ill-tempered jests in regard to General Pemberton and
when an order came from him, the courier who brought it was not out of hearing, before they made light of it and ridiculed the plan he proposed.[19]

By 9:00 a.m., the situation was more ominous as a second Federal
column was encountered moving along the Middle road in response
to which the Confederate commander was forced to deploy his entire army. Pemberton formed his divisions along a three-mile front
on a line running southwest to northeast which guarded both the
Raymond-Edwards and Middle roads and commanded the valley of
Jackson Creek. If the Federals were advancing along those two roads,
and those two roads only, Pemberton's position would be tough to
break. Unfortunately for the Pennsylvanian in gray, another powerful
Union column was pushing along the Jackson road toward his left
flank, undetected.

Positioned on the left, at the Crossroads, was a battle-tested
brigade of Alabamians commanded by Brig. Gen. Stephen D. Lee.
Concerned for the safety of his left flank and the unprotected crest of
Champion Hill 600 yards north of the Crossroads (Champion Hill
was the dominant feature of the battlefield rising 140 feet above the
surrounding area), Lee directed Lt. Col. Edmund Pettus—younger
brother of Mississippi's war governor, John J. Pettus—to reconnoiter
the Jackson road. A half-hour later, Pettus came riding back frantically waving his arms and informed Lee that the enemy was pushing
along the road from Bolton in large number. The perceptive Lee realized that if left unchecked, the Federals would turn his flank, capture Edwards, and cut the army off from its base in Vicksburg.

Notifying his division commander, Carter Stevenson, of this critical development, Lee shifted his brigade north to meet the enemy
threat. With sweat dripping off their faces, the Alabamians moved at
the double-quick and into position to cover the road and occupy the
bald crest of Champion Hill. Two guns of the Botetourt (Virginia)
Artillery were also with great difficulty wheeled into position on the
crest of the hill to support the infantrymen. The cannoneers from
Virginia quickly unlimbered their guns and dropped trail facing
north.

From his vantage point atop the hill, Lee watched in awe as the
Federal columns neared the Champion house, 800 yards away, and

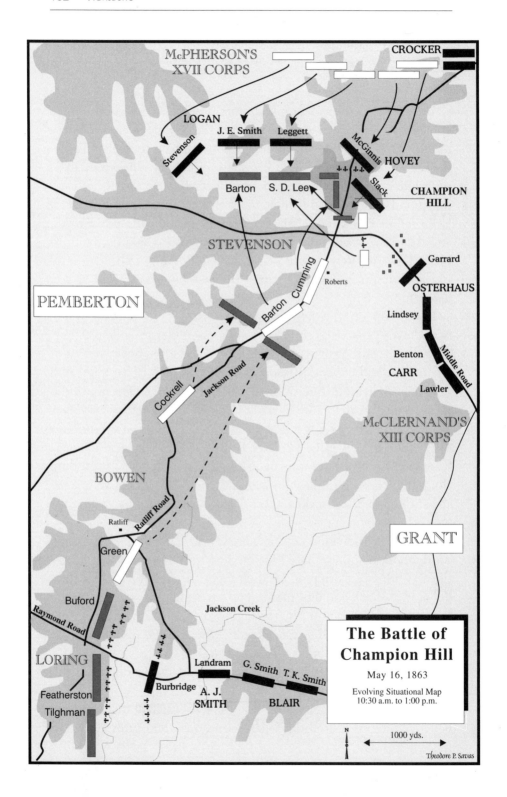

The Battle of Champion Hill

May 16, 1863

Evolving Situational Map
10:30 a.m. to 1:00 p.m.

1000 yds.

Theodore P. Savas

swung from column into line of battle. The enemy moved into position with man touching man, rank pressing rank, and line supporting line. Lee's men could see Union officers riding up and down the lines giving encouragement to their men and making sure that all was set for the advance. Bugle blasts and drum rolls were audible to the men on Champion Hill as they watched the Northern soldiers uncase their colors and fix bayonets in preparation for the advance.

There was little time to admire the pageantry of war, however, as Lee watched the Federal line continue to deploy and slowly extend beyond his left flank. Shifting his men to the left, Lee's line grew thin and gaps appeared between his regiments. Unable to shift adequately to meet the Federal threat and provide protection to Champion Hill, Lee requested assistance from the next brigade in line—a brigade of Georgians commanded by Brig. Gen. Alfred Cumming. Cumming, who had been in command of the brigade for only three days, responded to Lee's urgent request by dividing his available force and shifted several regiments to the salient at Champion Hill. The wary Georgian left two regiments and four guns of Capt. James F. Waddell's Alabama battery to guard the vital Crossroads (facing east against the Union threat on the Middle Road).

At 10:30 a.m., the Federals began the advance at a slow and steady pace. The soldiers from Alabama and Georgia watched as the enemy pushed their way through deep ravines and dense underbrush to close on their position. Cumming later wrote that "the attack broke upon us with great impetuosity and vehemence, in overwhelming force, and in a manner wholly unexpected and unlooked for." As the Confederate line opened fire, it became a source of anxiety to both Stevenson and Lee that the Federals would turn their left flank, which was in the air, and capture the bridge on Jackson Road over Bakers Creek. (Although the water of Bakers Creek was subsiding, the bridge was the only avenue of escape available to Pemberton's army at this point in time on May 16.)[20]

Reacting quickly to avert disaster, Stevenson ordered another brigade of Georgians, commanded by Brig. Gen. Seth Barton, to move cross-country from the Ratliff plantation road and into position on his left. Barton's men covered the distance at the double-quick and arrived without a moment to spare for, as he reported, "The enemy having turned Lee's left flank, were already in the timber, pressing vigorously forward." The Georgians drove in the enemy skirmishers, but were stopped cold when confronted by the enemy's line of battle. At first, boasted Joseph Bogle of the Fortieth Georgia, "We were handling the enemy in our immediate front in fine style. . . .though the bullets whizzed by us like a swarm of mad hornets." Within minutes, however, Barton's men were soon engulfed by a sea of blueclad soldiers and struggled to hold their ground.[21]

By 11:30, the troops were heavily engaged along the entire line from near Bakers Creek on the left to the crest of Champion Hill. Although the Southerners fought with grim determination and skill, they could not stem the Union onslaught. With a mighty cheer the Federals slammed into the Confederate line and a wild melee ensued in which clubbed muskets and bayonets were freely used. On the crest of Champion Hill the Southern line began to buckle and give way. Capt. John Johnston (nephew of Joseph E. Johnston) of the Virginia battery wrote: "Under a heavy charge we were run over, our infantry breaking, and our horses being shot down by the charging troops and by our own infantry." General Stevenson reported that "Nothing could protect the artillery horses from the deadly fire of the enemy. Almost all were killed, and along my whole line the pieces, though fought with a desperation on the part of both officers and men which I cannot praise too highly, almost all fell into the hands of the enemy." Sgt. Francis Obenchain from Virginia recalled, "They did not then kill all the horses. Some they shot and some they bayoneted. I begged them not to murder the men."[22]

Although the sounds of battle gave ample evidence of the magnitude of combat on his left, Pemberton had sent no support to Stevenson. With the collapse of the salient on Champion Hill early in the afternoon, Stevenson had no recourse but to fall back. Scrambling back through the dense woods and scattered fields, the Confederates sought to form a new line on the Jackson road. Despite the scene of panic as hundreds of frightened soldiers continued to stream to the rear, Stevenson, Lee, and others vainly attempted to rally their men. Although disheartened by the loss of his battery on Champion Hill, Sergeant Obenchain rode to the rear in search of help. "When I got through the woods," he later wrote, "I came upon some cleared land and there found Genl. Pemberton. He was alone." Obenchain asked him a question but no reply was offered. Instead

Pemberton told him, "I have ordered Bowen's and [Brig. Gen. Martin E.] Green's brigade in to drive the enemy & recapture the lost guns."[23]

With Stevenson's initial line shattered and the enemy astride the Jackson road between his army and the Bakers Creek bridge, the situation facing John Pemberton was critical. In an effort to reestablish his left and, thereby save his right, Pemberton ordered Bowen and Loring to counterattack and drive the Federals back. Both officers, following the example set earlier by Pemberton himself, refused to obey the order stating that they were in the presence of the enemy and would not move unless peremptorily ordered to do so. (Although their statements were accurate, neither division was then engaged in more than desultory firing.) A second time the courier was sent to the recalcitrant subordinates with the same instructions. Time, however, was of the utmost importance. Desperate to stave off disaster, Pemberton rode to the right himself and ordered Col. Francis M. Cockrell's brigade of Bowen's division to move at once.

Cockrell's Missourians were the finest combat troops in either army and had proven their metal on many hard-fought fields. With a large Magnolia blossom in one hand and sword in the other, Cockrell led his men to the left in a cloud of dust. Advancing on the run up the Ratliff plantation road, his men swept past the Isaac Roberts house, which served as Pemberton's headquarters. There was the army commander waving his straw hat urging the men forward. One Missourian who hurried along caught sight of the commanding general and noted, "We passed General Pemberton and staff standing in the road, almost in the edge of action. His manner seemed to be somewhat excited; he and his staff were vainly endeavoring to rally some stragglers, who had already left their commands."[24]

As they advanced to the sounds of battle, the rugged soldiers from Missouri were inspired by the novel appearance of a group of ladies who cheered them on by singing "Dixie." Ephriam Anderson of the Second Missouri Infantry recalled with pride that, "At the sight of this, a novel appearance on the battle-field, the boys shouted zealously, and I could not refrain from hallooing just once, expressive of my admiration for the perfect 'abandon' with which these fair creatures gave their hearts to the cause."[25]

Cockrell's men also had plenty of heart and, followed by the Arkansans and Missourians of Brig. Gen. Martin Green's brigade, slammed into the Federals near the Crossroads. The mass of soldiers clad in butternut and gray swept over the Crossroads and reclaimed the guns of Waddell's battery which had fallen to the enemy. At the point of bayonet, Bowen's determined fighters drove the Union troops before them back over the crest of Champion Hill. With reckless abandon the fiery Missourian drove his men beyond the hill toward the Champion house near which Federal teamsters could be seen frantically whipping their animals in a desperate effort to get the wagons away.

Confederate fortune, however, was short-lived; for moving into position to stem the gray tide were fresh Federal troops that formed line of battle astride the road and checked Bowen's vicious attack. "The battle here raged fearfully," wrote Anderson, who noted that "one unbroken, deafening roar of musketry was all that could be heard." Determined to hold the ground thus gained, Bowen sent an urgent plea for reinforcements. Tense moments passed as he waited for support, but Loring's men were nowhere in sight. Directed onto the wrong road, Loring's battle-hardened veterans would not arrive in time for the Southerners to capitalize on Bowen's success.[26]

As the Missourian desperately clung to his position, the ominous cry for ammunition rang out along his line. But there was none to be had as the ordnance wagons had left the area earlier in the day. In a frenzy, his men scrounged among the cartridge boxes of the dead and wounded in search of ammunition with little success. Faced with overwhelming numbers in front and threatened on the left, Bowen's stalwart fighters reluctantly began to yield ground inch by inch—yet hoping that Loring would arrive to even the contest.

All hope was suddenly dashed as the dreadful word quickly spread that the enemy had broken through the roadblock on the Middle road and were advancing in force toward the Crossroads. Risking total envelopment if he remained longer, Bowen disengaged and ordered his men to fall back. The remnant of his proud division streamed through the woods and scores of men threw down their weapons and accouterments in a race for survival. Barely reaching the Crossroads ahead of the enemy on the Middle road, the soldiers

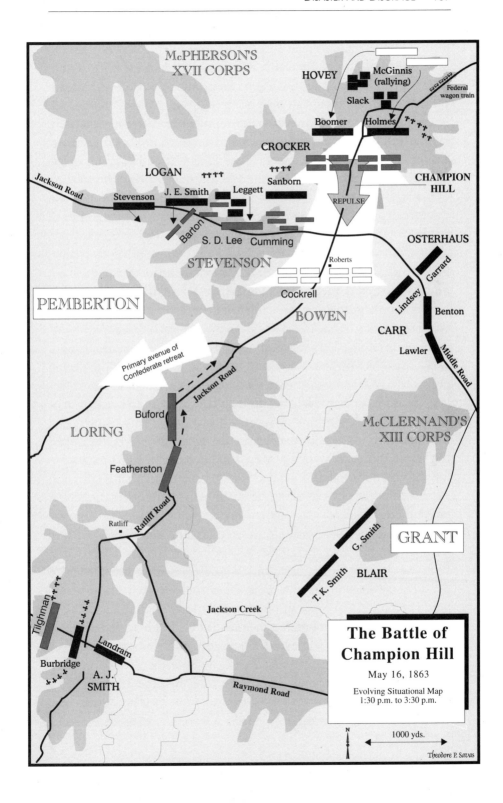

McPHERSON'S
XVII CORPS

HOVEY

McGinnis
(rallying)

Slack

Federal
wagon train

Boomer   Holmes

CROCKER

Jackson Road

LOGAN

Sanborn

CHAMPION
HILL

Stevenson   J. E. Smith   Leggett

REPULSE

Barton

S. D. Lee   Cumming

OSTERHAUS

STEVENSON

Roberts

Garrard

Cockrell

Lindsey

Benton

PEMBERTON

BOWEN

CARR

Lawler

Middle Road

Primary avenue of
Confederate retreat

Jackson Road

Buford

McCLERNAND'S
XIII CORPS

LORING

Featherston

Ratliff

Ratliff Road

G. Smith

GRANT

T. K. Smith   BLAIR

Tilghman

Jackson Creek

Landram

Burbridge

A. J.
SMITH

Raymond Road

**The Battle of
Champion Hill**

May 16, 1863

Evolving Situational Map
1:30 p.m. to 3:30 p.m.

N

1000 yds.

Theodore P. Savas

from Missouri and Arkansas had to run a gauntlet of flame as a murderous flank fire ripped through their ranks from the east. Unable to stem the tide of panic stricken men, Bowen rode to inform Pemberton of the disastrous turn of events.

Dealt a serious blow by the repulse of Bowen's division, Pemberton's army was now faced with annihilation as the enemy controlled not only the vital crossroads, but was in possession of the bridge across Bakers Creek on the Jackson road. At this critical stage of battle, Loring finally arrived with two of his three brigades and, on the run, deployed into line of battle on a ridge several hundred yards south of the Jackson road. Although disheartened by the sights which greeted his arrival, Loring was full of fight and prepared to charge. No sooner had the command "Forward" echoed down the line, however, when a member of Pemberton's staff rode up alongside Loring with an order for the army to fall back on Edwards—the day was lost.

Confederate soldiers were captured by the score as Federal troops swept over the Crossroads as a tidal wave and pushed after the fleeing gray masses. Stevenson's division was shattered and could not be relied upon for further service as his men fell back on Edwards in panic and confusion. Bowen's division had also been badly mauled, and even some of his men evidenced the demoralization which gripped the army. Although his troops were still effective, Bowen's men were low on ammunition and needed time to regroup. Loring's division alone was in fighting condition and was ordered to cover the retreat of Pemberton's army.

The task facing Loring was a difficult one. South of the Crossroads, his two brigades, led by Brig. Gens. Winfield S. Featherston and Abraham Buford, were opposed by brigades from five Federal divisions. In the presence of such overwhelming numbers, Loring held his men in position only long enough to force the enemy to deploy, then ordered them to fall back slowly. A similar situation existed on the Raymond-Edwards road where two Union divisions—that had remained inactive throughout the day—were now advancing in force against Tilghman's lone brigade. It was only a matter of time before Loring's troops were brushed aside and Pemberton's army destroyed.

Fortunately for the Confederate army, fatigue parties had worked throughout the day under the supervision of Maj. Samuel Lockett, chief engineer of the army, to construct a bridge across Bakers Creek on the Raymond-Edwards road. As the turbulent water subsided, they were also able to make the ford passable for artillery. With little semblance of order, Pemberton's men now crowded toward the only open avenue of escape as the setting sun cast lurid shadows over the bloody field of battle. Escape, however, was dependent on the ability of the rear guard to hold the enemy in check long enough for the army to cross.

One and one-half mile east of the creek, Tilghman's brigade was deployed astride the Raymond-Edwards road as the army's rear guard. The ridge on which his men were posted was the highest ground between the enemy and Bakers Creek. If the Federals seized his position, Tilghman realized that enemy artillery would command the bridge and ford and effectively cut the Confederate escape route. Knowing that he must hold his position at all hazards, the Marylander was determined to sacrifice his command, if need be, to save the army.

Tilghman's position west of the Coker house was naturally strong, being a low ridge which commanded a wide sweep of open ground. Strengthened by the six guns of Capt. James J. Cowan's Company G, First Mississippi Light Artillery and two guns of Company C, Fourteenth Mississippi Artillery Battalion under Capt. Jacob Culbertson, his position was difficult to turn and would prove costly to assault.

The redlegs from Mississippi opened with canister and sent the enemy scrambling for cover. Union artillery, however, quickly moved into position in front of the Coker house, dropped trail, and roared into action. The Federal guns pounded Tilghman's position with telling effect, yet the Mississippians manned their cannon with cool deliberation. Amid the crash of shot and shell, Loring rode up to Cowan and said, "I intend to save my Division as I have been cut off by defeat of Genl. Stevenson. I want your Battery to hold this position until sun down, or captured."[27]

Captain Cowan was somewhat startled when Tilghman suddenly dismounted, walked over to one of the guns and said, "I will take a shot at those fellows myself." As he aimed the cannon, enemy shells screamed past Tilghman, who remarked to the delight of his men, "They are trying to spoil my new uniform." His jest was prophetic for James G. Spencer of Cowan's battery recorded, "He then sighted the gun again & as he stepped back to order fire, a Parrott shell struck him in the side, nearly cutting him in twain." Tilghman's badly mangled body, escorted by his son and aide Frederick Tilghman, was taken to the Yeiser house (Hiawatha) where the Confederate brigadier was pronounced dead.[28]

Tilghman's sacrifice was not in vain as thousands of Confederate soldiers swarmed across Bakers Creek and reached Edwards. The badly shaken men of Carter Stevenson's division were first off the field and did not stop until they reached Bovina, west of the Big Black River. The remnant of Bowen's division was next to cross. Having suffered heavy casualties at Port Gibson on May 1, and greater casualties at Champion Hill, his division was but a shadow of its former self. Yet, Bowen's proud division was still an effective fighting force and was ordered by Pemberton to form line of battle west of Bakers Creek and hold the crossings for Loring to pass.

As his exhausted soldiers moved into position on the west bank of Bakers Creek, Federal troops crossed the stream on the Jackson road and pushed southwest toward the lower bridge. Outflanked, Bowen's position was soon made untenable as these Federals unlimbered artillery and shelled the crossings. The ever combative Missourian realized that he could no longer hold the crossings and sent an urgent message to Loring imploring him to save his own division. With a heavy heart, Bowen then turned his men toward Edwards and left Loring to his fate.

"My first determination was to force my way through by the ford," wrote Loring, who rode to the creek to make a quick reconnaissance. "Arriving there," he later reported, "it was found that our troops were gone, some of whom having been driven back upon us. The enemy's skirmishers were advancing, and a heavy force occupied the commanding ridge across the creek, his artillery playing upon the crossing." The situation was desperate! Adding to the degree of urgency, Loring observed that, "The enemy upon our right flank and rear had been re-enforced, so that we were enveloped upon three sides, leaving no road to move upon."[29]

Trapped east of the creek, Loring moved southwest and, guided by a local physician, searched for a favorable crossing point. Darkness, however, enveloped the fields as his men moved into the Bakers Creek bottom and their march slowed to a crawl over the muddy trail. To expedite their movement, the Confederates abandoned twelve cannon, along with their limbers and caissons, and seven wagon loads of ammunition—all of which fell into Federal hands the next day. As they reached the crossing east of Mount Moriah, Loring's men began to despair for the night sky was illuminated by fires ranging in Edwards. (Commissary supplies and munitions had been set afire by Pemberton's retreating army.) Loring mistakenly believed that the flames indicated the enemy was in possession of Edwards and thought it now impossible to rejoin the army. After a hasty consultation with his subordinates, he decided to push through the night in a southeasterly direction and the following evening reached Crystal Springs. The odyssey of Loring's division came to an end on May 19 as his weary soldiers arrived in Jackson—the same day that Grant's forces made their initial attempt to storm the Vicksburg stronghold.

Pemberton was unaware that Loring's division had been cut off by rapidly moving Union forces which occupied Edwards around midnight. Hoping to keep his army intact, the Confederate commander ordered Bowen's tired soldiers into the fortifications east of the Big Black River with the intention of holding the bridge long enough for Loring to cross. At 5:30 a.m. on May 17, however, the sound of artillery announced the arrival of enemy forces rather than Loring's division. After a brief reconnaissance, Union troops deployed into line of battle and with a mighty cheer swept over the Confederate fortifications driving Bowen's men in wild flight across the river. It proved another disastrous day for John C. Pemberton, the remnant of whose army fled for the cover of the Vicksburg defenses.

In the largest, bloodiest, most significant action of the Vicksburg campaign, Confederate casualties had been staggering: 381 killed, 1,018 wounded, and 2,441 missing out of 23,000 men engaged. Added to the grizzly human casualties, Confederate losses included

27 cannon, thousands of stands of arms, and numerous battleflags. Perhaps most devastating to Pemberton's army was the loss of Loring's division that materially reduced the force available for the defense of Vicksburg. Coupled with the loss of an additional 1,800 men and 18 cannon at the Big Black River, Pemberton's army had been defeated in detail and its morale shattered. The ultimate fall of Vicksburg was assured.[30]

In the most important action of his military career, John Pemberton had failed, and had failed miserably. Poor staff work, lack of intelligence, improper reconnaissance, and unsound tactics all contributed to the bloody defeat at Champion Hill; but above all, *"Indecision, Indedecision* [sic], *Indecision"* on the part of the Pennsylvanian in gray who commanded the Army of Vicksburg was the reason for failure. Although others must shoulder a portion of blame for Confederate defeat, the responsibility must rest on the commanding general on whom history would heap ignominy and shame. No one realized this more than John Pemberton himself who commented as he rode from the Big Black River toward Vicksburg: "Just thirty years ago I began my career by accepting a cadetship at the U.S. military academy. And, today, that same date, that career is ended in disaster and disgrace."[31]

For all practical purpose it was, but it was a disaster that would affect an entire nation and her people.

CHAPTER SIX

THE FIRST HONOR AT VICKSBURG

The 1st Battalion, 13th U.S. Infantry

From the outbreak of hostilities in April 1861, it was clear to President Abraham Lincoln and his advisors that sizeable land and naval forces were required to "pocket" the key city of Vicksburg and regain control of the Mississippi River. The administration had already taken steps to augment the Regular army by the addition of several regiments, and had assembled numerous volunteer forces for the drive downriver from Cairo, Illinois. Of the mighty host thus assembled and destined for glory, one unit in particular would surpass all others in attaining fame in the operations for Vicksburg, the 1st Battalion, 13th United States Infantry—the Regulars.

The regiment was constituted by President Lincoln on May 4, 1861. Its remarkable career, which began near St. Louis, Missouri, at Jefferson Barracks, continues today. During the campaigns to gain control of the Mississippi River and its major tributaries, the men of the 1st Battalion, 13th United States Infantry would see action at Chickasaw Bayou in December 1862, and at Arkansas Post in January 1863. It was, however, in the spring of 1863 that this unit established a reputation befitting its first commander, Col. William T. Sherman, and earned the distinction of "First at Vicksburg."[1]

The year 1863 was ushered in with feverish activity as Maj. Gen. Ulysses S. Grant, commander of the Union Army of the Tennessee, seized upon Federal naval supremacy on the inland waters to transfer his force from Memphis to Milliken's Bend and Young's Point, Louisiana, on the great river upstream from Vicksburg. He also stationed troops farther north at Lake Providence, Louisiana. During the winter months, Federal forces stockpiled tremendous quantities of food, clothing, medicine, ammunition, and countless other items in preparation for the spring campaign aimed at Vicksburg. Grant also orchestrated a series of ill-fated bayou expeditions, or experiments as he called them, the object of which was to reach the rear of Vicksburg. During this phase of the operations, the Regulars of the 1st Battalion, 13th U.S. Infantry, participated in the nearly disastrous Steele's Bayou Expedition.[2]

By late March, the roads in the lower Mississippi River Valley began to dry which enabled Grant to launch his army on a bold march south through Louisiana. To divert Confederate Lt. Gen. John C. Pemberton's attention from his principal movement, Grant sent Sherman up the Yazoo River toward the northern flank of Vicksburg's defenses, while the other corps of his army marched down the Louisiana side of the Mississippi River, first to Hard Times, then to Disharoon's plantation, thirty-five miles below Vicksburg. To complete this initial phase of the campaign, the Union fleet under the command of R. Adm. David Dixon Porter passed below the Vicksburg batteries on the nights of April 16 and 22, and the batteries of Grand Gulf on the evening of the 29th. By the end of April, all was in readiness to cross the river and move on Vicksburg from the south and east. Sherman's troops were to rivet Confederate attention north of Vicksburg while Grant crossed the river below the city.

The Regulars were commanded by Capt. Edward C. Washington, grand nephew of George Washington, and attached to Col. Giles Smith's brigade, Maj. Gen. Frank Blair's divi-

Capt. Edward Washington
Vicksburg National Military Park

sion, of Sherman's XV Corps. The officers and men who comprised the 1st Battalion, were eager for action and disappointed at being left behind to make a demonstration while the rest of the army moved to cross the Mississippi River. The demonstration which took place near Snyder's Bluff on April 30-May 1, was less than impressive, and the men of the battalion saw little activity during this charade. The Regulars were anxious to join in the more active operations. Yet, they were only further disappointed when Blair's division was left to guard the supply bases in Louisiana, while Sherman's two remaining divisions hastened to join Grant.[3]

On April 30-May 1, 1863, the Union commander hurled his army across the mighty river and onto Mississippi soil to begin the inland campaign aimed at Vicksburg. The Federal beachhead was secured as Confederate troops were driven from the fields and forests west of Port Gibson. With the initiative firmly in hand, Grant pushed to the northeast, deep into Mississippi. A sharp engagement was fought on May 12 near the village of Raymond and Union forces were again victorious. Sherman's corps, less Blair's division, joined the main column at Little Sand Creek, and on May 14 helped to seize Jackson.

Having finally been relieved of duty at Milliken's Bend, the Regulars rushed to join their comrades in Mississippi. On May 11, Captain Washington's men gave a rousing cheer as they crossed over the river from Hard Times to Grand Gulf. The stalwart men of the battalion, along with two of Blair's three brigades pushed out of Grand Gulf on the morning of May 12 escorting a large supply train consisting of 200 wagons. The weather was warm and the roads dusty. Water along the route was scarce and, in the intense heat, the soldiers suffered with parched throats. The cumbersome wagons slowed the march to a crawl and the column was compelled to make frequent halts. The line of march took the men from Grand Gulf through Willow Springs, to Rocky Springs, Old Auburn, and into Raymond where they arrived on May 15.[4]

By the time Ed Washington and his Regulars tramped into Raymond, Jackson had been captured and was being effectively neutralized by the other units of Sherman's corps. Grant's main columns were pushing west with a view of concentrating on Edwards Station, mid-way between Vicksburg and Jackson.

Confederate forces, however, under Pemberton's personal command, were in Edwards and a major battle appeared imminent.

Early on the morning of May 16, Grant was appraised of Pemberton's location and troop strength by two civilian employees of the Southern Railroad. Reacting quickly to the intelligence, the Union commander pushed his columns over three parallel roads covering a broad front while maintaining supporting distance. The Regulars moved out of Raymond at sunrise and took up the line of march on the direct road to Edwards Station. By mid-morning the rugged footsoldiers of the battalion had covered nine miles when they heard the sound of firing to their front. Pemberton and his army were making a stand near Bakers Creek, the salient point of his line resting on Champion Hill. Although the field was bitterly contested as the battle swayed back and forth, the Regulars saw but little action and suffered no casualties. In this, the bloodiest action of the Vicksburg campaign, Grant's numerical superiority and errors by Pemberton and his two ranking generals enabled the Federals to prevail and the Confederates were driven from the field.[5]

With but little rest, the Regulars were on the road at daylight on May 17. Giles Smith, the brigade commander, reported that "the ground everywhere evidencing the hast with which the retreat of the enemy had been made, it being strewn with ammunition, muskets, wagons, caissons, and, in a field near the road, eleven pieces of artillery were found, which had been abandoned by the enemy." The soldiers pushed forward with confidence and by noon were on the banks of the Big Black River at Bridgeport.[6]

The battalion was greeted by the sharp crack of musketry which announced the presence of Confederate sharpshooters on the opposite bank. Skirmishers were deployed and returned the lethal fire. Artillery was also run forward, dropped trail, and sprayed the opposite bank with canister. In quick order, the Southerners were compelled to surrender and the river was cleared for crossing. By nightfall, a pontoon bridge was laid and the men of Blair's division crossed safely. The 1st Battalion, 13th U.S. Infantry was among the first units to cross, and the men bivouacked two miles west of the river on the plantation of Mary Brooks.[7]

Earlier that day, farther to the south, the grayclad columns were in full retreat toward Vicksburg and its fortifications. The Confederates stopped in an effort to hold the bridges over the Big Black River to await Maj. Gen. William W. Loring's division which had been cut off during the retreat from Champion Hill. Grant, however, moved with great speed and, on the 17th, spearheaded by Brig. Gen. Michael Lawler's brigade of McClernand's corps, stormed the Confederate works and compelled the Southerners to burn the bridges. Pemberton's army, badly shaken, ran for the cover of Vicksburg defenses.

On through the long day and into the evening marched the weary soldiers of Pemberton's army. Singly and in small groups, with no sense of order or discipline, the men filed into the rifle-pits and turned to meet Grant's rapidly approaching army. A medley of sounds filled the night air as the Confederates readied their defenses: officers shouted orders, teamsters whipped their animals and dragged artillery into position, and, as the soldiers worked with picks and shovels, some men cursed while others prayed. Throughout the night, the ringing of axes was constant as additional trees were felled to strengthen fortifications, clear fields of fire, and form abatis in their front. Work continued at a feverish pace and, by sunrise, the city was in a good state of defense.

The familiar sound of reveille shattered the morning stillness at an early hour on the 18th, and the Regulars were on the road at daybreak. Although the day was warm, Captain Washington and his battalion covered nine miles by 9:30 a.m., and had reached the junction of the Bridgeport and Benton roads. A halt was made for the troops to rest and eat their rations. Fires were started and the men enjoyed a relaxing cup of coffee.[8]

With buoyant spirits, the troops eagerly resumed the march early in the afternoon. As the Northerners neared Vicksburg, Companies A (Capt. Charles Ewing) and C (Capt. Frank Muhlenberg) of the 13th U.S. Infantry were deployed as skirmishers and felt for the Confederate rear guard. Contact was made two miles from the city along the Graveyard Road and continued to within 100 yards of the Vicksburg defenses, when pursuit was called off. Later that same night the Regulars were again sent forward to relieve the pickets of Col. Thomas Kilby Smith's brigade, and there they remained till early morning.[9]

There was little sleep that night as orders were carried from army headquarters to the various units, and dispositions made for the assault planned for May 19. Grant believed that a quick and powerful thrust would give him possession of the fortress city, but, perhaps he moved too quickly. His army was strung out between Vicksburg and the Big Black River. Consequently, when time for the attack arrived, Sherman's corps alone was in proper position.

The morning of the 19th brought the sharp crack of musketry between pickets and sharpshooters. The men boiled their coffee and ate hardtack while artillery pieces were wheeled into position and brought to bear on the Confederate works less than a quarter mile away. The people and defenders of Vicksburg were about to experience war in all its horror.

Pemberton's defense line ran for more than eight miles and formed a huge perimeter around the city with both flanks resting on the river. The Confederate defenses were a series of large earthworks connected by rifle-pits and parapets dotted by embrasures for artillery. The line was formidable! Northeast of Vicksburg, guarding the Graveyard Road approach to the city, was the 27th Louisiana Redan on the north and the Stockade Redan to the south. Sherman's task was to reduce these strongholds and open the roadway to Vicksburg.[10]

The XV Crops was formed with Blair's division on the left in the following order: Col. Thomas Kilby Smith's brigade on the left, astride the Graveyard Road; Col. Giles Smith's brigade in the center; and Brig. Gen. Hugh Ewing's brigade on the right. After the lines were formed, the troops marched to the crest of a hill, ordered "In place-rest," and there the sturdy veterans under Ed Washington waited for the artillery to open on the Confederate works.[11]

To soften up Pemberton's lines, Grant ordered an artillery bombardment to precede the attack of his infantry. Accordingly, at 9:00 a.m. the cannon opened a sporadic fire to get the proper range, then maintained a vigorous fire for hours. The sound of the guns was deafening. The ground shook as the artillerymen hurled solid shot and shell at the city's defenses and the thick clouds of smoke which rose from the guns shrouded the fields which made it virtually impossible to see. The Confederates crouched behind their defenses and made scant reply to the fire of Wood's, Barrett's, and Hart's Illinois batteries.[12]

As the artillery continued its fire, the Regulars made final preparations for the assault. The infantrymen steadied their nerves, placed bayonets on their rifles, and dressed their lines. Giles Smith's brigade was arrayed with the 6th Missouri on the right, five companies of the 113th Illinois—right center, 116th Illinois—left center, seven companies of the 1st Battalion, 13th United States Infantry on the left, and the 8th Missouri in reserve.[13]

At 2:00 p.m., all the artillery pieces in position fired three volleys in rapid succession, the signal for the charge. Capt. Edward Washington, commander of the battalion, turned to his men, drew his sword, and gave the commands in quick order: "Attention, Shoulder Arms, Battalion Forward, Charge Bayonets, Double Quick- March." The Regulars, 250-strong, went forward in splendid array with their bright colored banners snapping in the breeze above them. The regimental standard was carried by Sgt. Robert M. Nelson of Company B, and the national colors by Sgt. James E. Brown of Company C. Both men were determined to plant their colors atop the parapets of Vicksburg.[14]

Once over the crest, the Confederate works came into view looming ominously against the skyline. Between the surging blue tide and the city's defenses the terrain was difficult to traverse being a deep, steep ravine filled by obstructions designed to disrupt their advancing lines. Sgt. Washington W. Gardner of Company C described the scene: there were "fallen tree tops facing us, many of the limbs sharpened, and a wire strung to strike us about the knees or below and throw us on those sharpened limbs." In addition, there were tree stumps, a dense growth of brush and cane, holes covered with dried grass, a rail fence, and, off to the right, a large frame house, outbuildings, and a cornfield.[15]

The entrenched Southerners were ready. Inside the Stockade Redan was the veteran 36th Mississippi under Col. William W.

Witherspoon, anchoring the left of Brig. Gen. Louis Hebert's brigade. About 2:00 p.m., responding to the massing of Federal troops opposite the 27th Louisiana Lunette and the Stockade Redan complexes and the ensuing advance, Col. Francis M. Cockrell sent his Missouri Brigade forward to bolster the defenses. Col. A. C. Riley's 1st Missouri and Col. James McCown's 5th Missouri quickly joined the Mississippians in side the redan and along the poplar stockade. The 3rd Missouri, under Col. W. R. Gause, fell in behind, ready to reinforce weak spots in this sector of the Confederate defenses.[16]

Shortly after the advance started, Confederate artillery and small-arms fire began taking its toll as it ripped into the advancing lines tearing gaps that could not be filled. Casualties mounted at an alarming rate, especially among the color guard. Cpl. Noble Warwick was the first of the color guard to fall, being hit "just after passing the crest." As he lay upon the ground in pain, Warwick watched his comrades advance. Years later he wrote, "Corporal Slate of G Co. was the next wounded of the Color Guard shot through both thighs." In the hail of fire, Sergeant Brown and the national colors were among the next to fall. A member of the battalion who witnessed the colors drop to the ground noted that the gallant Brown "fell dead pierced by a ball through the head." During the assault, Cpls. Daniel Payne and Edward Maher, both of Company C, would also be killed while carrying the national standard, along with fourteen others killed or wounded.[17]

As the charge of the Regulars swept through the cornfield north of Graveyard Road, the first line of obstructions was reached. The tangled mass of cane, brush, and trees presented an "almost impassable" barrier and disrupted the advancing blue lines 50 yards from their starting point. The advance continued as the Union troops filtered through the abatis one by one or in small groups, but all order was lost.[18]

The Confederate fire was devastating and pinned down several units. So that the advance might continue, the 8th Missouri was halted at the top of the ravine and blazed away at the defenders of Vicksburg. Under this protective fire, the brigade again pushed forward and sought shelter at the bottom of the ravine. Captain Washington led his men down the steep ravine to the next line of

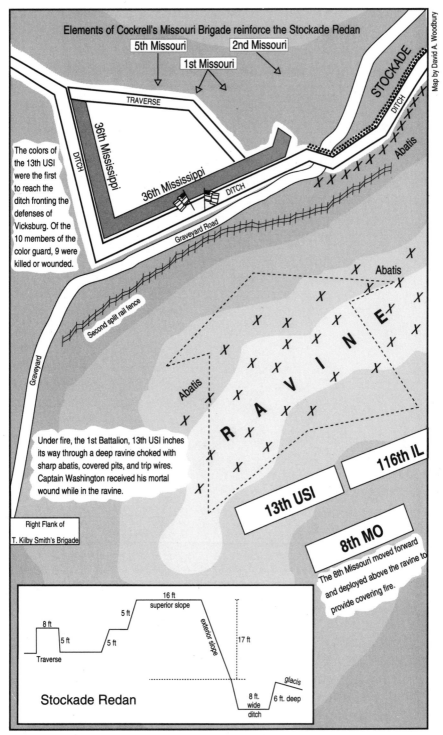

Attack on the Stockade Redan, May 19, 1863

Ravine through which the 13th U. S. I. charged in their attack against the Stockade Redan. The Redan is visible in the upper left. *Photo by C. Bowie Lanford, Vicksburg National Military Park.*

obstructions. Gardner recalled, "Our comrades were now falling around us at every step, some killed instantly, others having an arm or a leg shot off, and wounds of all descriptions." Casualties became heavy and the regimental surgeon set up a temporary hospital between the lines in the shelter of the ravine.[19]

View from the Stockade Redan. The 13th U. S. I. formed for the advance along the ridge line at the top of the photograph and advanced up the ravine toward the camera. A monument to Captain Washington, who received a mortal wound in the ravine, can be seen in the left foreground. *Photo by C. Bowie Lanford, Vicksburg National Military Park.*

Not only was Giles Smith's attack faltering, but, to his left, Kilby Smith's brigade was also having a difficult time. His five regiments formed in two lines and pushed down the Graveyard Road toward the Stockade Redan. A deadly crossfire raked their advance and brought most of the bluecoats to a halt far short of their objective with their lines bleeding and torn.[20]

With momentum waning, brigade, regimental, and company commanders attempted to rally and reform their men. It proved a difficult task because of the intensity of the Confederate fire and the rough terrain, alignment had been lost. As confusion spread, regiments became intermixed. To get the men moving again, Captain Washington and the color-bearers advanced to the rail fence at the base of the slope. As the line resumed its forward movement, the fearless Washington was cut down while scaling the fence. Seeing the captain fall, Sergeant Nelson immediately ran to his side and asked if there was anything he could do for him. Realizing that his wound was mortal, Washington slowly unfastened his sword belt, took out his pocketbook and watch, and asked that Nelson give them to the next officer in command.[21]

In spite of Washington's loss, the Regulars continued their determined advance up the hill toward the northface of Stockade Redan. On hands and knees the men clawed their way up the hillside. As they neared the Confederate works, they came under the fire of their infantry and artillery. Still, they continued. Pvt. Charles H. Smart of Company C recalled, as he climbed the hill, "I saw John A. Phelan, a private of Company C, raise his gun two or three times and endeavor to draw a bead on some object in our rear." When asked what he was trying to do, Phelan replied, "There is a fellow back there on the hill, who loads his gun, sticks it over the log behind which he is concealed and fires away, regardless of where his shot takes effect, and if he puts his head above that log I'll kill him."[22]

A handful of Federals cleared the rail fence. This was the final obstruction between them and the Confederate line as they clambered up the hill. A private carrying the national flag was shot through the head, and the colors fell once more. Captain Ewing seized the standard and, waving it defiantly above him to inspire the men, moved forward.[23]

Within twenty-five yards of the redan, Ewing was overcome by exhaustion and sat on a stump to catch his breath. The young captain, however, continued to wave the flag as the blue tide swept up the hill. Finally at the top, several men made a dash for the ditch fronting the Confederate works, one of them being Sergeant Nelson with the regimental colors. Among those swarming over the top and first into the ditch was Sergeant Gardner of Company C. Nelson was immediately behind him and thrust the flagstaff into the outer wall of Stockade Redan. The regimental standard of the 13th United States Infantry was the first Northern colors planted on the exterior slope of the works surrounding Vicksburg.[24]

While standing on the stump urging his men forward, Captain Ewing had his right thumb shot off and the "Stars and Stripes" fell to the ground. A member of the battalion who stood nearby grasped the flag, jumped into the ditch, and planted the standard on the exterior slope. The Regulars had carried both their colors to the enemy's works and there they proudly waved side by side in the bright afternoon sun.[25]

Once in the ditch, the Federals began digging holes in the bank with their bayonets for the purpose of scaling the bastion's exterior slope and waited for reinforcements. At that moment, as the remainder of the First Brigade crept toward Stockade Redan, Kilby Smith's brigade resumed its advance. Down Graveyard Road surged men from Ohio, Illinois, and Indiana. A few men from the 83d Indiana and the 127th Illinois also reached the ditch and planted their flags. The majority of the brigade, however, was pinned down less than 50 yards from the Confederate works and, at such close range, the lethal exchange of fire continued.[26]

As the men of the battalion struggled up the hill on hands and knees toward the ditch, Hugh Ewing's brigade came into position for the assault. With a fury, he let loose his four regiments on the 27th Louisiana Lunette. Several times his men surged through the ravine and up the hill, only to be stopped within 30 yards of their goal. Ewing's losses were frightful! Unable to reach their goal, his men sought shelter in the base of the ravine.[27]

The Federal battle lines had been stopped. Heavy casualties made another assault by Blair's division impractical without support. Lt. J. A. Boies of Company H was sent to the rear to ask Sherman for orders and reinforcements. En route, an artillery projectile severed a leg and he soon died.[28]

With no assistance in sight, the brigades began to withdraw. The handful of men in the ditch were left to fend for themselves in what one of the Regulars termed a "living grave." Private

Smart of Company C noted with anguish, "I expected every minute would be our last." In the heat of battle he recalled seeing "a Confederate musket held in a vertical position behind the Redan." Years later he wrote:

> Resting my musket on the fence at the full cock and pointed at the Confederate gun, I picked up a piece of a limb of a tree about a foot long and an inch and a half in diameter and threw it at the musket, striking it fair and square. As it did so, the man holding the musket raised up in full sight, when I pressed the trigger of my Springfield. The Confederate threw up both his hands falling backwards.[29]

Hand grenades were tossed back and forth between the men behind the works and those in the ditch. Confederate demands for surrender were met by the sharp crack of a musket. A lieutenant of the battalion, who made it to the ditch, was bold enough to grab the national colors and hold it as high as he could. The spearhead was shot off and the tassels and ribbons fell to the ground. One Southerner even attempted unsuccessfully to seize and pull in the colors.[30]

Realizing that it was useless to scale the redan, the men in the ditch decided to wait until the sun set then withdraw as best they could under cover of darkness. As soon as it was dark, the men mounted the bank behind them on the north side of the redan and scrambled down into the ravine. On his way back, Pvt. James Kephardt of Company C spotted a wounded officer and carried him to the rear and medical treatment. For his action, Kephardt became a recipient of the Medal of Honor.[31]

As darkness blanketed the fields, the sounds of battle slowly faded into silence, only to be replaced by the cries of the wounded. Dead and wounded were thickly strewn among the stalks of corn, in the ravines, and on the slope leading to Stockade Redan. Casualties had been high, especially in Giles Smith's brigade. The Regulars alone lost 7 out of 12 officers and 64 enlisted men for a total of 71 out of 250 engaged. It had been a frightful day![32]

Under cover of darkness, several men of Blair's division returned to the bloodstained fields to search for killed or wounded comrades. Confederates also came out of their works to gather in the Union wounded that were close to their lines. One of the

Federals thus removed was Capt. Edward Washington. Pvt. J. V. Kearns of Company H recalled that as his party neared the enemy's works, the Confederates called out that they had Captain Washington in their hands and that he was dying.[33]

To prevent further removal of the Union wounded by their comrades, a detachment of Confederates set the frame house between the lines on fire. The light from this blaze burned for hours and exposed the fields and hollows for all to see. None the less, search parties continued their work and brought in several privates and Lt. Joseph L. Horn of Company D.[34]

The search, however, failed to locate the national colors and led the Regulars to believe that the cherished banner had been captured. The regimental and national colors were borne form the enemy's works by Sergeants Nelson and Edley respectively. Nelson arrived safely back in camp with 4 bullet holes in his clothes, 18 bullet holes in the flag, and 2 pieces of canister and 1 minie ball in the staff. Edley, however, did not make it back. Around 3:00 a.m., as the men sat by their campfires reflecting on the days events, an exhausted private staggered into camp dragging the national colors behind him. Upon examination, the flag was found to contain 56 bullet holes and the staff had been broken in three parts; ample support of Sergeant Garner's claim that "men never stood a hotter fire."[35]

The next day, May 20, the regiment was drawn up in line once more. As General Sherman and his staff rode by, the corps commander called to Capt. Charles C. Smith, now in command of the battalion. With sadness in his voice, Sherman asked, "Is that all that was left of the 13th? Are either of the color Sergeants saved?" "Yes, General," was the captain's response, "Sergeant Nelson." Sherman answered, "Well, we can give him something better," and Nelson was made quartermaster sergeant.[36]

The corps commander gave his former command "something better" as General Orders No. 64 issued on August 15, 1863, from department headquarters read:

> The board find[s] the Thirteenth United States Infantry entitled to the first honor at Vicksburg, having in a body planted and maintained its colors on the parapet with a loss of 43.3-10 per cent including the gallant Commander Washington who died at the parapet. Its conduct and loss the board, after a

careful examination believe unequaled in the army and respectfully ask the General commanding the department to allow it the inscription awarded— "First at Vicksburg."37

Capt. Frank Muhlenberg of Company C later wrote with firm conviction that, "No men did more when they faced shot and shell that memorable afternoon than did the officers and men of that gallant Battalion, and its sacrifices were most glorious and heroic to protect the country for which they fought." The Regulars of the 1st Battalion, 13th United States Infantry were so proud of the honor bestowed upon them that they adopted the slogan as their unit motto. To this date, the soldiers of the 13th United States Infantry proudly wear emblazoned on their shoulder patch the honor awarded: "First at Vicksburg."38

Chapter Seven

Spades Are Trump

Siege Operations

His nose bloodied in the assault on May 19, 1863, Maj. Gen. Ulysses S. Grant, commander of the Union Army of the Tennessee, remained undaunted. Three days later, confident that the city would fall in the face of a determined assault, he again hurled his footsoldiers against the fortifications of Vicksburg. Throughout the day on May 22, repeated Union charges were driven back with fearful loss. By day's end, hundreds of men in blue laid dead or dying upon the field and "fortress Vicksburg" stood defiant.

In the two assaults against Vicksburg, the Union army lost 659 men killed, 3,327 wounded, and 155 missing. The dead were left lying exposed and the bodies soon began to bloat and turn black under a scorching Mississippi sun. The stench was sickening! The ghastly sight and smell prompted the Confederate commander, Lt. Gen. John C. Pemberton, to write Grant on May 25, "in the name of humanity I have to propose a cessation of hostilities for two hours and a half, that you may be enabled to remove your dead and dying men." Grant reluctantly acquiesced and at 6:00 p.m. white flags of truce appeared all along the line. As the gruesome task of the burial details was conducted, men in blue and gray mingled between the works. Two and a half hours later, the flags were taken down and everyone ran for cover. The siege of Vicksburg was on.[1]

The ease with which his assaults were repulsed convinced the Federal commander to lay siege to the city. On May 25, by order of General Grant, Lt. Col. John A. Rawlins, the army's assistant adjutant-general, issued Special Orders Number 140 directing:

> Corps commanders will immediately commence the work of reducing the enemy by regular approaches. It is desirable that no more loss of life shall be sustained in the reduction of Vicksburg and the capture of the garrison. Every advantage

will be taken of the natural inequalities of the ground to gain positions from which to start mines, trenches or advance batteries. The work will be under the immediate charge of corps engineers, corps commanders being responsible that the work in their immediate fronts is pushed with all vigor. Capt. F. [Frederick] E. Prime, chief engineer of the department, will have general superintendence of the whole work. He will be obeyed and respected accordingly.

In compliance with these orders, corps engineers working under Captain Prime's direction drove thirteen approaches at various points toward the Confederate fortifications.[2]

The work of driving forward these approaches was for weeks the focus of siege operations. Yet, such activity drew little attention from the Northern newspapermen who covered the actions of Grant's army. As the reporters (as well as their readers) considered siege operations monotonous and mundane, little was written about the principal activity of the Union army at Vicksburg. Even the soldiers themselves considered such duty as boring and left only sketchy accounts of their daily labors. Consequently, historians and writ-

Maj. Gen. John A. Logan
Generals in Blue

ers have seldom detailed approach operations in their publications on the Vicksburg campaign.

In order to provide a comprehensive understanding of the Vicksburg Campaign, this essay addresses the engineering aspects of siege operations by detailing the efforts on Logan's Approach. Named to honor Maj. Gen. John A. Logan, commander of the Third Division, XVII Corps, it was the most successful of the approaches dug by the Federal soldiers during the siege and was carried forward along the Jackson road.

At daybreak on May 26, in accordance with instructions from corps headquarters, General Logan detailed a 300-man fatigue party to open the approach. Working under the direction of Capt. Andrew Hickenlooper, chief engineer of the XVII Corps, the fatigue party broke ground approximately 150 feet southeast of the Shirley House (referred to as the White House by the soldiers of both armies) and

Capt. Andrew Hickenlooper
Brevet Brigadier Generals in Blue.

400 yards east of its objective—the Third Louisiana Redan. The soldiers worked with picks and shovels and, although the approach trench was eight feet wide and seven feet deep, progress was rapid. (The Vicksburg bluffs are formed of loess soil, a fine-grained silt or clay, which made digging easy.) By day's end, the soldiers had carried the approach several hundred feet.

The fatigue party was protected from Confederate small arms fire by a sap roller which, in this case, consisted of a railroad flatcar on which was stacked 20 bales of cotton. The flatcar was pushed slowly ahead of the fatigue party while the men behind threw the dirt to either side providing flank protection. In this fashion they were able to drive the approach forward with little fear of Confederate sharpshooters.

Captain Hickenlooper turned the approach south on the morning of May 27 to avoid a deep ravine and followed a ridge back to the Jackson road. Pleased with the progress thus far achieved, the engineer reduced the number of men in the fatigue party by one-third. By May 29, the approach had reached Jackson Road and was turned west. "Every man in the investing line became an army engineer day and night," recalled one Federal infantryman who labored behind the sap roller under the hot sun. "The soldiers got so they bored like gophers and beavers, with a spade in one hand and a gun in the other."[3]

By June 3 the approach had been carried to a commanding knoll, 130 yards east of its objective. Union soldiers quickly established an advance breaching battery on the knoll which was designated "Battery Hickenlooper." The battery contained two 24-pounder

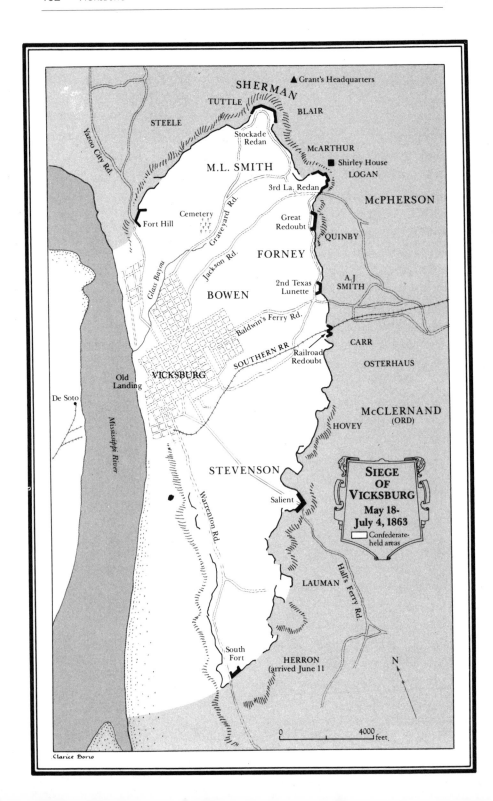

Siege of Vicksburg
May 18-July 4, 1863

Confederate-held areas

Clarice Borio

howitzers and one 6-pounder gun which roared into action on June 6. Two weeks later, two 30-pounder Parrotts, rifled guns, were added to Battery Hickenlooper and soon pounded a breach in the earthen parapet of the Third Louisiana Redan.

The energetic Captain Hickenlooper continued to push the approach forward and by June 8 was within 75 yards of the redan. Confederate sharpshooters began to make life uncomfortable for the men in the fatigue party and Union sharpshooters responded with a vengeance and deadly accuracy. Lt. Henry C. Foster of the 23d Indiana Infantry, known as "Coonskin," for he wore a coonskin fur cap, was among the better shots in the army. Under cover of darkness, and with the assistance of his fellow Hoosiers, Foster built a tower of railroad ties in the road just east of Battery Hickenlooper. "Coonskin's Tower," as it was called, enabled Union sharpshooters to see over the Confederate parapets. From their perch, Foster and his comrades picked off Confederate soldiers with ease.

Confederate artillery roared into action in an effort to destroy the tower. But, the Southern guns were quickly smothered by more numerous and heavier Union artillery. The defenders of Vicksburg were further discouraged to discover that small arms fire was ineffective against the tower. The minie balls they fired either flew harmlessly around the corners or embedded in the thick ties. As a result, Coonskin's tower stood for the duration of the siege.

The tower made a novel appearance on the field of battle and it became a popular attraction. As Union soldiers were rotated on and off the firing line, many curious infantrymen visited the tower in their spare time and asked Foster for permission to climb to the top. So many, in fact, that the famous sharpshooter started charging an admission of twenty-five cents. Thus during the siege, not only did Foster embellish his reputation as a marksman, but added significantly to his army pay.

One of the more frequent visitors to the tower was no less an individual than General Grant. The Union commander was in the habit of riding along the lines in the uniform of a common private so as not to draw attention to himself from Confederate marksmen. The only insignia of rank that he wore were the two stars on each of his shoulders.

Closer and closer the advancing earthworks came. Photographers Armstead & Taylor of Corinth made this image of a section of the lines called the gap, and behind it an observation post dubbed Coonskin Tower. To the defenders it became increasingly clear that time was against them. *Vicksburg National Military Park*

One day, the commanding general was atop the tower foolish exposing himself by resting his elbows on the ties while looking out through his binoculars. A Confederate soldier spotted him, but, not knowing who he was, began yelling at Grant rather than shoot, telling him to get his head down or get it shot off. The man's captain, hearing the obscenities being used, looked across the way to see at whom they were directed and recognized Grant. Instead of telling the soldier to shut up and shoot, the captain reprimanded him for using offensive language with an officer—even though that officer was the enemy. Hearing all this and realizing the danger he was in, Grant quickly descended the tower and was spared to lead the Union to victory at Appomattox and eventually gain White House.

By June 16, the head of the approach was within 25 yards of the Confederate works. Night shifts were discontinued by Captain Hickenlooper as a precautionary measure and two additional lines of rifle pits were thrown up to provide protection for the fatigue parties. The approach trench finally reached the exterior slope of the redan on June 22 and volunteers were called for to commence mining operations.

At 9:00 a.m. on June 23, 35 volunteers, all of whom were former coal and lead miners, began work on the mine. Working in two shifts of three reliefs each, the miners dug a gallery three feet by four feet into the face of the redan. The tunnel was drifted in 45 feet and a smaller gallery extended another 15 feet. Two other galleries were then run out on either side of the main shaft at an angle of 45 degrees for a distance of 15 feet.

The sounds of the digging were audible to the Confederates inside the redan. Realizing what the Union soldiers were doing, the Confederates sank a countermine in hope of locating and destroying the tunnel before a mine could be charged or detonated. At the bottom of the countermine the air was stifling. Yet, the Southerners made out the conversations of Union soldiers digging opposite them. Sounds, however, travel differently under ground than they do on the surface and although the Confederates could hear conversations, they could not tell from which direction or from what distance the sounds were coming. On the morning of June 25, the digging opposite them stopped as the Federal miners completed their task without incident and the mine was quickly packed with 2,200 pounds of black powder.

The mine was set to be detonated at 3:00 p.m. that same day and preparations were made to follow up the explosion with an infantry assault. Throughout the morning and into the afternoon troops moved into position and readied themselves for the attack. Grant joined Maj. Gen. James B. McPherson, commander of the XVII Corps, at Battery Hickenlooper to observe the explosion. Once all was in readiness, the fuses were lit.

Tension ran high in both Union and Confederate lines as 3:00 p.m. came and went, yet there was no explosion. Nervous soldiers wondered if "volunteers" would be ordered into the tunnel to investigate the cause of the delay as the clock reached 3:15 p.m., 3:20 p.m., then 3:25 p.m., and still all was quiet.

Suddenly at 3:28 p.m. the ground began to swell, there was a muffled thud, then a loud explosion as dirt rose to the very heavens. Nathan M. Baker, a chaplain in the 116th Illinois who witnessed the explosion, likened it to an "immense fountain of finely pulverized earth" and noted that the column of dirt was "mingled with flashes of fire and clouds of smoke, through which could occasionally be caught glimpses of dark objects—men, gun carriages, shelters, and so on." Before the dirt settled, Captain Hickenlooper and his pioneers charged into the crater to clear the way for the charging infantrymen. While the engineer and his men cleared away debris, the 45th Illinois raced forward and Sgt. Henry H. Taylor, planted the Stars and Stripes upon the enemy's works. Taylor became a recipient of the Medal of Honor for his conspicuous action on June 25.[4]

Scores of Union soldiers poured into the crater determined to exploit the breach in the Confederate works while Southern troops responded to the emergency with equal determination to block their advance on Vicksburg. The ensuing battle raged for hours during which men fought with clubbed-muskets, bayonets, and fists. As the sun sank in the western sky, fleeing from the scene of carnage, the crater slowly filled with the bodies of the dead and wounded, men in blue and gray. And yet, the troops were still locked in bitter combat as darkness enveloped the bloody field.

Throughout the long, horrifying night, Union and Confederate soldiers hammered away at one another in a grim struggle for possession of the crater. Without respite, the fighting continued as the sun rose on June 26 and fresh troops were thrown into the fray. As the morning wore on, Grant came to realize that success had eluded him once again and that afternoon ordered McPherson to recall the troops. The fighting at the Third Louisiana Redan lasted more than 20 hours. Fortunately for the Federals, their casualties were minimized by darkness during much of the fighting and Grant lost 34 men killed and 209 wounded. In the melee which swirled around the crater, the defenders of Vicksburg held firm at a cost of 21 killed and 73 wounded.[5]

Captain Hickenlooper immediately began construction of another gallery on June 26. The shaft, drifted by miners under what remained of the redan, was completed on July 1 and packed with 1,800 pounds of powder. Confederates again sank a countermine in a futile effort to locate the enemy's tunnel, this time utilizing eight blacks to do the digging. On July 1, at 3:00 p.m., the mine was detonated and seven of the blacks were killed instantly. One, however, a man named Abraham, was blown into the air and landed behind Union lines. A Northern soldier recalled, "one Negro was thrown a 150 feet, lighting on his head and shoulders, scarcely hurting him. He attempted to run back, but a half dozen leveled muskets brought him back." One soldier even had the audacity to ask the poor man "How high did you go?" to which he responded, "Dunno, massa, but t'ink about t'ree mile." (Abraham became an instant celebrity and for the few remaining days of the siege, some enterprising soldiers placed him in a tent and charged an admission for their curious comrades to see America's first man in space.)[6]

The mine explosion on July 1 was not followed by an infantry assault—it was not necessary. For Grant, who on June 30 had been appraised by his chief engineer that all of the Union approaches were within 5 to 120 yards of the Confederate lines, any additional loss of life would be but a "useless effusion of blood." He realized that a few more days of digging would drive all the approaches to their objectives at which time thirteen mines could be positioned and detonated simultaneously. This was the moment that he and his soldiers had been working toward throughout the siege. Plans were thus initiated to widen the approaches to permit the passage of infantry and artillery to the front, planks and sandbags were readied to throw across the ditches fronting the Confederate works, and the troops were shifted into position for the attack scheduled by Grant for July 6.[7]

All his preparations were rendered useless as within 48 hours of the July 1 explosion, white flags appeared along the lines and Generals Pemberton and Grant met near the Jackson road to discuss the surrender of Vicksburg. On July 4, at 10:00 a.m., the valiant defenders of Vicksburg marched out of their works and stacked their arms. The "Gibraltar of the Confederacy" at last fell.

General Pemberton was and continues to be severely criticized for surrendering Vicksburg on July 4. One fact few historians point out, however, is that had he not surrendered when he did, he might have lost Vicksburg in the assault that would have been launched by Grant on July 6. The Confederate commander fully understood the dire situation in which the Federal approaches had placed his army after weeks of siege and acted on the only option available to him. Thus to appreciate the many facets of this complex campaign, it is crucial to understand that the fortress city on the Mississippi River did not fall in the face of determined assault, nor were the gallant defenders of Vicksburg brought to their knees by a lack of food and water. Rather, spades were trump as the capitulation of Vicksburg was made inevitable by the unrelenting efforts of Union engineers and their fatigue parties who labored on the approaches in the scorching heat of a Mississippi sun.

CHAPTER EIGHT

SHUT UP AS IN A TRAP

Citizens Under Siege

Unfortunately, most works on the Vicksburg Campaign focus almost exclusively on the military operations centered on the fortress city and fail to address a key element in the equation—namely, the civilian population of Vicksburg, these men, women and children who experienced war in all its horrors during the long 47 days of siege. Who were these people and what is their story?

This story belongs to such people as Emma Balfour, an attractive Vicksburg socialite and her husband William a prominent physician; Mary Loughborough from Missouri who followed her soldier-husband James across the great river and was trapped in the doomed city; Margaret Lord whose

---

Emma Balfour
Balfour House

---

husband was rector of Christ Episcopal Church, the cornerstone of which had been dedicated by Bishop Leonidas Polk in 1839—and thousands more whose names and stories of hardship and suffering are forgotten or unknown. Collectively they were the citizens of Vicksburg, nearly 5,000 in number in 1860 when civil war tore the nation asunder, a war which fate cruelly dictated would directly impact their lives more so than people in any other American city, North or South.

Situated on the east bank of the Mississippi River, the city was founded by and named for the Rev. Newitt Vick, a Methodist minister from Virginia who in 1812 first viewed the "Father of Waters" from the heights on which the city now stands. But it was the silent water of the great river which gave birth to the town and nourished its soil. Through industry and thrift those who followed Vick tamed the land and traditionally yielded a bountiful harvest. An abundance of wood, cotton, and foodstuffs soon ushered in brisk and profitable trade with cities and towns along the river and its tributaries. The steamboats which plied the river at Vicksburg came from New Orleans, Memphis, St. Louis, Louisville, Cincinnati, and Pittsburgh and brought prosperity to the "City on the Hill" which grew in wealth and charm to become by 1860 one of the larger cities in Mississippi and was considered by many among the most beautiful in the South.

Situated high atop the bluffs overlooking the river, Vicksburg attracted people from throughout the region and beyond, each one of whom added a new dimension to the city. Variety came to characterize the people and their city. "By 1860," noted one historian, "the hills were tiered with buildings—long, low warehouses lay along the waterfront; three blocks up from the river the best stores and shops lined Washington Street, farther away from the river, Greek Revival homes, shielded by fences and hedges, stood aloof from the streets, [and] less pretentious houses were stacked along the hillsides." The most prominent structure was the Warren County Court House built—by slave labor—on the highest hill in Vicksburg. Completed in 1858, the courthouse symbolized not only the city's prominence as the county seat, but proclaimed to the world that Vicksburg was a bold, confident, and dynamic community—traits that would lead the city during the war and sustain her people in their darkest hour.[1]

Although noted for its charm and beauty, it was the people who gave Vicksburg its identity, its flavor. They were a mixture of people from across the South with a sprinkling of Northerners and immigrants from more than a score of foreign lands. This diversity was reflected in every aspect of community life from architecture to clothing, social customs to religion, and made Vicksburg unique among the towns along the river. "These people together with the agricultural community served by Vicksburg, supported almost one hundred shops, banks, stores, factories, and business houses of one sort or another," noted historian Peter Walker. In his classic study of the city entitled *Vicksburg: A People at War 1861-1865,* Walker writes: "Wholesale grocers, commission merchants, and cotton brokers held the largest business interests in the city. Druggists, gunsmiths, tailors, jewelers, insurance salesmen, publishers, bookbinders, carriagemakers, stove- and boilermakers, photographers, bakers, confectioners, nurserymen, liquor dealers, and dressmakers catered to the legitimate wants and wishes of the community." Professional men as well were abundant in Vicksburg where lawyers, doctors, and teachers all made a good living. The city was also home to political figures of renown on both the state and federal levels.[2]

On the eve of civil war, Vicksburg boasted six newspapers which covered the gamut of political views, including *The Daily Citizen* edited by J. M. Swords which, during the Siege of Vicksburg, would be printed on wallpaper. Four fire companies—the Washington, Constitution, Phoenix, and Independent—provided amusement to the people as they raced one another to fires and sometimes even put them out. There were churches and civic organizations to suit any denomination or interests and hotels and brothels to fit any pocketbook.

There was a cosmopolitan air to the community where the merchants and professional men ruled. Their position and the city's wealth were enhanced with the arrival of the railroad in the 1830s. By 1860, the iron rails connected Vicksburg with Jackson and points eastward to the Atlantic seaboard. From Jackson, connecting lines ran north to Memphis and south to New Orleans. Across the great river the rails stretched over Louisiana on their way to Texas. The sustained economic growth provided by the railroads promised a bright future for Vicksburg.

But throughout the ante—bellum period the railroads could not compete with the steamboats and the heartbeat of the town emanated from the docks along the waterfront. There slaves, free men of color, and Irish immigrants unloaded the precious cargoes of finished products and luxury items such as silks, china, glassware, and wines, and loaded the boats high with cotton—the "white gold" of the fertile lower Mississippi River Valley. Vicksburg and her people enjoyed a special bond with the river—it was their river and every aspect of community life depended on the silent, majestic water. Sara Dorsey of Louisiana recognized and understood that bond and referred to the citizens of Vicksburg as "the keepers of the River." But, just as the river gave life to the town, it would bring the instrument of Vicksburg's destruction.[3]

As the nation drifted to the brink of civil war, the citizens of Vicksburg watched with mounting anxiety as the threat of secession spread as wildfire across the South. Due to the city's unique demographics and its reliance on the river, Vicksburg was more conservative in its political views than most other Southern towns. As the secession crisis reached a fever pitch, the citizens of Vicksburg went to the polls in November of 1860 and in expressing their pro-Union sympathy cast their votes for John Bell for president.

The election of the Republican candidate, Abraham Lincoln, as president, however, spurred the fire-eaters and secessionists throughout Mississippi and across the South to lead their states out of the Union. As Mississippians contemplated the momentous issue of secession, in Vicksburg, Marmaduke Shannon editorialized in the *Daily Whig*:

> The die is cast...Abraham Lincoln is President of the United States. . . .What is [our] duty in this crisis in our national affairs. . . .Shall [we] follow the rash and mad advice which the Governor of this State...urge? We do not mean to rebel against the Government because an obnoxious man has been made President! We do not mean to raise the standard of resistance. . . .Let others do what they will, for us, we will stand by the Union, the Constitution, and the laws.[4]

Still hopeful that secession, and the war which would probably follow, could be avoided, the citizens of Vicksburg elected pro-Union delegates to the Secession Convention that convened in Jackson in January 1861. Their voice, however, could not stem the tide of passion which engulfed the state and on January 9, Mississippi became the second state to secede. Church bells rang in joyous chorus across Mississippi, but the news of secession was met passively in Vicksburg with mixed emotion reflective of the divided sympathies of her people. But the citizens of Vicksburg were Mississippians first and would slowly close ranks in support of the state.

The firing on Fort Sumter on April 12, 1861, followed by President Lincoln's call for troops, crushed all hopes for reunification or peaceful secession. For good or ill the citizens of Vicksburg found themselves at war in which their city would be the target of enemy guns. Defense of their homes was paramount and the citizens of

Vicksburg unified in common cause. J.M. Swords, editor of *The Daily Citizen*, expressed the sentiments of the townspeople as he wrote, "We can and will whip the Black Republican...hordes...if they ever attempt to subjugate the South."[5]

An English visitor to the city in that spring of excitement noted in his diary that "war fever is rife in Vicksburg." The men who flocked to the colors came from all walks of life and represented every strata of Vicksburg society. Among the companies that were formed from Vicksburg and Warren County were the Volunteer Southrons, Vicksburg Sharpshooters, Jeff Davis Rebels, Hill City Cadets, Warren Rifles, and the Brierfield Defenders. With dreams of glory and heroism dancing about in their heads off to war they went with little comprehension of the horrors they were about to experience. Knowing that in war the only certainty is death, one Vicksburg merchant, the firm of Catching + Porter advertised "our stock of Mourning Goods was never so complete" and their shelves carried a full line of "black organdie, black silk grenadine, black mosambique, black silk mitts, black kid gloves, and black lace veils." There would be far greater need for these items than the citizens of Vicksburg could have imagined in the spring of 1861. Scores of men would never return from the bloody fields of battle, scores more would be wounded and maimed for life—but all would be changed forever.[6]

By year's end the citizens of Vicksburg began to feel the economic impact of war as fewer steamboats tied up at the city's waterfront, and those that did carried mostly war supplies. Goods were still abundant, but rose rapidly in price—unemployment also climbed. The Benevolent Society was formed by caring citizens who operated a "Free Market" to feed the families of the poor and unemployed. The Ladies Hospital Association, sewing clubs, and an array of other organizations were formed to meet the specific needs of the people in Vicksburg and the soldiers who were stationed in and around the city. The use of homespun clothing and food substitutes were a clearer sign of the war's economic impact as the holiday season passed to begin a new year.

The year 1862 ushered in calamity for Confederate forces responsible for the defense of the Mississippi River. A series of defeats at Forts Henry and Donelson and in the bloody battle at Shiloh brought the tragedy of war to Vicksburg as hundreds of wounded soldiers arrived in town by train or steamboat. Many of the townspeople watched as the soldiers, some of whom were their own sons, were unloaded and taken to the hospitals which were soon filled to capacity. Mahala Roach, who helped care for the men, recorded that "It was a sad sight, and makes us realize that the war is near us indeed."[7]

Most citizens, however, basked in a false sense of security as Vicksburg was still 200 miles from the nearest enemy force. That sense of security was shattered in late April as the ships of David Glasgow Farragut's West Gulf Blockading Squadron bombarded and passed Forts Jackson and St. Philip which resulted in the fall of New Orleans. The loss of New Orleans shocked the citizens of Vicksburg who now realized that there was nothing between them and the Federal fleet only five days steaming time away. With the enemy expected daily in Vicksburg, Mahala Roach observed that "bustle and confusion reigned everywhere" as people prepared to flee the city. Another resident, Anne Broidrick, wrote that the people, "walked the streets aimlessly, as one does when troubled, with bowed heads and saddened mien. It was like the slaying of the first born of Egypt. Sorrow was in every house."[8]

In Vicksburg, preparations for war began in earnest as the city took on increased significance. Jefferson Davis, himself a resident of Warren County, referred to Vicksburg as "the nailhead that held the South's two halves together." On May 1, Mansfield Lovell's troops that had evacuated New Orleans by train poured into Vicksburg and began construction of batteries overlooking the Mississippi River. As the soldiers labored on the fortifications, the Union fleet slowly steamed upriver. Baton Rouge fell on May 8, Natchez four days later, and on Sunday, May 18, the advance flotilla of Farragut's fleet arrived below Vicksburg.[9]

In response to a demand for surrender, Lt. Col. James. L. Autry, the post commander at Vicksburg, wrote defiantly that "Mississippians don't know, and refuse to learn, how to surrender to an enemy." Incensed by this response, Federal officers ordered their gun crews to open fire upon the city. "Men, women and children, both black and white, went screaming through the streets," recalled one panic-stricken citizen as the shot and shell crashed into buildings or landed in the city streets. Thousands of frightened citizens fled the city or sought shelter in caves that they had dug into the hills to escape the hail of iron that rained down upon Vicksburg from mid–May, all through June, and into late July. Such actions kept civilian casualties to a minimum, the only fatality among the populace was Mrs. Patience Gamble who was decapitated by a shell.[10]

By late July, Farragut's squadron, wracked with sickness and plagued by rapidly falling waters, withdrew from Vicksburg to safer, deeper water below Baton Rouge while the ironclads, timberclads, and rams returned upriver to Helena and Memphis. The naval siege of Vicksburg ended. The city had withstood its first test under fire and editor Shannon wrote with pride in the pages of his *Daily Whig*, "In the midst of all this, Vicksburg, proud, gallant little Vicksburg, firm as the eternal hills on which she reposes, gazes boldly and defiantly upon her enemy." One resident who watched the fleet withdraw noted with jubilation, "What will they say [in the] North now about opening the Mississippi River; huzzah for Vicksburg," but added, "9 groans for New Orleans."[11]

During the calm which followed the naval siege, Vicksburg was turned into a powerful bastion by construction of a ring of forts connected by a line of trenches and rifle–pits. Guarding all land approaches to the city, the line of works was formidable but, without adequate numbers of cannon or troops to man the line, Vicksburg remained vulnerable. The sense of vulnerability fueled the fears of those in the city as, by year's end, Federal forces were again in motion toward Vicksburg.

In response to the developing threat, President Davis, accompanied by Gen. Joseph E. Johnston, arrived in Vicksburg on December 21 to bolster the morale of the people and inspect Pemberton's army. The president was impressed by the strength of the fortifications which ringed the city. Johnston, however, declared the line of earthworks to be nothing but an elaborate trap and warned that certain disaster awaited the army which manned Vicksburg's defenses.

Davis's visit was short and the assurances he provided failed to assuage the fears of those who lived in the "Hill City," while Johnston's keen military instincts only provided the citizens with ominous prophecy. The mayor and board of alderman at least took a more pragmatic step and passed a resolution which called for a day of "Humiliation, Fasting and Prayer to Almighty God, that Vicksburg may be spared from the Hand of the Destroyer."[12]

The destroyer, in the form of Maj. Gen. William T. Sherman and his Union Expeditionary Force from Memphis, soon arrived. On Christmas Eve, the ranking officers of the Vicksburg garrison attended a gala ball hosted by Dr. William Balfour and his wife Emma. Unaware of Sherman's approach, the officers, dressed in their finest uniforms, danced the night away with the belles of Vicksburg. Suddenly, the music and dancing stopped when a courier covered in mud burst into the room and handed a warning message to the Confederate commander. Maj. Gen. Martin Luther Smith, then in command of the garrison, exclaimed, "This ball is at an end; the enemy are coming down the river, all non-combatants must leave the city." The garrison was called to arms and prepared to do battle.[13]

Christmas Day passed quietly in Vicksburg as the Federals ate their feast of hardtack and coffee aboard transports moored near Milliken's Bend. But the following day, the Union flotilla steamed up the Yazoo River and landed Sherman's men at the mouth of Chickasaw Bayou north of town. Fighting escalated on December 27 and 28 as the Federals probed for an opening in the Confederate defenses. On Monday, December 29, Sherman ordered his troops to attack saying "we will lose 5,000 men before we take Vicksburg, and may as well lose them here as anywhere else." In the battle which ensued, Union troops were bloodily repulsed and the citizens of Vicksburg breathed a sigh of relief that their prayers for deliverance had been answered.[14]

Life slowly returned to a semblance of normalcy during the winter of 1862-63. Prices in town continued to escalate and the scarcity of goods became more painful. The influx of refugees and soldiers who poured into Vicksburg pushed the over-strained supply system to the breaking point. Business throughout the city was sharply curtailed because of limited resources. Butchers, for example, opened their shops only half a day as the shelves were empty. One woman complained, "I got with difficulty two chickens," and noted that "An egg is a rare and precious thing." Luxury items, however, even salt, were available to those who could afford them. Kate Stone's mother purchased some silk with which to make a dress and grumbled that the material had "cost a pretty penny."[15]

Although it had been a bleak Christmas day, the new year was ushered in with the promise of hope. But as yet another year of war began, a more dangerous, determined foe prepared to advance on the fortress city and the people of Vicksburg watched in trepidation as Grant marshaled his forces across the river at Young's Point and Milliken's Bend.

The campaign began in earnest in late March 1863 as Grant set his army in motion. Unaware of the enemy's movements in Louisiana, those in Vicksburg, citizens and soldiers alike, were caught off guard on the dark, moonless night of April 16 when the Union fleet steamed into action. The townspeople were startled from their sleep by the sound of heavy guns and witnessed gunboats and transports pass the batteries. Mary Loughborough wrote of the terror of that night: "We could hear the gallop, in the darkness, of couriers upon the paved streets; we could hear the voices of the soldiers on the riverside. The rapid firing from the boats, the roar of the Confederate batteries, and, above all, the screaming, booming sound of the shells, as they exploded in the air and around the city." By morning light all was quiet again and the citizens went about their daily routines as if nothing had happened.[16]

Oddly enough, the people of Vicksburg garnered little information on the events which unfolded around them as the Union army crossed the Mississippi River and pushed deep into the interior of their state. It was not until the 16th of May, when the roar of the cannon at Champion Hill echoed through the city streets, that they realized the proximity of their danger. Uncertainty and fear crept into their hearts, but few would accept as truth the rumors of disaster and defeat which spread as wildfire throughout town.

Sunday, the 17th of May, dawned bright and clear. "The birds are singing as merrily as if all were well," recorded Emma Balfour. "The flowers are in perfection, the air heavy with the perfume of cape jasmine and honeysuckle, and the garden bright and gay with all the summer flowers." "Yet in all the pleasant air and sunshine of the day," wrote another woman, "an anxious gloom seemed to hang over the faces of the men: a sorrowful waiting for tidings, that all knew now, would tell of disaster. There seemed no life in the city; sullen and expectant seemed the men—tearful and hopeful the women." Such hope, however, was in vain.[17]

The insightful Mrs. Balfour noted with a tinge of shame, that "all save the spirit of man seems divine." Indeed, for on that Sunday morning the armies again clashed along Big Black River, just nine miles from Vicksburg. The struggled resulted in the wild flight of Pemberton's army toward the city and its perimeter of forts. In Vicksburg, Mary Loughborough watched in horror as the soldiers clad in butternut and gray reached the city and recorded for posterity the events of that day as she wrote "...in all the dejected uncertainty, the stir of horsemen and wheels began, and wagons came rattling down the street—going rapidly one way, and then returning, seemingly, without aim or purpose: now and then a worn and dusty soldier would be seen passing with his blanket and canteen; soon, straggler after straggler came by, then groups of soldiers worn and dusty with the long march."[18]

Emma Balfour also witnessed the flood of soldiers who streamed into Vicksburg and wrote with trembling hand: "I hope never to witness again such a scene as the return of our routed army! From twelve o'clock until late in the night the streets and roads were jammed with wagons, cannons, horses, men, mules, stock, sheep, everything you can imagine that appertains to an army—being brought hurriedly within the intrenchment." Nothing like order prevailed among the troops as divisions, brigades and regiments were broken and separated. Hundreds of men had no weapons, entire batteries had been abandoned in the field at Champion Hill and along the line of Big Black River. "As the poor fellows passed," she noted, "every house poured forth all it had to refresh them. . . .Poor fellows, it made my heart ache to see them, for I knew from all I saw and heard that it was want of confidence in the General commanding that was the cause of our disaster." Late that night she confided to her diary the fears of many in Vicksburg writing, "What is to become of all the living things in this place when the boats commence shelling—God only know—shut up as in a trap—and thousands of women and children—who have fled here for safety."[19]

On May 19 and again on the 22d, Grant hurled his army against the city's defenses only to be repulsed with the loss of more than 4,000 men. During the assaults, the citizens of Vicksburg were introduced to war in all its horror as shot and shell fell in the city streets and crashed through their homes. Public buildings soon filled to capacity with the wounded of both armies and the stench of death was ever-present. Adding to misery of their daily lives were swarms of flies which feasted on the carcasses of man and beast.

spirit of the Vicksburg women and
woman whose remarkable strength
boasted with pride, "Rather than let
us any suffering, I would be content

many in the early days of siege; but
y after weary day, week after bloody
weaken. Civilians soon realized that
ath of the battlefield. Although fig-
casualties, the harsh reality was that
ldren died victims of war.   Mrs.
rnal the death of one child:

he most heartrending screams and moans.
d into a cave about a hundred yards from
the poor woman believed, in safety, she
ve. A mortar shell came rushing through
the earth above the sleeping child—oh!
ing in the upper part of the little sleep-
cent life without a look or word of pass-
art.[24]

those in Vicksburg regardless of
o child, playing in the yard, had
The discovery ended in death for
g it, had innocently pounded the
d, showing as the white smoke
f a life that to the mother's heart

that the only time the shelling
ts ate their morning, noon, and
intervals when silence reigned,
red into a false sense of security
Often they were trapped on the
d and had to dodge the deadly
r of the caves. Not all, however,
ughborough captured one such

The defenders of Vicksburg, posted behind stout fortifications, had
stood defiant in the face of a powerful and determined foe. Unable to
take the city by storm, Grant began siege operations to reduce
Vicksburg and its garrison into submission by attrition. Throughout
the month of May and into June Union soldiers slowly extended
their lines to the left and right until they invested the beleaguered city.
Once the investment was completed, Pemberton's garrison was effectively cut off from all supply and communications with the outside
world. For the citizens and soldiers trapped in Vicksburg, life soon became a terrifying quest for survival. They had to subsist solely on what
they had stockpiled in Vicksburg prior to the siege. With each passing
day those supplies dwindled until they were nearly exhausted.

In order to conserve what food supplies were on hand, Pemberton
ordered the daily ration for his soldiers cut to three-quarter the standard issue, then to half, then to quarter. Rations were then cut again,
and yet again, and yet again. By the end of June the garrison was issued only a handful of peas and rice per man per day. It was hardly
enough to keep one alive, but it was all they had. Water too, became a
scarce commodity and by late June had to be rationed.

Disease began to spread rapidly through the ranks. Dysentery, diarrhea, malaria, and various fevers all took a heavy toll of human life and
were more certain of death than were Union sharpshooters. As the
siege progressed, a steady stream of men, first by the score, then hundreds, could be seen to lay their weapons aside and walk or crawl as
best they could to the hospitals in Vicksburg. Public buildings were
filled to capacity and many handsome private residences were converted to hospitals. But even there, there was no succor as medicines
were in short supply. Each day the "dead wagons" made the rounds of
the hospitals and the dead were brought out in ever increasing number and carried to their long rest and interred in the city cemetery
northeast of town.

Adding to the horrors caused by shortages of food and water,
Union land and naval batteries shelled the city and its defenses.
Powerful batteries were established along the siege lines as Federal ar-
tillerists placed 220 cannon, many of which were rifled guns, and
bombarded the fortress city night and day. R. Adm. David Dixon
Porter also moved his gunboats into position to engage the

Confederate river batteries and stationed mortar scows on the far side of De Soto Point, opposite Vicksburg. The large 13-inch mortars could hurl a 218-pound ball one-half mile into the air which, at the height of its trajectory, blocked out the sun. When the bombs, as they were called by the citizens of Vicksburg, crashed to earth the explosion created a crater almost fifteen feet deep. There appeared to be no safety anywhere.

Life under siege soon translated into life under ground as citizens and soldiers alike dug deep into the loess hills and hollowed out rooms in which to live. At first, those who fled to the caves found the conditions abhorrent. "When we went in [to the cave] this evening and sat down," recorded one resident of town, "the earthy, suffocating feeling, as of a living tomb, was dreadful to me. I fear I shall risk death outside rather then melt in that dark furnace." Mrs. Balfour wrote in similar terms of her experience: "As all this rushed over me and the sense of suffocation from being underground, **the certainty** that there was no way of escape, that we were hemmed in, caged—for one moment my heart seemed to stand still." It was a feeling that she and others would grow accustomed to over the next six weeks.[20]

Mary Loughborough, whose husband James was an officer in Pemberton's army, was forced underground with her daughter to seek shelter from the artillery projectiles which fell like rain upon the city. Of her experience she lived to write:

> The caves were plainly becoming a necessity, as some persons had been killed on the street by fragments of shells. The room that I had slept in had been struck by a fragment of a shell during the first night, and a large hole made in the ceiling. I shall never forget my extreme fear during the night, and my utter hopelessness of ever seeing the morning light. Terror stricken, we remained crouched in the cave, while shell after shell followed each other in quick succession. I endeavored by constant prayer to prepare myself for the sudden death I was almost certain awaited me. My heart stood still as we would hear the reports from the guns, and the rushing and fearful sound of the shell as it came toward us. As it neared, the noise became deafening; the air was full of the rushing sound; pains darted through my temples; my ears were full of the confusing noise; and, as it exploded, the report flashed through my head like an electric shock, leaving me in a quiet state of terror the most painful that I can imagine—cowering in a corner, holding my child to my heart—the only feeling of my life being the chocking throbs of my heart, that rendered me almost breathless. As singly as they fell short, or beyond the cave, I was aroused by a feeling of thankfulness that was short of duration. Again and again the terrible fright came over us in that night.[21]

account, but they little know
children if they expect this."
would be taxed to the limit, s
them know that they are caus
to suffer martyrdom!"[23]

Her sentiments were shared
as the bombardment continue
week, even the resolute began
they were not immune to the
ures vary as to the total of civi
innocent men, women, and
Loughborough recorded in he

> Sitting in the cave, one evening, I h
> I was told that a mother had taken
> us; and having laid it on its little b
> took her seat near the entrance of
> the air, and fell with much force, er
> most horrible sight to the mother-
> ing head, and taking away the youn
> ing love to be treasured in the moth

The dreaded bombs preye
gender, race, or age. "A little
found a shell," recalled one res
the child who "in rolling and
fuse; the terrible explosion fo
floated away, the mangled rem
had possessed all of beauty and

A Confederate soldier obs
stopped was when Federal ar
evening meals. During these
many who lived in Vicksburg
and ventured forth from their
city streets when the shelling
projectiles as they raced for th
reached safety. The observant M
tragedy writing:

A young girl, becoming weary in the confinement of the cave, hastily ran to the house in the interval that elapsed between the slowly falling shells. On returning, an explosion sounded near her—one wild scream, and she ran into her mother's presence, sinking like a wounded dove, the life blood flowing over the light summer dress in crimson ripples from a death-wound in her side, caused by the shell fragment.[26]

The sufferings of those in Vicksburg would haunt for the remainder of her days one woman who clung to life in the caves. "The screams of the women of Vicksburg were the saddest I have ever heard," she later wrote of those who lost loved ones to Union shells. "The wailings over the dead seemed full of heart-sick agony. I cannot attempt to describe the thrill of pity, mingled with fear, that pierced my soul, as suddenly vibrating through the air would come these sorrowful shrieks!—these pitiful moans!—sometimes almost simultaneously with the explosion of a shell."[27]

During one of the more intense periods of shelling, Margaret Lord, wife of the Rev. Dr. William Lord, rector of Christ Church, tried to comfort her daughter Lida as the

Rev. William Lord
Vicksburg 47 Days of Siege

family crouched in the basement of their house of worship. "Don't cry my darling," she soothed the child assuring her that "God will protect us." The little girl could not be calmed sobbing, "But, momma, I's so 'fraid God's killed too!"[28]

The shelling and constant fear of death wore heavily on the nerves of the soldiers in the trenches as it did citizens such as Lida Lord. "Another day like the past twenty-one as one day could be like another," complained Lt. William Drennan in the pages of his diary on June 9, 1863. "Monotony does not convey all the sameness of these days imposes on one. There is a tension of nerves, an extreme anxiety, as you have experienced for a few moments and that you have felt—had you to endure it long, it would craze you." Two days later he wrote of the scepter which overshadowed the monotony of events in Vicksburg and made the days so difficult to bear. "The mortality here at this time is very great; hardly a day passes but I see dozens of men carried to their last homes. They are buried in a trench with a blanket for a shroud. Coffins can not be had for all of them. Graves are dug today for use tomorrow."[29]

Citizens and soldiers alike came to fear that death was certain should the siege continue throughout the summer. Everywhere they looked evidenced the destructive power of the besieging army the grip of which was slowly strangling them into submission. "How blightingly the hand of warfare lay upon the town!" observed Mary Loughborough whose memory of life in the once magnificent city of Vicksburg seemed but a dream. Food supplies dwindled and, just as with the soldiers who stood steadfast in the trenches, the citizens of Vicksburg came to stare at starvation. Prices for all commodities were exorbitant as goods of any kind were practically non-existent. By the end of June, one could walk through the market places along Washington Street and see "skinned rats" hanging for sale. The shortages of even life's basic necessities were made painfully more apparent as *The Daily Citizen*, Vicksburg's leading newspaper, came to be issued on wallpaper.[30]

Yet, in the midst of suffering and death, there was new life. At least two children were born in caves during the siege. In honor of the circumstances which greeted his arrival into the world, one boy was christened William Siege Green. For the newborn babies, their parents, and all others in Vicksburg, there were also reasons for hope. Surely the authorities in Richmond would not forsake a city as significant as Vicksburg was to the Confederacy. Knowing that Gen. Joseph E. Johnston had been sent to Mississippi by President Davis to rescue Vicksburg and its besieged garrison, relief was on their minds and their constant prayer was for deliverance.

But that deliverance never came and the sands of time expired. On the hot afternoon of July 3, white flags of truce appeared along the lines. A trio of officers in gray, led by General Pemberton, rode out from the city along the Jackson Road and beyond the defense line. Riding to meet them was a cavalcade of officers in blue led by General Grant. The two generals, however, failed to come to terms during this meeting, but agreed to a cessation of hostilities and continued communication through an exchange of notes. Late that night, Grant sent in his final terms which were accepted by Pemberton in the pre-dawn darkness on the Fourth of July.

The Siege of Vicksburg was over, word of which spread quickly among the civilian population as the first streaks of dawn brightened the sky. The morning was deathly quiet and as the people of Vicksburg grappled with emotions, the valiant defenders of the city marched forth from their works, stacked their arms, unbuckled their accouterments, and furled their flags. Those who had remained steadfast to the end broke down and shed tears unashamedly as

Lucy McRae
Vicksburg 47 Days of Siege

they returned to their works to await what fate held in store for them.

Venturing from the caves that had sheltered them through the long ordeal of siege, the citizens slowly returned to their homes to await their own fate at the hands of Union occupation forces. Young Lucy McRae was moved to tears by the sights which enveloped her as she reached the family home on Main Street accompanied by her younger brother. "How sad was the spectacle that met our gaze," she wrote, "arms stacked in the center of the streets, men with tearful eyes and downcast faces walking here and there; men sitting in groups feeling that they would gladly have given their life-blood on the battlefield rather than hand over the guns and sabers so dear to them." Echoing those sentiments was Margaret Lord who with a heavy heart watched as "Our poor soldiers came in a continuous stream past the house, so pale, so emaciated, and so grief stricken, panting with the heat and Oh! saddest of all, without their colors and arms."[31]

When informed by her husband James that Vicksburg had surrendered, Mary Loughborough wandered from her cave for the first time in days. "On the hill above us the earth was literally covered with fragments of shell—Parrott, shrapnel, canister." She was amazed that anyone had escaped the missiles of destruction which rained down upon the city for weeks, and recorded in her journal that, "Minie balls lay in every direction, flattened, dented, and bent from the contact with trees and pieces of wood in their flight. The grass seemed deadened—the ground ploughed into furrows in many places; while scattered over all, like giants' pepper, in numberless quantity, were the shrapnel balls."[32]

Despite the appalling sights, for those who had survived the constant bombardment by Union cannon and heavy mortars, the most stunning sensation was silence. "It seems to me I can hear the silence, and feel it, too," gently breathed Dora Anderson. "It wraps me like a soft garment; how else can I express this peace?" Resigning herself to the silence, Mary Loughborough expressed the sentiment of many in Vicksburg as she sighed, "Amen."[33]

Residents who had fled the city prior to the siege slowly returned that day. Ida Barlow was one who returned to Vicksburg on July 4 and noted: "Starving men, women and children with rags hanging to them stalked the streets in utter despair. They had given all for their country, and had naught left but a feeble claim on life and this they were ready to give also." Truly, they had lost most everything but life itself and the will to survive. Kate Stone, who returned to a home laid desolate by war, typified the spirit of those who resumed life in and around Vicksburg. "We must bear our losses as best we can," she boldly proclaimed. "Nothing is left but to endure."[34]

And they would endure—

CHAPTER NINE

TO RESCUE GIBRALTAR

Efforts of the Trans-Mississippi Confederates to Relieve Fortress Vicksburg

In the spring of 1863, from when the Vicksburg Campaign began to unfold until the city was invested, Confederate forces in the Trans-Mississippi Department were presented with an opportunity to defeat or at least hinder Federal movements aimed at the capture of the river fortress. Late to grasp the opportunity, Southerners struck at Union supply enclaves in Louisiana. Their principal effort resulted in failure at the Battle of Milliken's Bend on June 7—an action that was only the second major engagement in which blacks fought in the uniform of United States soldiers. Few historians, however, make any mention of these operations in their discussions of the Vicksburg Campaign. The following essay presents that seldom-told chapter of the Vicksburg drama.

On March 29, 1863, Maj. Gen. Ulysses S. Grant boldly launched his Union Army of the Tennessee on a march south through Louisiana from his base camps at Milliken's Bend and Young's Point. In characteristic fashion and with grim determination, Maj. Gen. John A. McClernand of the XIII Corps was ordered to open a road from Milliken's Bend to New Carthage on the Mississippi River below Vicksburg. It was Grant's intention to search for a favorable crossing point below the Confederate stronghold and transfer the field of operations to the area south and east of Vicksburg. The movement started on March 31, and thus the Vicksburg Campaign began in earnest.

At the same time, Union Maj. Gen. Nathaniel P. Banks massed a force of 15,000 men at Berwick Bay, west of New Orleans, and prepared to launch a drive up the Bayou Teche aimed at Alexandria, Louisiana. In response to these developing threats, Confederate Lt. Gen. E. Kirby Smith, in command of the Trans-Mississippi

Maj. Gen. John G. Walker
Generals in Gray

Department, sought to augment his forces in Louisiana. On April 14, Smith ordered the Texas Division of Maj. Gen. John G.

Walker to march from Pine Bluff, Arkansas, to Monroe, Louisiana, from which point it could be thrown against either Grant or Banks.

The Federal threats, however, developed rapidly. On April 16, part of the Union fleet commanded by R. Adm. David Dixon Porter successfully fought its way past the batteries of Vicksburg with the loss of only one transport and headed toward a rendezvous with Grant somewhere below the city. The next day, April 17, McClernand's XIII Corps, the vanguard of the Union army, began to concentrate at New Carthage, while the eager foot soldiers of Maj. Gen. James B. McPherson's XVII Corps took up the line of march south from Milliken's Bend, to where they had been shuttled by boat from Lake Providence.

Kirby Smith kept abreast of these developments and anxiously awaited the arrival of Walker's Texans. Unbeknownst to Smith, the Texans had not yet received their marching orders.

In Arkansas, the officers and men of Walker's Texas Division had for weeks been marching and countermarching between Little Rock and Pine Bluff. One Texan angered by the senseless routine stated emphatically that the division had been "used up to accomplish nothing." Another Texan, far more philosophical, wrote, "It was generally believed amongst the troops that Gen. [T. H.] Holmes was advised by the Medical Board to give Walker's Division enough of exercise. This may be the object of our marching and countermarching between Little Rock and Pine Bluff." Either way, the Texans were eager for a fight and welcomed the orders directing them to Louisiana.[1]

John George Walker, the popular commander of the Texas Division, was born on July 22, 1822, in Cole County, Missouri. Commissioned directly into the United States Army in 1846 by President James K. Polk, Walker was appointed a first lieutenant in a company of mounted rifles and served during the Mexican War. He remained in the army and later served in California, Oregon, and New Mexico attaining the rank of captain by 1861. At the outbreak of hostilities between the states, Walker was on duty at Fort Union in New Mexico. On July 31, 1861, he resigned from United States service and was immediately commissioned colonel of the 2d Virginia Infantry. Rising rapidly through the ranks, he was named a brigadier general on January 9, 1862, in which rank he exercised both brigade and division command. In cooperation with "Stonewall" Jackson's command, Walker led a division in one of the more remarkable concentrations in the annals of war at Harpers Ferry where his troops occupied Loundon Heights. Two days after the September 15 surrender of Harpers Ferry, he experienced savage fighting at Antietam.

Promoted to major general on November 8, 1862, Walker was transferred to the Trans-Mississippi Department and in January assumed command of the Texas Division then encamped at Little Rock. One Texan wrote that General Walker "soon became very popular with them his presence was always hailed with the wildest enthusiasm by both officers and soldiers." Joseph P. Blessington of the 16th Texas Infantry recalled that Walker "gave us our first lesson in the field in the face of the enemy, and of all the generals in command of the Confederate troops, he was the most untiring, vigilant, and patient. No commander could surpass him. Devoid of ambition, incapable of envy, he was brave, gallant, and just." The Houston *Telegraph* noted that the new commander was "Laborious, systematic, painstaking, unostentatious—working himself according to a rigid standard of duty, and exacting the like from others." Yet, a more objective evaluation written by Edwin C. Bearss characterizes Walker as "competent but unimaginative."[2]

Walker's Texas Division consisted of four brigades, three of Texans and one of Arkansans commanded respectively by Henry E. McCulloch, James M. Hawes, Horace Randal, and James C. Tappan. A brief examination of these commanders is in order.

Henry E. McCulloch was the younger brother of Confederate Brig. Gen. Ben McCulloch who was killed at Elkhorn Tavern.

Brig. Gen. Henry McCulloch
Generals in Gray

Henry was born in Rutherford County, Tennessee, on December 6, 1816. Twenty years later he moved to Texas and settled in Guadalupe County. During the Mexican War he served as a captain in a company of Texas Rangers and, afterwards, served in both houses of the state legislature. In 1859, President James Buchanan appointed him a United States marshal for the eastern district of Texas.

At the outbreak of the war in 1861, Henry McCulloch was commissioned colonel of the 1st Texas Mounted Rifles and, for a short time, commanded the Department of Texas. Appointed a brigadier general on March 14, 1862, he assumed command of the troops in East Texas. Later that same year, he was ordered to Little Rock and given command of the Texas Division. During his tenure of command the division saw little action; and upon Walker's assignment, McCulloch reverted to brigade command. His brigade consisted of the 16th, 17th, and 19th Texas Infantry, the 16th Texas Cavalry (dismounted), and Capt. William Edgar's four gun-battery of light artillery. McCulloch's Brigade was considered the elite of the Texas Division and would perform the most creditable service in the operations to relieve Vicksburg.[3]

Turning to James M. Hawes, the records show him to be a native of Lexington, Kentucky, born on January 7, 1824. A West Point graduate, class of 1845, Hawes stood 29 in a class of 41. He saw action in Mexico where he won two brevets for gallant and meritorious service and, yet, declined one of them. He later taught infantry and cavalry tactics and mathematics at West Point; and, like George S. Patton of World War II fame more than 60 years later, served a tour at the

French cavalry school at Saumur. Upon his return from France, he was sent to Kansas and was there during the border disturbances of the 1850s.

Hawes resigned his commission on May 9, 1861, and in June was elected colonel of the 2nd Kentucky Cavalry. At the request of Albert Sidney Johnston, he was appointed a brigadier general in the Provisional Army to rank from March 5, 1862. Hawes commanded the cavalry in the Western Department during the Shiloh operations. Afterwards, at his own request, he was relieved of the cavalry and assumed command of an infantry brigade in John C. Breckinridge's division. In October 1862, he was sent to the Trans-Mississippi Department where on April 24, 1863, he was given command of a brigade in the Texas Division. The 12th, 18th, and 22nd Texas Infantry, 13th Texas Cavalry (dismounted), and Capt. Horace Halderman's four-gun battery of light artillery composed his brigade.[4]

The other brigade of Texans was commanded by Col. Horace Randal. A native of Tennessee, born in 1833, his family joined a host of thousands who put "G.T.T." on their doors and "Gone to Texas." Randal was a graduate of the United States Military Academy class of 1854. His performance at the Point, however, was less than brilliant and he graduated 45 in a class of 46. He served in the infantry and then in the dragoons on the frontier. On February 27, 1861, he resigned his commission as a second lieutenant in the U.S. Army only to be disappointed by the offer of similar commission in the Confederate service. Randal importuned President Jefferson Davis for higher rank and was quick to point out that he had commanded the cavalry in Lincoln's inaugural parade. (Personally, this writer cannot think of a more solid qualification for higher rank.)

Failing to gain what he considered a more appropriate rank, the ostentatious Randal fought as a private in Virginia. He later became a lieutenant and aide-de-camp on the staff of Maj. Gen. G. W. Smith. In 1862, however, he was named colonel of the 28th Texas Cavalry (at that time dismounted for lack of horses), and later that same year was assigned brigade command in the Texas Division then at Little Rock. His brigade consisted of the 11th and 14th Texas Infantry, 6th Texas Cavalry Battalion (dismounted), 28th Texas Cavalry (still dismounted), and Capt. J. M. Daniels four-gun battery of light artillery. One Texan thought Randal a "distinguished officer" who, in action, "seemed ubiquitous as he screamed his orders here and there, always urging his men on the foe."[5]

Brig. Gen. James C. Tappan's Brigade of Arkansans would not participate in the operations about to be discussed and, therefore, neither the brigadier or his men will be evaluated in this essay.

In Louisiana, Union threats continued to ominously unfold. On April 19, Kirby Smith implored General Holmes to "Please hasten Walker's movements." Yet, it was not until the 23rd, after a loss of four valuable days, that orders were issued for the Texans to proceed without delay to Monroe. On April 24, the Texans broke camp and took up the line of march south toward Louisiana. The men marched at a leisurely pace for the weather was excessively warm and water along the route was scarce. Walker's command received a warm reception at Monticello where, as one soldier proudly recalled, "the ladies were on the sidewalk waving their handkerchiefs as a token of admiration for the Texas boys."[6]

Although finally en route, the Texans were losing the battle with time. On April 29, Porter's gunboats bombarded the Grand Gulf defenses in preparation for a landing by Grant's troops. The fleet silenced the guns of Fort Wade, but could not quiet those of Fort Cobun. Ever adaptive, Grant disembarked his men from the transports and marched them five miles farther down the Louisiana shore. That evening, Porter's fleet ran past the Confederate batteries and rendezvoused with Grant at Disharoon's plantation. The next day as the Texans prepared to cross the state line into Louisiana, a far more significant crossing was being made as Grant hurled his army across the mighty river and onto Mississippi soil. A band aboard the flagship *Benton* struck up "The Red, White, and Blue" as Grant's infantrymen came ashore. In the largest amphibious operation in American history up to that time, Grant landed 22,000 men and began the inland campaign to capture Vicksburg.

Once ashore, Grant's forces pushed rapidly inland and marched through the night. In the early morning hours of May 1, Confederate resistance was encountered west of Port Gibson. In a furious battle which raged throughout the day, Union soldiers fought with grim determination to secure their beachhead on Mississippi soil while Confederate soldiers struggled with equal determination to drive the invaders into the river. As the contest raged in unabated fury, Walker's

Division crossed the state line north of Monroe, marched three miles, and bivouacked for the night. As the Texans bedded down for the night, their comrades were in full retreat from Port Gibson.

Although victory at Port Gibson secured his beachhead and forced the Confederate evacuation of Grand Gulf, Grant was concerned about his supply and communications line which ran a distance of sixty-three miles from Milliken's Bend to Hard Times. He realized that it was vulnerable and, if cut, could embarrass or even terminate his operations in Mississippi. Therefore, on May 3, he ordered a road cut from Young's Point to Bowers' Landing which would not only shorten his line considerably, to only twelve miles, but afford greater protection to the vital supplies his army needed to conduct the inland campaign against Vicksburg.

One can here already see the opportunity for Confederates in the Trans-Mississippi Department to deal Grant a crippling blow slipping away.

That same day, May 3, Walker's command camped on Bayou Bartholomew northeast of Ouachita City. The following day, the Texans reached Trenton on the Ouachita River opposite Monroe—less than two days march from Grant's Mississippi River enclaves. The Texans, however, settled into camp at Trenton and remained there from May 5 to 9. During this time frame, Grant's presence in Louisiana constantly diminished and only four regiments, plus recently recruited blacks, remained to guard Milliken's Bend and the supply line through Richmond.

On May 9, Brig. Gen. Paul O. Hébert, Confederate commander in northeastern Louisiana, requested assistance from Walker to launch an attack on Milliken's Bend. Although Walker favored the idea, "orders were imperative" to embark his command and move toward Alexandria. Hébert pleaded for just one brigade, yet only gained assurances from Walker that as soon as Banks was taken care of he would return to cooperate in an attack on Grant's bases.[7]

Lt. Gen. John C. Pemberton, in Mississippi, also recognized the urgency to destroy Grant's exposed line of supply. On May 9 he wired Smith: "You can contribute materially to the defense of Vicksburg and the navigation of the Mississippi River by a movement upon the line of communications of the enemy on the western side of the river." He emphasized, "To break this would render a most important service."

Smith, however, more concerned with developments affecting his own department, hesitated to act upon Pemberton's request.[8]

On May 10, Walker's Texans, having learned of the evacuation of Alexandria, returned to Trenton. Immediately upon disembarkation, Hawes' and Randal's brigades started overland toward Natchitoches to assist Maj. Gen. Dick Taylor then falling back from Alexandria toward Shreveport. McCulloch's Brigade, however, remained in Trenton until May 16.

On May 12, during McCulloch's inactivity at Trenton, Federal forces opened the road from Young's Point to Bowers' Landing; while in Mississippi, Grant's troops handed the Confederates another defeat in the Battle of Raymond, and on May 14, captured the Mississippi capital of Jackson.

Not wishing to detach combat troops for occupation duty, Grant applied the torch to Jackson then turned his army west toward its true objective—Vicksburg. En route from Jackson to Vicksburg, Grant's army inflicted devastating casualties on Pemberton's force in the bloodiest action of the Vicksburg campaign at Champion Hill on May 16. That same day, McCulloch's Brigade took up the line of march toward Campti 116 miles west of Monroe. Thus, the only Confederate force capable of crippling Grant's supply line in Louisiana moved away from this vulnerable target.

On May 17, as the Texans tramped westward, Grant soundly defeated Confederate forces at the Big Black River Bridge and hurled Pemberton's army back into the defenses of Vicksburg. Having witnessed the debacle at the Big Black River and the wild flight of his troops, Pemberton dejectedly stated to his chief engineer, "Just thirty years ago I began my military career by receiving my appointment to a cadetship at the U.S. Military Academy, and to-day—the same date—that career is ended in disaster and disgrace."[9]

The Confederate army fell back into Vicksburg without semblance of order or discipline. The men moved about singly or in small groups. Hundreds of men had no weapons, entire batteries had been abandoned in the fields at Champion Hill and at Big Black River Bridge. It was this demoralized mass of men which prepared to resist the Union onslaught at Vicksburg.

On May 19, Grant re-established contact with the fleet on the Yazoo River at Haynes' and Snyder's bluffs and began to replenish dangerously depleted supplies of food and ammunition. Having re-established contact with the fleet, Grant assured himself an uninterrupted line of supply and communications via the Mississippi and Yazoo rivers. Two days later when a road was opened from the Yazoo bases to the army besieging Vicksburg, it became immaterial whether or not the Confederates attacked the bases at Milliken's Bend and Young's Point.

Lest Walker's command is left marching westward, the Texans' saga must continue.

On May 22, the Texans reached Campti and all three of Walker's brigades were united. That same day, Grant's second assault on fortress Vicksburg was repulsed with severe losses. Four days later, on May 26, the Texans moved via

Maj. Gen. Richard Taylor
Generals in Gray

transports toward Alexandria which had been abandoned by Banks, who sought greater laurels at Port Hudson.

Walker's Division did not remain long in Alexandria for on May 28 the men headed toward Perkins' Landing on the Mississippi River downstream from Vicksburg. Three days later, on May 31, McCulloch's Brigade formed line of battle and attacked a lone Union regiment (the 60th Indiana) at Perkins' Landing. The Federals, however, managed to escape thanks to the timely arrival of the ironclad *Carondelet* and a transport which evacuated the Hoosiers. In this minor skirmish, their first of the campaign, the Texans lost 1 killed and 6 wounded.

At this important juncture, Taylor desired to use Walker's Division in an advance on Berwick Bay, overrun the LaFourche, and threaten New Orleans. Taylor, however, was overruled by Kirby Smith who directed him to strike at the Federals in Madison Parish. Taylor opposed

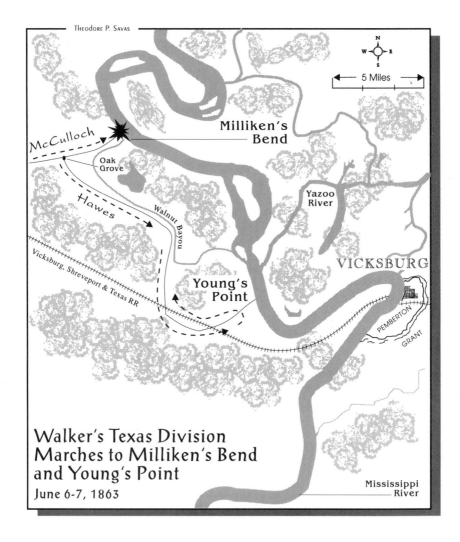

Theodore P. Savas

Walker's Texas Division Marches to Milliken's Bend and Young's Point
June 6-7, 1863

the idea and later wrote, "Remonstrances were to no avail. I was informed that all the Confederate authorities in the east were urgent for some effort on our part in behalf of Vicksburg, and that public opinion would condemn us if we did not *try to do something.*" Taylor insisted "that to go two hundred miles and more away from the proper theatre of action in search of an indefinite something is hard; but orders are orders."[10]

In accordance with his orders, Taylor reluctantly directed the Texans to Richmond, Louisiana. Taylor himself went on ahead of the Texans and reached Richmond at dusk on June 5. He immediately set about gathering intelligence concerning the enemy dispositions and troop strengths at Milliken's Bend and Young's Point. Much of the data gained by Taylor was provided by Lt. Col. Isaac F. Harrison of the 15th Louisiana Cavalry Battalion. Some of it was correct, and some was not. Harrison, for example, grossly underestimated enemy troop strength at both points; and faulty intelligence played a key role in the Confederate plan of action.[11]

The Texans tramped into Richmond at 10:00 a.m. on June 6, where they cooked rations and rested for several hours. Walker was informed of the enemy's dispositions and briefed on the plan of action. Taylor's plan called for Walker's Division to launch simultaneous assaults on the enemy at Milliken's Bend and Young's Point, while a combat patrol led by Col. Frank Bartlett of the 13th Louisiana Cavalry Battalion attacked the Federal enclave at Lake Providence.

On June 6, as the Confederates planned for action, the Federals at Milliken's Bend made a reconnaissance in the direction of Richmond. The Federals had been monitoring the increased Confederate activity and feared an attack on Milliken's Bend was imminent. Consequently, Brig. Gen. Elias S. Dennis, commander of the District of Northeast Louisiana, ordered Col. Hermann Lieb to make a reconnaissance to-ward Richmond.

Lieb was a feisty soldier. Born in Switzerland, he emigrated to the United States and settled in Illinois. At the outbreak of the war, he en-listed for ninety days as a private in Company B of the 8th Illinois Infantry. Upon reorganization of the regiment in July of 1861, Lieb was elected captain and the following year was promoted to major. He saw action at Fort Donelson and at Shiloh. During the operations now under discussion, he was colonel of the 9th Louisiana Infantry (African Descent) and commanded the post at Milliken's Bend.[12]

At 2:00 a.m., on June 6, Lieb moved out with his own regiment and several companies of the 10th Illinois Cavalry. His force pushed to within three miles of Richmond when they made contact with Confederates. After driving in the pickets, Lieb became apprehensive and decided to return to Milliken's Bend. When half-way to the post, Lieb's men were surprised to see the Illinois troopers dashing up in

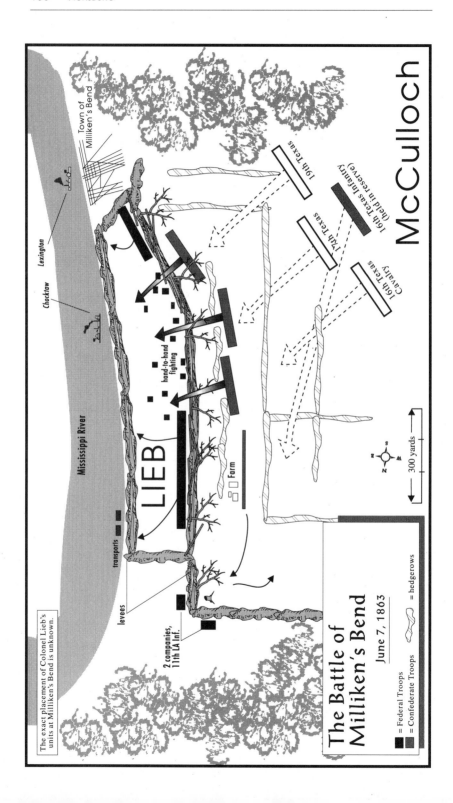

The exact placement of Colonel Lieb's units at Milliken's Bend is unknown.

McCulloch

19th Texas

16th Texas Infantry (held in reserve)

17th Texas

16th Texas Cavalry

Town of Milliken's Bend

Lexington

Chocktaw

Mississippi River

transports

LIEB

hand-to-hand fighting

Farm

levees

2 companies, 11th LA Inf.

N

S

E

W

300 yards

The Battle of Milliken's Bend

June 7, 1863

■ = Federal Troops
■ = Confederate Troops

〰 = hedgerows

their rear, hotly pursued by Confederate cavalry. Reacting quickly, Colonel Lieb deployed his regiment into line. A single volley sufficed to drive off the Confederates. Convinced that his post was in danger, Lieb requested reinforcements. In response to the colonel's urgent request, the 23rd Iowa (a white regiment) was hurried from Young's Point to Milliken's Bend; and the ironclad *Choctaw* was sent by Admiral Porter to provide additional support. That night, the Federals fortified their camp by constructing abatis and barricades of cotton bales. Confidence bred by these preparations, Lieb had his men under arms at 3:00 a.m. on June 7.[13]

The Confederate plan of action called for a night march. The Texans left Richmond at 6:00 p.m., on June 6, in hopes of arriving at the enemy camps at sunrise. One Texan recorded the march with these words:

> In sections four abreast, and close order, the troops took up the line of march, in anticipation of meeting almost certain death, but with undaunted, unquailing spirits. In breathless silence, with the high glittering stars looking down upon them, through dark and deep defiles marched the dense array of men, moving steadily forward; not a whisper was heard—no sound of clanking saber, or rattle of canteen and cup.[14]

At Oak Grove plantation the road forked, the left fork led to Milliken's Bend, the right to Young's Point. Walker sent McCulloch's Brigade toward Milliken's Bend and Hawes' Brigade toward Young's Point, while he remained at Oak Grove with Randal's Brigade as a general reserve.

McCulloch's Brigade, 1,500—strong, arrived within one and one-half miles of Milliken's Bend at 2:30 a.m. with cavalry scouts deployed in front. Union picket fire scattered the Confederate cavalrymen who fell back precipitously before the unexpected resistance. In the darkness and confusion, the cavalrymen were then fired upon by McCulloch's skirmishers. Fortunately, no men were injured, although they did lose two horses killed and a third wounded. McCulloch quickly deployed his brigade into line of battle with Col. Richard Waterhouse's 19th Texas Infantry on the right, Col. R. T. P. Allen's 17th Texas Infantry in the center, and Lt. Col. E. P. Gregg's 16th Texas Cavalry (dismounted) on the left. Col. George Flournoy's 16th Texas Infantry was held in reserve.

As the Federal pickets began falling back, Lieb placed his men on the levee behind cotton bales. His units consisted of the 8th, 9th, 11th, and 13th Louisiana Infantry Regiments (African Descent), 1st Mississippi Infantry (African Descent), and the 23d Iowa Infantry totaling 1,061 men. The black troops were recently recruited, poorly trained, and poorly armed. In many cases, they were also poorly led. But, they had the advantage of position and were supported by the guns of the powerful ironclad *Choctaw*.

McCulloch placed his Texans into line of battle astride the Richmond road and proceeded to drive the Federal pickets, who were positioned behind a succession of thick hedges. One Texans wrote, "It was impossible for our troops to keep in line of battle, owing to the many hedges we had to encounter, which it was impossible to pass, except through a few gaps that had been used as gates or passways." Once passed the hedgerows, McCulloch reformed his brigade within twenty-five paces of the main Federal line. Shouting, "No quarter for the officers, kill the damned abolitionists, spare the niggers," the Texans scaled the levee and closed on the enemy. A withering volley stunned the Southerners, but the poorly trained blacks were unable to reload their cumbersome weapons before the Texans were upon them. McCulloch reported, "The line was formed under a heavy fire from the enemy, and the troops charged the breastworks, carrying it instantly, killing and wounding many of the enemy by their deadly fire, as well as the bayonet." The brigadier noted, "This charge was resisted by the negro portion of the enemy's force with considerable obstinacy, while the white or true Yankee portion ran like whipped curs almost as soon as the charge was ordered."[15]

Clubbed muskets and bayonets were freely used as the Texans surged over the cotton-bale breastworks atop the levee. Joseph P. Blessington of the 16th Texas recalled, "The enemy gave away and stampeded pell-mell over the levee, in great terror and confusion. Our troops followed after them, bayoneting them by hundreds." Sweeping through the Federal encampment, McCulloch's men raced toward the second levee next to the river. Their efforts to gain the levee, however, were driven back repeatedly by the deliberate fire of *Choctaw's* big guns.[16]

Unable to cross the levee, McCulloch's men mopped-up isolated pockets of resistance and plundered the Federal camp. The brigadier sent an urgent request to Walker for reinforcements, but before help arrived, McCulloch spotted a second gunboat, the venerable timber clad *Lexington*, coming upriver. Realizing that his troops were no match for gunboats, and without waiting for Walker's arrival, McCulloch ordered a withdrawal to Oak Grove plantation.[17]

In the engagement at Milliken's Bend, McCulloch's Brigade suffered losses of 44 killed, 131 wounded, and 10 missing. The Texans, however, inflicted 652 casualties on the Federals of which number 101 were killed, 285 wounded, and 266 captured or missing.[18]

Confederate reports and correspondence relative to the bloody fighting at Milliken's Bend refer to the circumstances surrounding the capture of armed negroes. Kirby Smith, after hearing that black soldiers had been captured, wrote to Richard Taylor, "I hope this may not be so, and that your subordinates. . . may have recognized the propriety of giving no quarter to armed negroes and their officers. In this way we may be relieved from a disagreeable dilemma."[19]

The situation was perplexing for Taylor, Smith, and Confederate civil authorities. The fate of these blacks and of their white officers who were also captured continues to be a source of controversy. An examination of the *Official Records* reveals that on August 12, 1863, Maj. Gen. Henry Halleck forwarded to Grant a copy of a newspaper article which appeared in the *Missouri Democrat* (date unknown) which reads as follows:

> The following is given upon the authority of Lieutenant Cole, of the Mississippi Marine Brigade:
>
> The day after the battle of Milliken's Bend, in June last, the Marine Brigade landed some 10 miles below the [Milliken's] Bend, and attacked and routed the guerrillas which had been repulsed by our troops and the gunboats the day previous. Major [James M.] Hubbard's cavalry of the battalion, of the Marine Brigade, followed the retreating rebels to Tensas Bayou, and were horrified in the finding of skeletons of white officers commanding negro regiments, who had been capture by the rebels at Milliken's Bend. In many cases these officers had been nailed to the trees and crucified; in this situation a fire was built around the tree, and they suffered a slow death from broiling. The charred and partially burned limbs were still fastened to the stakes. Other instances were noticed of charred skeletons of officers, which had been nailed to slabs, and the slabs placed against a house which was set on fire by the inhuman demons, the poor sufferers having been roasted alive until nothing was left but charred bones. Negro prisoners recaptured from the guerillas confirmed these facts, which were amply corroborated by the bodies found, as above described. The negroes taken were to be resold into slavery, while the white officers

were consumed by fire. Lieutenant Cole holds himself responsible for the truth of the statements.[20]

Grant, who had previously heard and investigated rumors that both whites and blacks captured at Milliken's Bend had been hung, wrote Halleck on August 29 that he considered the newspaper extract "entirely sensational." On June 22, Grant had sent Cols. Thomas Kilby Smith and John Riggin to deliver a note of inquiry to Richard Taylor concerning these rumors. Taylor, replying five days later, wrote that "had any officer or negro been hung the fact must come to my knowledge, and the act would most assuredly have met with the punishment it deserved." Taylor assured Grant that if any such atrocities occurred, he would deal "summary punishment" on the perpetrators. The Union commander was satisfied with Taylor's reply and wrote, "I am now truly glad to hear your denial." As no official complaint was filed by the Lincoln administration, it appears that Federal authorities could find no direct evidence to support accusations such as those which appeared in the Missouri *Democrat*.[21]

As the rugged veterans of McCulloch's Brigade battled with the Federals at Milliken's Bend on June 7, 1863, their fellow Texans of Hawes' Brigade moved against Young's Point. Provided with local guides and intelligence reports from Taylor, Hawes' Brigade, 1,400-strong, had left Richmond at 7 p.m. on June 6. The brigadier later wrote, "I found these guides inefficient and useless to me." Lack of reconnaissance led the brigade to consume seventeen hours to march eleven miles because the men had to halt for four and one-half hours at Walnut Bayou as a bridge was out and scouts had to search for a suitable crossing point. Instead of arriving at dawn as was planned, the brigade reached the vicinity of Young's Point at 10:30 a.m. Hawes recalled, "After taking position in the woods, I found about 500 of my men rendered unfit for duty from exhaustion, occasioned by the excessive heat. About 200 of these 500 had to be carried to the rear."[22]

Informed that his men could approach the Federal camp through woods, Hawes was shocked as his command debouched onto a level plain which he stated was "destitute of trees and brush, in full view of a large camp of the enemy, situated below Young's Point, about 1 1/2 miles distant from my lines." As the Texans advanced across the fields, they could see Federal reinforcements arrive by transports supported by gunboats. Realizing that the chances for success had disappeared, Hawes ordered his troops to retire. And so Confederate efforts at Young's Point also ended in failure.[23]

In reporting the action of June 7, Taylor wrote, "I regret exceedingly that I am unable to report results commensurate with the force employed on this expedition. Much greater loss ought to have been inflicted upon the enemy, and the stores which he burned ought to have been captured for our use." His report, however, became bitter as he attempted to place blame for failure on others. He wrote, "Brig.-Gen. McCulloch, his officers, and men displayed great bravery, but injudicious handling of the troops prevented the attainment of the results which were anticipated." His report continued, "In this affair Gen. McCulloch appears to have shown great personal bravery, but no capacity for handling masses."[24]

Dick Taylor wrote at great length to absolve himself from blame as evidenced by his report to Smith:

> I beg the lieutenant-general commanding to believe that I used every personal exertion in order to insure success. Myself and staff acted as pioneers, bridge-builders, scouts, quartermasters, and commissaries. General Walker's division was suddenly and secretly thrown within 6 or 8 miles of the enemy's line of camps on the Mississippi River, information of the most reliable character furnished to it of the enemy's strength and position, which in every instance was fully verified. Nothing was wanted but vigorous action in the execution of the plans which had been carefully laid out for it to insure such success as the condition of affairs would admit; besides, the division commander had weeks before expressed to the lieutenant-general commanding his ardent desire to undertake this or a similar expedition. Unfortunately, I discovered too late that the officers and men of this division were possessed of a dread of gunboats such as pervaded our people at the commencement of the war. To this circumstance and to want of mobility in these troops are to be attributed the meager results of the expedition.[25]

In similar fashion, John Walker attempted to clear his command of blame. The division commander wrote of McCulloch's effort that "nothing could have been more admirable than the gallantry displayed by officers and men, and the failure of complete success was owing principally to the want of local knowledge and the incompetency of the guides."[26]

McCulloch used even stronger language to defend his actions. The brigade commander wrote:

> I was entirely misinformed by our guide with regard to the ground over which we had to advance. Instead of finding it a smooth, open field without obstructions, I found the ground exceedingly rough, covered with small running briars and tie-

vines, through which infantry could scarcely march, and so much cut up with
ditches and obstructed with hedges that it was impracticable to make any well-reg-
ulated military movement upon it; and, under all the circumstances, I would not
have been the least surprised if we had made an entire failure; and nothing but the
best and bravest fighting, under the providence of God, could have crowned our efforts with even partial success.[27]

The recriminations continued for years. As late as 1879, Taylor
maintained his "I told you so" attitude. In his work *Destruction and
Reconstruction*, he wrote, "As foreseen, our movement resulted, and
could result, in nothing."[28]

Blame, however, must also be shared at higher levels of command.
The rigid Confederate department structure which separated areas of
command along the Mississippi River created a disunified response to
Federal efforts aimed at Vicksburg and Port Hudson. In discussing
Generals Pemberton and Smith, Ed Bearss writes, "The two generals
were far more concerned about enemy threats to their administrative
regions than cooperating to embarrass or defeat the Yankees."
Indecision characterized the actions of both men during these operations.[29]

Other roots of failure can be identified: lack of railroads in the Trans-
Mississippi Department hampered Confederate troop movements and
prevented a rapid concentration of available manpower; lack of enthu-
siastic leadership on the part of Dick Taylor; poor positioning of his
troops by John Walker; lack of intelligence, poor reconnaissance, and
inefficient guides. The list goes on and on.

Could their efforts have been successful? Historian Bearss believes
that, "If undertaken at an earlier date, in late April or early May, a slash-
ing Southern onslaught against one or more of General Grant's
Louisiana enclaves or his long, exposed supply line west of the great
river might have jeopardized the Union campaign." Bearss goes on to
state, "It was only after Pemberton's army was under siege, and the situation had become desperate that the trans-Mississippi soldiers were
committed. And when they were, it was too little too late."[30]

Indeed, efforts of the trans-Mississippi Confederates to relieve
fortress Vicksburg were too little too late. The Texas Division had
marched to the brink of glory during the Vicksburg Campaign in the
spring of 1863. But, at the critical moment, did not seize the opportunity to deal Grant a crippling blow which may very well have altered
the outcome of the Civil War and changed the course of this nation's
history. For John Walker and his "Greyhounds," that opportunity came
but once.

CHAPTER TEN

TRIUMPH AND DEFEAT
Vicksburg Surrenders

The golden rays of the morning sun swept across the sky ushering in what promised to be a typical Mississippi summer day. Rising with the sun, the heat and humidity soon became oppressive and stifling clouds of dust which stirred with each step of man or beast made it difficult to breathe. An eerie silence settled over the city, a silence only characteristic of the muddy water which flowed relentlessly past the town toward the sea. The citizens of Vicksburg enjoyed the quiet of the morning. Their pride, hope, and dreams would not permit them to accept the quiet as being ominous. But it was, for the fate of their city, of their nation, was being decided on that morning—July 3, 1863.

The time was 10:30 a.m. when two horsemen rode out from the besieged city. With soldierly bearing they performed their humiliating task. Under a white flag of truce they delivered a letter requesting that an armistice be granted in order to arrange terms for the capitulation of the city and its garrison. It was the forty-sixth day of siege for the citizens and soldiers of Vicksburg. Their limits of endurance had been reached.

To those who wondered at the silence, it seemed an eternity since May 17 when the army staggered back into the city's defenses from the line of the Big Black River. On that day, confusion and disorder prevailed among the ranks as the soldiers clad in butternut and gray filed into the trenches around Vicksburg. Stunned by a series of bloody defeats, there were many heard to say, "It's all Pem's fault," referring to the Confederate commander, Lt. Gen. John C. Pemberton. A Northerner by birth, he was distrusted by many in the ranks and even by some of his ranking subordinates who viewed their plight as treachery. To bolster the morale of his soldiers and respond to his critics, the general proclaimed to the army:

> You have heard that I was incompetent, and a traitor; and that it was my intention to sell Vicksburg. Follow me, and you will see the cost at which I will sell Vicksburg. When the last pound of beef, bacon, and flour, the last grain of corn, the last cow and hog and horse and dog shall have been consumed, and the last man shall have perished in the trenches, then, and only then will I sell Vicksburg.[1]

But, that time had come. By the end of June the garrison was subsisting on a handful of peas and rice issued once a day per man. Even their water was rationed which fueled the spread of disease. Dysentery, diarrhea, malaria, and various fevers spread rampant through the ranks, all of which took a heavy toll of human life and were far more certain of death than the enemy in blue that surrounded Vicksburg. Thousands of men were in the hospitals and Pemberton's line was stretched dangerously thin. Those who stood to the trenches bore mute testimony to the rigors of siege as their eyes were glazed over and their cheeks were hollow. You could count their every bone!

The conditions in Vicksburg affected the soldiers mentally as well as physically. Desertion was commonplace and the army was ripe for mutiny. A letter received by Pemberton on June 23 reflected the temper of the army. Entitled "Appeal for Help," the note pled "If you can't feed us, you had better surrender us, horrible as the idea is, than suffer this noble army to disgrace themselves by desertion." Stating that "The emergency of the case demands prompt and decided action on your part," the note read by Pemberton was signed "Many Soldiers." Faced with the alternatives to surrender or cut his way out, Pemberton too, began to despair. But, by July 1, only one alternative was left. [2]

The decision to capitulate was based upon the consensus of division and brigade commanders; but ultimately, the responsibility for the decision lay on one man—General Pemberton. A Pennsylvanian by birth, the Confederate commander believed that he might obtain favorable terms on July 4. "I know my people," he told his subordinates, in reference to Northerners. He believed them to be a vainglorious lot and that the Federals would give generous terms should he be willing to surrender the city on the great national holiday. With

The Union Army passing the courthouse as it took possession of Vicksburg on July 4, 1863. *From a wartime sketch.*

this in mind, he opened communications with Maj. Gen. Ulysses S. Grant, commander of the Union Army of the Tennessee.

Grant's answer was painfully terse, "The useless effusion of blood you propose stopping by this course can be ended at any time you may choose, by an unconditional surrender of the city and garrison." With Union land and naval forces as a cordon around Vicksburg, Grant was master of the situation. He had fought too long and hard to demand anything less than unconditional surrender. He owed these terms to himself and to his army.[3]

In the company of his staff, Pemberton received Grant's response. He had hoped for more favorable terms—terms to which he believed the valiant defenders of Vicksburg had a right. In the quiet of his headquarters, however, all hopes were dashed and the Pennsylvanian in gray was "reduced to the ignominy that awaits a defeated leader." Accepting his fate, Pemberton prepared to meet Grant later in the day to discuss the capitulation of Vicksburg.[4]

Shortly before 3:00 p.m. all was astir along the Jackson road, east of Vicksburg, where soldiers of the contending armies were separated by only a few feet. White flags once again appeared along the Confederate works and firing quickly came to a halt. From the east came a group of horsemen in blue led by Grant. "It was a glorious sight to officers and soldiers on the line where these white flags were visible," wrote the Union commander, "and the news soon spread to all parts of the command." Grant continued:

> The troops felt that their long and weary marches, hard fighting, ceaseless watching by day and night, in a hot climate, exposure to all sorts of weather, to diseases, and, worst of all, to the gibes of many Northern papers that came to them saying all their suffering was in vain, that Vicksburg would never be taken, were at last at an end and the Union sure to be saved.[5]

Accompanied by a score of officers, orderlies, and his twelve- year-old son Fred, Grant rode with confidence along the line amidst the wild cheers of his men. Fred observed that his father "betrayed no excitement." Even in victory the Union commander was a plain, simple, unassuming man who viewed his role in this great drama as duty and nothing more. "Soon a white flag appeared over the enemy's works," recalled Fred, "and a party of Confederates were seen approaching."[6]

The smaller group of horsemen in gray who approached from the west was led by Pemberton. He was accompanied by the two men who had delivered his note to Grant earlier in the day—Maj. Gen. John S. Bowen (his most capable subordinate) and Lt. Col. Louis Montgomery. The ride from his headquarters to the front lines was one of the longest rides made by the Confederate general and those with him. These men were slowed in their journey for the road was "hideously gashed and gutted" from the Union artillery fire that had rained down upon the city for six weeks.[7]

This solemn group of men shared few words as they rode toward destiny. Rather, they were lost in thought. Pemberton must have looked back on a military career which spanned thirty years. A graduate of West Point and veteran of the Mexican War, in which he earned two brevets for gallantry, he had resigned his commission at the outbreak of the Civil War and offered his services to the Confederacy. That service had been faithfully executed, yet he feared that his career was about to end in "disaster and disgrace." Those with him heard him say, "I feel a confidence that I shall stand justified to my Government if not to the Southern people. . . should it be otherwise—the consolation of having done the only thing which in my

Grant and Pemberton meet under oak tree to discuss surrender terms. Union soldiers destroyed the tree for souvenirs. *From Library of Congress Collection*

opinion could give security to Vicksburg and to the surrounding country. . . will be reward enough." The consolation of which he spoke was soon to be his only reward.[8]

The Confederate horsemen rode out beyond their works and dismounted. Walking forward, they met the Union officers and shook hands. Grant recalled, "Pemberton and I had served in the same division during part of the Mexican War. I knew him very well, therefore, and greeted him as an old acquaintance." Nothing, however, could put the Confederate general at ease and he appeared "much excited."[9]

Pemberton inquired of Grant his terms for the capitulation of Vicksburg. In reply, his opponent said that he had no terms other than unconditional surrender. The Confederate commander remarked, "Then, sir, it is unnecessary that you and I should hold any further conversation; we will go to fighting again at once." Shaken by Grant's insistence on an unconditional surrender, Pemberton exclaimed, "I can assure you, sir, you will bury many more of your men before you will enter Vicksburg." He then emphasized that he had supplies and munitions to last an indefinite period.[10]

But Grant knew different for Confederate deserters spoke freely of hunger and their lack of ammunition. Seeing through this bravado and hopeful that the surrender could be consummated, Grant proposed a conference between the subordinate officers then present to discuss surrender terms. While the officers discussed arrangements for the possible capitulation of Vicksburg, the two commanders walked off to the side, sat in the shade of a stunted oak tree, and talked privately with one another.

The meeting ended. No agreement had been reached on terms of surrender. It was, however, settled that Grant would send a letter by 10:00 p.m. stating his final terms. It was further agreed that all hostilities would end and not be renewed until correspondence between the two commanders ceased. Mounting their horses, the generals then returned to their respective commands.

Rumors spread like wildfire throughout the city and among the soldiers of both armies. Conjectures were various, but it was commonly believed that surrender had been decided upon. Capt. George H. Hynds of the 31st Tennessee Infantry wrote, "I believe we have been sold and Pemberton is now giving a bill of sale for us and receiving his reward. It is hard to be sold and not to get part of the purchase money." The thought of surrender held no appeal for Lt. William Drennan either, for he wrote, "Oh! it is heart-sickening, for should Vicksburg be surrendered and we be taken prisoners, I have no idea that we shall see outside of prison walls for months—perhaps not during the war. A prison has no charms for me and I still hope that they parole."[11]

The heat of the afternoon was oppressive. At 5:00 p.m. the last gun was fired in defense of Vicksburg. Chaplain William L. Foster of the 35th Mississippi recalled, "I heard the shrill note of the artillery-man's bugle. It was the first time I had heard the blast of the bugle during the siege. In a moment our canon [sic] ceased firing. The enemy beyond the river also ceased & stillness again rested upon the peaceful bosom of the father of waters."[12]

Silence reigned over the besieged city. To Lt. Richard L. Howard of the 124th Illinois Infantry:

> The silence began to be fearfully oppressive. For so many long days and nights it had been a continuous battle. Not a minute but the crack of the rifle or the boom of the cannon had been in our ears. And much of the time it had been deafening. Now it was still, absolutely still. . . . It was leaden. We could not bear it; it settled down so close; it hugged us with its hollow, unseen arms till we could scarcely breathe.

The silence gave rise to mixed emotions for the soldiers of both armies. To the men in blue, it brought relief that their toil would soon end and hope that victory was near. For the Confederates it brought deeper despair and anxiety that their struggle and immense sacrifice had been in vain. As expressed by Chaplain Foster, the gallant defenders of Vicksburg felt in their hearts that it was "a painful silence, foreboding evil," which hung over the doomed city.[13]

Indeed, Vicksburg was a doomed city. Grant recalled, "When I returned to my headquarters I sent for all the corps and division commanders with the army immediately confronting Vicksburg. . . . I informed them of the contents of Pemberton's letter, of my reply, and the substance of the interview, and that I was ready to hear any suggestion." It was, according to Grant, "the nearest approach to a 'council of war' I ever held."[14]

The Union commander favored unconditional surrender. Some of his officers, however, argued that such terms would tie up Federal land and naval forces until the prisoners could be transported northward to prisons. Instead, it was recommended that the garrison be paroled which would clear Union forces for immediate service. Recognizing the validity of their advice, Grant informed R. Adm. David Dixon Porter, commander of the Union naval forces operating against Vicksburg, of his plans:

> I have given the rebels a few hours to consider the proposition of surrendering; all to be paroled here, the officers to take only side-arms. My own feelings are against this, but all my officers think the advantage gained by having our forces and transports for immediate purposes more than counterbalance the effect of sending them north.[15]

These would be welcome terms to Pemberton and his weary soldiers as Confederate morale had been destroyed by the length and hardships of the siege. To complete this work, Union officers all along the line ordered "some discreet men [placed] on picket to-night to communicate to the enemy's pickets the fact that General Grant has offered, in case Pemberton surrenders, to parole all the officers and men, and permit them to go home from here." Many Southern soldiers would be quick to accept this generous offer and leave for home shortly after the city capitulated.[16]

At 10:00 p.m., Pemberton received Grant's amended terms. After scanning the note, he submitted it for deliberation to a council of his generals. His own inclination was to reject these terms. Yet, the Confederate commander acquiesced in the opinion of his generals who, with but two exceptions, favored acceptance of Grant's terms. After hearing the vote of his officers, Pemberton calmly, but with deep emotion addressed his subordinates assembled at army headquarters on Crawford Street:

> Well, gentlemen, I have heard your votes and I agree with your almost unanimous decision, though my own preference would be to put myself at the head of my troops and make a desperate effort to cut our way through the enemy. That is my only hope of saving myself from shame and disgrace. Far better would it be for me to die at the head of my army, even in a vain effort to force the enemy's lines, than to surrender it and live and meet the obloquy which I know will be heaped upon me. But my duty is to sacrifice myself to save the army which has so nobly done its duty to defend Vicksburg. I therefore concur with you and shall

offer to surrender this army on the 4th of July.[17]

It was a bitter pill for Pemberton and those with him to swallow, but their sense of duty demanded nothing less of them. With a heavy heart, the Confederate general then dictated a letter to Grant which read in part:

> In the main, your terms are accepted; but in justice both to the honor and spirit of my troops, manifested in the defense of Vicksburg, I have to submit the following amendments, which, if acceded to by you, will perfect the agreement between us:

> At 10 a.m. to-morrow I propose to evacuate the works in and around Vicksburg, and to surrender the city and garrison under my command, by marching out with my colors and arms, stacking them in front of my present lines, after which you will take possession.

Ever mindful of the people of Vicksburg, whose words of encouragement had helped sustain his army during its ordeal and by their noble suffering had inspired his defense, Pemberton also requested that the rights and property of citizens be respected.[18]

Midnight passed as the officer carrying Pemberton's proposal rode out from the city. Behind Union lines, Grant, unable to sleep, sat at his writing table while his son Fred was "sitting on my little cot." The young boy later wrote of that fateful morning, "Presently a messenger handed father a note. He opened it, gave a sigh of relief, and said calmly, `Vicksburg has surrendered.'"[19]

One final exchange of notes, however, was necessary before the agreement was consummated. "The amendment proposed by you cannot be acceded to in full," replied Grant. "I can make no stipulations with regard to the treatment of citizens and their property. While I do not propose to cause them any undue annoyance or loss, I cannot consent to leave myself under any restraint by stipulations." Pressuring his opponent, the Union commander went on to state, "Should no notification be received of your acceptance of my terms by 9:00 a.m., I shall regard them as having been rejected, and shall act accordingly."[20]

Enough blood had been shed in the defense of Vicksburg. In the early morning hours Pemberton wrote Grant, "I have the honor to acknowledge the receipt of your communication of this day, and in reply to say that the terms proposed by you are accepted." In accordance with those terms, white flags appeared along the city's defenses at 10:00 a.m. and the garrison of Vicksburg marched out of their entrenchments, stacked their arms, and furled their cherished banners.[21]

The Siege of Vicksburg was ended which dimmed hopes of Southern independence. But for President Lincoln, who joyfully exclaimed upon receipt of the news that "The Father of Waters again goes unvexed to the sea," it was a "Glorious Fourth" as the Union would now surely be preserved.[22]

EPILOGUE

Martial music echoed through the streets of Vicksburg as columns of Union infantry with colors uncased converged on the Warren County Courthouse on July 4, 1863. Church bells pealed a thunderous ovation and the heavy tread of troops with steady cadence reverberated among the buildings. Adding to the medley of sounds were the high-pitched steam whistles of the Union fleet as R. Adm. David Dixon Porter's gunboats, gaily bedecked with flags fluttering in the breeze, rounded to along the city's waterfront.

A crowd assembled around the courthouse and watched with mixed emotions as the Confederate flag, which had flown from the cupola as a symbol of defiance, was lowered and replaced by the Stars and Stripes. Tears flowed freely down the cheeks of those who were now vanquished and of those for whom it was "de year ob jubilo." But when the music stopped and the crowd dispersed, one fact was clear—Vicksburg was now an occupied city and, with the surrender of Port Hudson on July 9, the Mississippi River would be open to navigation.

The significance of this event was recognized immediately across the nation. In the North, newspapers heralded the triumph as being one of the war's great victories. Some even claimed that it was the most decisive campaign ever waged in American military history— and justly so. In a period of only 13 weeks, Grant had inflicted more than 9,000 battle casualties during the course of the campaign, and upon the surrender of Vicksburg on July 4, captured 172 pieces of artillery, 50,000 shoulder weapons, and 29,491 officers and men—a staggering combination of men and material that the South could not replace. Demonstrating that he was one of history's great battle captains, Grant had accomplished this remarkable feat while suffering the loss of only 10,142 men killed, wounded, and missing. Francis V.

Greene, a leading military historian of the late nineteenth and early twentieth centuries, writes emphatically in his book *The Mississippi*: "We must go back to the campaigns of Napoleon to find equally brilliant results accomplished in the same space of time with such a small loss."[1]

Throughout the South, people viewed the loss of Vicksburg as the death knell of the Confederacy. In addition to the loss of the garrison and its war material, the South was now split in two along the line of the Mississippi River and vital supply routes were cut which linked the Confederate heartland to the vast trans-Mississippi region. Coupled with the Federal blockade of Southern ports on the Atlantic and Gulf coasts, that eventually slowed to a trickle the arrival of essential war materials from Europe on which the armies of Robert E. Lee and Braxton Bragg relied upon to conduct offensive operations, the South was encircled by Federal forces. Now surrounded in the coils of the giant anaconda, the Confederacy could not long endure.

The summer of 1863 marked a turning point in the American Civil War as across the broad spectrum of conflict the armies of the North and South clashed in bloody combat. In Mississippi, Tennessee, Virginia, and Pennsylvania the lifeblood of a nation was poured out upon the earth as brothers fought one another in defense of ideals held dear. As Grant slowly established his lines around Vicksburg, the Confederate Army of Northern Virginia, under the redoubtable Gen. Robert E. Lee, pushed north across Maryland and into Pennsylvania. The campaign on which so many Southern hopes rested, climaxed in a three-day struggle at Gettysburg during which more than 51,000 soldiers, Union and Confederate, were casualties of war. Lee's army was forced to retreat south of the Potomac; its offensive might virtually destroyed. Upon reflection of the turn of events in July 1863, Col. Josiah Gorgas, chief of the Confederate Ordnance Bureau, lamented: "Yesterday we rode on the pinnacle of success—today absolute ruin seems to be our portion. The Confederacy totters to its destruction."[2] Twenty-one months later, the inevitability of Appomattox Court House ended the greatest tragedy in American history.

It may interest the reader to learn the individual destiny which awaited the principal actors in the Vicksburg drama who were subjects of these essays. Here are but a few:

—**David Glasgow Farragut**, whose ships of the West Gulf Blockading Squadron attempted to bombard Vicksburg into submission based solely on the might of their naval guns, was promoted to rear admiral on July 16, 1862, for his service on the Mississippi River. His most famous action came on August 5, 1864, at Mobile Bay when, lashed to the mast of his flagship *Hartford*, he coined the most famous statement in naval history as he shouted to his men, "Damn the torpedoes, full-speed ahead!" Elevated to vice admiral on December 23, 1864, Farragut became the nation's first admiral on July 25, 1866. He died on August 14, 1870, having spent virtually his entire life in the United States Navy.[3]

—**Lt. Col. James L. Autry,** who boldly responded to the U.S. Navy's demand for surrender by stating that "Mississippians don't know, and refuse to learn, how to surrender to an enemy," had been born in the village of Hayesborough, near Nashville, on January 8, 1830. That day, cannon were booming in Nashville as the citizens celebrated the anniversary of the Battle of New Orleans. Autry was raised in Holly Springs, Mississippi, and entered the practice of law with L. Q. C. Lamar who, following the Civil War, became Secretary of the Interior and a justice on the U.S. Supreme Court. At the outbreak of hostilities between the states, he entered service as a lieutenant in the Home Guards of Marshall County which became Company B, 9th Mississippi Infantry. Elected lieutenant colonel upon formation of the regiment, Autry was later transferred to the 27th Mississippi. Following service as post commander at Vicksburg, he returned to the command of his regiment and on December 31, 1862, was "pierced through the head by a minnie ball" while charging Federal cannon at Stones River. Upon learning of the death of her son, Martha Wyche Autry wept. "My poor boy!," she cried, "The first sound that ever came to him was the booming of cannon, and it was the last sound he ever heard."[4]

—**Maj. Gen. John A. McClernand,** the crusty commander of the Union XIII Corps which led the march down the west side of the river in the opening phase of the campaign, became an object of Grant's ire and was relieved of his command at Vicksburg on June 18, 1863. Although he was eventually restored to command in 1864 and led the XIII Corps during the latter stage of the ill-fated Red River Campaign, his military career was over. Following service in the field, he returned to the arena of politics, but never again exercised the powerful influence he once held in Congress. The recalcitrant general led a long and active life and finally succumbed to the effects of dysentery on September 20, 1900. McClernand lived long enough to see the field of his most stirring triumph and stinging defeat turned into a national military park on the grounds of which the people of Illinois erected a magnificent equestrian statue in his honor. Ironically, there are no monuments on the hallowed ground at Vicksburg in honor of either James B. McPherson or William T. Sherman, the corps commanders whom Grant credited in securing victory.[5]

—**Col. Benjamin Grierson,** the former music teacher who led what Sherman called the "most brilliant expedition of the Civil War" as his raiders severed the Southern Railroad of Mississippi then raced for the safety of Union lines at Baton Rouge, became a national hero and was elevated to brigadier general. His reputation, however, suffered in 1864 as he served under a string of "less able commanders" and was involved in the debacle at Brices Cross Roads on June 10, 1864, when Union forces were routed by Nathan Bedford Forrest. Grierson remained in the Regular Army following the Civil War and served as colonel of the 10th United States Cavalry, comprised of black troopers known as "Buffalo Soldiers." His career ended in 1890 when he retired as a brigadier general. His 30-year career in the cavalry seems all the more remarkable when one recalls that when a boy he had been kicked in the head by a horse and almost died. Ben Grierson had grown up hating horses.[6]

—**Sgt. Richard Surby,** leader of the Butternut Guerrillas during Grierson's Raid who was wounded at Wall's Bridge and captured by the Confederates, was sent to a hospital in Magnolia. One month later he began the long journey to Richmond, Virginia, where he was incarcerated at Libby Prison. Following exchange, Surby wrote, "As we left City Point I bade farewell to Southern hospitality. I have no desire to taste its sweets again." He rejoined his regiment on October 13, 1864, at Collierville, Tennessee, after an absence of five months and thirteen days. Promoted to hospital steward, he served with his regiment, the 7th Illinois Cavalry, until mustered out on November 4, 1865.[7]

— Brig. Gen. John S. Bowen, the bold and daring fighter whose Southerners stood defiant at Grand Gulf as Porter's gunboats bombarded the fortifications on April 29, and whose men fought with such grim determination at Port Gibson on May 1 and at Champion Hill on May 16, contracted dysentery during the siege. On the morning of July 3, as he rode beyond the works under a flag of truce to seek an audience with Grant, the fiery Missourian was gaunt from the debilitating effects of the disease. Shortly after the surrender, Bowen was forced by weakness to a hospital bed where his wife attempted to nurse him back to health. His former neighbor in St. Louis, General Grant, offered the services of Federal doctors, but Bowen preferred to stay with his men. On July 12, as his Missourians took up the line of march from Vicksburg to the parole camps in Enterprise, Mississippi, and Demopolis, Alabama, the general was conveyed in an ambulance. Jostled over poor roads, his condition worsened and, on the following day, John Bowen breathed his last. Interred near the village of Raymond, his body was removed in 1881 to Cedar Hill Cemetery in Vicksburg where his remains now rest in an unmarked grave.[8]

— Maj. Gen. James B. McPherson, the young, handsome, and personable commander of the XVII Corps, was praised by Grant and Sherman for his actions during the Vicksburg campaign and promoted to brigadier general in the Regular Army. Yet, the inexperience and timidity he demonstrated on the fields at Raymond and Champion Hill would be evidenced on other fields and, although he rose to command of the Army of the Tennessee, McPherson's actions never justified the confidence that his superiors had in him. On July 22, 1864, he was killed in action near Atlanta—the only Union army commander killed during the Civil War.[9]

— Brig. Gen. John Gregg the fiery Texan who bitterly contested the field at Raymond on May 12 and conducted the rearguard action at Jackson two days later, had been a member of the Texas secession convention in 1861 and elected to the Provisional Confederate Congress. He resigned from Congress to take up the sword and became a feared and respected combat officer. Following the Vicksburg campaign, he fought at Chickamauga and then commanded the famed Texas Brigade in Lee's army at the Wilderness and during the Overland campaign of 1864. Just as with his opponent in the Battle of Raymond, James B. McPherson, Gregg was destined to fall in action. His death came on October 7, 1864, as he valiantly led his men in fighting along the Charles City Road. In his report to the secretary of war, Robert E. Lee wrote, "The brave General Gregg, of the Texas brigade, fell dead at the head of his men." His loss was mourned by both Lee and the Confederacy.[10]

—**Maj. Gen. William W. Loring,** whose feud with John Pemberton did not bode well for the Confederates in the Battle of Champion Hill, had been the youngest colonel in the Army of the United States at the time of his resignation in 1861. He deeply resented being a subordinate in Confederate service to men who had been his junior in the old army. This led to a history of strained relationships between Loring and his superior officers, including a bitter feud with Stonewall Jackson early in war which resulted in Loring's transfer to Mississippi. Despite these difficulties, he was the senior ranking major general in Confederate service at war's end. In 1869, Loring accepted a commission as brigadier general in the service of the Khedive of Egypt and, in the company of other former Confederate officers, gained the promotions and decorations he craved.[11]

—**Maj. Gen. William T. Sherman,** commander of the XV Corps whose troops—most notable of whom were the rugged veterans of the 1st Battalion, 13th U.S. Infantry—vainly assailed the Stockade Redan on both May 19 and 22, understood the totality of war to a greater degree than most of his contemporaries. Recognizing that the morale of the civilian population which supported armed resistance to the government must be crushed in order to end the rebellion, Sherman would implement his concept of total war—rehearsed during the Meridian campaign—as he pushed through Georgia on his "March to the Sea." Thus, while in Virginia, Grant beat Lee, in Mississippi, Georgia, and the Carolinas, Sherman defeated the South. With the exception of Washington himself, Sherman is maybe the best known American soldier. Therefore, it is ironic that there are no monuments to William Sherman on any of the battlefields on which he fought during the Civil War.[12]

—**Maj. Gen. John A. Logan,** the former Democratic congressman from Illinois whose troops won renown at Raymond and

Champion Hill, has been characterized as the "Union's premier civilian combat general." Distinguishing himself during the Vicksburg campaign, for which service he became a posthumous recipient of the Medal of Honor, Logan rose to command of the XV Corps and, in the wake of McPherson's death at Atlanta, temporarily led the Army of the Tennessee. Due to his political background, he was superseded by a West Pointer and grew to hate academy graduates. Logan returned to Congress and served in both the House and Senate where he championed veterans' issues. In 1884 he rose to the pinnacle of his illustrious career when he was the Republican nominee for vice-president on the unsuccessful ticket with James G. Blaine.[13]

—**Capt. Andrew Hickenlooper,** former captain of the 5th Ohio Battery who served as chief engineer of the XVII Corps during the Vicksburg campaign and directed the construction of Logan's Approach and the mining of the Third Louisiana Redan, was awarded a gold medal by the board of honor for the corps. He was later appointed as chief of artillery for the Army of the Tennessee, a post for which his civil engineering and surveying background made him ideal. A man of many talents and interests, he became the president of the Cincinnati Gas Light and Coke Company following the war and wrote a number of technical books on gas and electricity. Entering the arena of politics, he first served as a U. S. Marshal for the Southern District of Ohio and rose to become lieutenant governor.[14]

—**Mary Loughborough,** the brave young woman from Missouri who followed her soldier-husband James into Vicksburg where she lived in a cave during the siege, became an accomplished writer/editor in the post-war era. The diary she maintained during the siege was first published in 1864 by Appleton & Company of New York. *My Cave Life in Vicksburg* was an instant success and is one of the most widely quoted works on the Siege of Vicksburg. Following her husband's death, Mary edited and published a monthly periodical, *Southern Ladies Journal,* and wrote several other works. Her accomplishments are all the more noteworthy as she established her status while raising four children. Mary Loughborough died on August 26, 1887, one day after her fiftieth birthday.[15]

—**Emma Balfour,** the prominent Vicksburg socialite and wife of Dr. William Balfour who hosted the gala Christmas ball in 1862 that was interrupted by the arrival of the Federal invasion armada, also maintained a diary of her trials and tribulations experienced during the Siege of Vicksburg. Her words provide us with a gripping account of life underground where the citizens of Vicksburg fled to escape the constant bombardment of Union guns. She faced the burden and shame of occupation and Reconstruction as bravely as she did the Federal shells which damaged her home. Today, her house is a tour home in which the Christmas ball is reenacted each year.[16]

—**John George Walker,** whose Texans stormed the Union supply enclave at Milliken's Bend, led the Texas Division through the Red River Campaign during which operations his actions could again be characterized as "competent but unimaginative." On June 17, 1864, he assumed command of the District of West Louisiana. Later that same year, he was given command of the District of Texas, New Mexico, and Arizona, where, relegated to the backwaters of conflict, Walker ended the war in obscurity. He fled to Mexico rather than accept parole, but later returned to the United States and won political appointment. He served as U.S. consul general in Bogota, Columbia, and later as special commissioner to the South American republics on behalf of the Pan-American Convention.[17]

—**Gen. Joseph E. Johnston,** commander of the so called Army of Relief, who in truth abandoned the garrison of Vicksburg, refused to accept any blame for the loss of the Confederate bastion on the Mississippi River. His strategic withdrawal in the face of Sherman's advance on Atlanta in 1864 was masterful, but resulted in his removal from command. Two months after being restored to command by Lee, Johnston surrendered what was left of his army to Sherman in April 1865. He served one term in the House of Representatives following the Civil War and was appointed Commissioner of Railroads by President Grover Cleveland. Johnston spent the balance of his life clinging desperately to what proved an inflated reputation. His *Narrative of Military Operations*, published in 1874, failed to quiet his critics, and, although a stamp was issued in his honor by the U.S. Postal Service in 1995, he remains one of the more controversial generals in American history.[18]

—**Frederick D. Grant,** son of Ulysses who accompanied his father throughout the Vicksburg campaign, went on to West Point where his career was less than stellar. He resigned from the service in 1881, became U.S. Minister to Austria and later served as police commissioner of New York City. Appointed a brigadier general of Volunteers at the outbreak of war with Spain, Fred remained in the service until his death in 1912 having become a major general.[19]

We finally come to the two most prominent figures of the campaign, their very names have become synonymous with triumph and defeat:

—**Lt. Gen. John C. Pemberton,** the ill-fated commander of the Vicksburg army who knew and accurately predicted the "obloquy which I know will be heaped upon me" for surrendering Vicksburg on of all days, July 4, resigned his commission, accepted a lower rank, that of lieutenant colonel, and served the Confederacy faithfully until the very end. Following the war, he tried his hand at farming near Warrenton, Virginia, on land given to him by his ever-loving mother. In this endeavor he also failed. Returning to his native Philadelphia, Pemberton quietly lived out the remainder of his life with dignity and died on July 13, 1881. His death was largely ignored in the South. Relegated to obscurity, biographer Michael Ballard writes of Pemberton's as being "the saddest fate." Perhaps, but in 1917 the Federal government erected a monument to John Pemberton on the grounds of Vicksburg National Military Park, which is more than can be said for Joe Johnston, Braxton Bragg, or a host of other Confederate generals who met with defeat during the Civil War. The weathered bronze statue of Pemberton is virtually all that reminds us of the Pennsylvanian in gray who followed his heart and offered his sword in defense of the woman he loved.[20]

—**Maj. Gen. Ulysses S. Grant**, who, against the advice of his subordinates, took great risks throughout the campaign, was launched into national prominence for his victory at Vicksburg. Proving his critics wrong, Grant finally gained the recognition that was his due and was promoted to major general in the Regular Army. Called to Washington in the late winter of 1864, he was elevated to lieutenant general and given command of all Union armies. Battling his way to the gates of Richmond and Petersburg, he compelled Lee to evacuate the Confederate capital and on April 9, 1865, received the surrender of yet another Southern army. Although Grant later served two terms as president of the United States, he is best remembered for his service as a general during the Civil War. Throughout his life, he remained a plain, simply, unassuming man of impeccable honesty who was loyal to his family, his country, and his fellow soldiers. That loyalty is best expressed by a photograph of Grant sitting on the porch at Mount McGregor in New York. Fighting a losing battle with throat cancer, he sat in a chair with his legs crossed, wearing his glasses and a stove pipe hat, a scarf wrapped around his neck, and without murmur of complaint, raced to finish his memoirs—sale of which would leave his family financially secure. His manuscript, which stands as a tribute to service faithfully performed, was finished on May 23, 1885. With firm hand he wrote from the heart: "These volumes are dedicated to the American soldier and sailor." Two months later, Grant died.[21]

The triumph and defeat which was the Vicksburg campaign determined the outcome of the Civil War from the ashes of which a stronger, unified nation emerged. Years later, as the generation which fought the great conflict responded to the final roll call, a grateful nation sought to preserve the fields where soldiers from the North and the South "gave the last full measure of devotion." In February 1899, Vicksburg National Military Park was established by the Congress to commemorate the campaign, siege, and defense of Vicksburg. Today, the park encompasses 1,800 acres, including the grounds of Vicksburg National Cemetery, and boasts of 1,324 monuments, markers, tablets, and plaques which make Vicksburg one of the more densely monumented battlefields in the world. The magnificent sculptures of stone and bronze which dot the park landscape make Vicksburg, in the words of one Civil War veteran, "the art park of the world." It is truly a fitting memorial to the soldiers and sailors in blue and gray who struggled at Vicksburg in the campaigns of 1862-1863. Their service is best summed by the words inscribed on the Pennsylvania Monument:

> Here brothers fought for their principles;
> Here heroes died for their country;
> and a united people will forever cherish the
> precious legacy of their noble manhood.[22]

ENDNOTES

CHAPTER ONE
"Unvexed to the Sea"
An Overview of the Vicksburg Campaign

1. Lloyd Lewis, *Sherman Fighting Prophet* (New York, 1932), pp. 252; U.S. War Department, *The War of the Rebellion: The Official Records of the Union and Confederate Armies,* 128 vols. (Washington, D.C., 1890-1901), series I, vol. 30, pt. 3, p. 694. Hereinafter cited as *OR*. All references are to series I unless otherwise noted.
2. David Dixon Porter, *Incidents and Anecdotes of the Civil War* (New York, 1885), pp. 95-96.
3. Jerry Korn, War on the Mississippi (Alexandria, 1985), p. 16.
4. *OR* 31, pt. 3, p. 459; *OR* 24, pt. 1, p. 22; John C. Pemberton, *Pemberton: Defender of Vicksburg* (Chapel Hill, 1942), p. 261.
5. U.S. War Department, *Official Records of the Union and Confederate Navies in the War of the Rebellion,* 31 vols.(Washington, D.C., 181895-1929), series 1, vol. 18, pp. 782-783.
6. *OR* vol. 17, pt. 1, p. 613.
7. John Fiske, *The Mississippi Valley in the Civil War* (New York, 1900), p. 225.
8. Samuel H. Lockett, "The Defense of Vicksburg," in Robert U. Johnson and Clarence C. Buel, eds. *Battles and Leaders of the Civil War,* 4 vols. (New York, 1884-1889), vol. 3, p. 488.
9. Diary (copy) of Emma Balfour, Diary Collection of Vicksburg National Military Park.
10. *The Story of the Fifty-fifth Regiment Illinois Volunteer Infantry in the Civil War 1861-1865,* edited by Edwin C. Bearss, (Huntington, 1993), pp. 237-240.
11. *OR* 24, pt. 1, pp. 276-277.
12. Osborn H. Oldroyd, *A Soldier's Story of the Siege of Vicksburg* (Springfield, 1885), p. 35.
13. Henry Steele Commager (editor), *The Blue and Gray: The Story of the Civil War as Told by Participants,* 2 vols. (Indianapolis, 1950), vol. 2, p. 677.

CHAPTER TWO
"The Only Viable Option"
Grant's March Through Louisiana

1. John Fiske, *The Mississippi Valley in the Civil War* (New York, 1900), p. 225.
2. Edwin C. Bearss, *The Vicksburg Campaign,* 3 vols. (Dayton, 1985-1986), vol. 2, p. 21.
3. Ulysses S. Grant, *Personal Memoirs of Ulysses S. Grant,* 2 vols. (New York, 1885), vol. 1 pp. 358-359.
4. *OR* vol. 24, pt. 3, p.168. 5. Oran Perry, "Perry Tells Story of the Siege of Vicksburg," *The Vicksburg Evening Post,* June 16, 1926.
6. Ephraim McD. Anderson, *Memoirs: Historical and Personal; Including the Campaigns of the*

First Missouri Confederate Brigade, edited by Edwin C. Bearss (Dayton, 1972), p. 284.

7. Ibid, p. 285.

8. *OR* 24, pt. 1, p. 634.

9. *OR* 24, pt. 3, p. 797.

10. Charles E. Wilcox, "With Grant at Vicksburg, from the Civil War Diary of Captain Charles E. Wilcox," edited by Edgar L. Erickson, *Journal of the Illinois Historical Society*, Vol. XXX, 1938, p. 467.

11. *OR* 24, p. 627.

12. *History of the Forty-sixth Regiment Indiana Volunteer Infantry*, September, 1861–*September, 1865*, compiled by committee (Logansport, 1888), p. 56.

13. Unidentified source, miscellaneous files (XV Corps), Vicksburg National Military Park.

14. *The Story of the Fifty-fifth Regiment Illinois Volunteer Infantry in the Civil War, 1861-1865*, compiled by a committee (Clinton, 1887), p. 231.

15. *OR* 21, pt. 1, p. 141.

CHAPTER THREE:
"Playing Smash With the Railroads"
The Story of Grierson's Raid

1. Edwin C. Bearss, *The Vicksburg Campaign*, 3 vols. (Dayton, 1985-1986), vol. 2, p. 129.

2. *FM 100-5 Operations*, 5 May 1986, Headquarters, Department of the Army, Washington, DC, pp. 91, 94, 95.

3. Ibid., pp. 53, 95.

4. *OR* 24, pt. 3, p. 45.

5. Ibid., p. 50.

6. Ibid., p. 58.

7. Ibid., p. 95

8. Ibid.; *OR*, 17, pt. 2, p. 396.

9. Stephen A. Forbes, "Grierson's Cavalry Raid," Illinois State Historical Society, *Transactions*, (Springfield, 1907), p. 27.

10. Ibid., p. 28

11. *OR* 24, pt. 3, p. 185.

12. Ibid., pp. 196-197; William H. Leckie and Shirley A. Leckie, *Unlikely Warriors: General Benjamin H. Grierson and His Family*, (Norman, 1984), p. 84.

13. Leckie, *Unlikely Warriors*, p. 84.

14. *OR* 24, pt. 3, p. 185.

15. Forbes, "Grierson's Cavalry Raid," p. 28.

16. Leckie, *Unlikely Warriors*, pp. 10-11.

17. Ibid., p. 12.

18. Ibid., p. xiii

19. Ibid., p. 59.

20. *Report of the Adjutant General of the State of Illinois*, vol. VIII, (Springfield, 1901), p. 3.

21. Forbes, "Grierson's Cavalry Raid," p. 29; Dave Roth, "Grierson's Raid," *Blue & Gray Magazine*, Vol. X, Issue 5, (Columbus, 1993), p. 19.

22. *Report of the Adjutant General of the State of Illinois*, vol. VIII, (Springfield, 1901), p. 8; *OR*, vol. 24, pt. 1, p. 29.

23. Richard Surby, *Grierson Raids*, (Chicago, 1865), p. 145; *OR*, vol. 17, pt. 1, p. 495; *Roster and Record of Iowa Soldiers in the War of the Rebellion*, vol. 4, (Des Moines, 1910), pp. 215–224.

24. Surby, *Grierson* Raids, pp. 13, 142.

25. Ibid., p. 113.

26. Ibid., p. 20.

27. Samuel L. Woodward, "Grierson's Raid, April 17th to May 2d, 1863," pt. 1, *Journal of the United States Cavalry Association*, vol. XIV, No. 52, (1904), p. 686.

28. Forbes, "Grierson's Cavalry Raid," p. 7; Surby, *Grierson Raids*, p. 20.

29. Woodward, "Grierson's Raid," pp. 689–690; Benjamin H. Grierson, *Record of Services Rendered the Government, 1863,* (privately printed n.d.), p. 102, cited in D. Alexander Brown, *Grierson's Raid* (Urbana, 1962, reprint) pp. 32–33.

30. *OR* 24, pt. 1, p. 523.

31. Surby, *Grierson Raids*, p. 35.

32. Forbes, *Grierson's Raid*, p. 9.

33. Woodward, "Grierson's Raid," p. 694; Forbes, "Grierson's Cavalry Raid," p. 18.

34. Surby, *Grierson Raid*, p. 47.

35. Woodward, "Grierson's Raid," p. 698.

36. Forbes, *Grierson's Raid*, p. 32.

37. Surby, *Grierson Raids*, p. 65.

38. Forbes, *Grierson's Raid*, pp. 17-18.

39. Brown, *Grierson's Raid*, p. 149.

40. Ibid., p. 153.

41. Surby, *Grierson Raids*, p. 69.

42. Woodward, "Grierson's Raid, April 17th to May 2d, 1863," pt. 2, *Journal of the U.S. Cavalry Association*, vol. XV (1905), p.100.

43. Grierson, *Record of Service*, p. 106.

44. Forbes, *Grierson's Raid*, p. 22.

45. Surby, *Grierson Raids*, p. 110

46. Woodward, "Grierson's Raid," pt. 2, p. 105.

47. Forbes, *Grierson's Raid*, p. 24

48. Ibid., p. 23.

49. Grierson, *Record of Service*, p. 108.

50. Brown, *Grierson's Raid*, p. 218

51. Forbes, *Grierson's Raid*, p. 6.

52. *OR* 24, pt. 1, p. 34; Brown, *Grierson's Raid*, p. 223.

CHAPTER FOUR
"The Inland Campaign Begins"
The Battle of Port Gibson

1. Ulysses S. Grant *Personal Memoirs of U.S. Grant*, 2 vols. (New York, 1885), vol. 1, pp. 480–481.

2. Charles B. Johnson, *Muskets and Medicine; or Army Life in the Sixties* (Philadelphia, 1917), pp. 78-79.

3. Samuel C. Jones, *Reminiscences of the Twenty-second Iowa Volunteer Infantry* (Iowa City, 1907), p. 29.

4. Henry Clay Warmoth, "The Vicksburg Diary of Henry Clay Warmoth: Part II," edited by Paul H. Hass, *Journal of Mississippi History*, Vol. XXXII, p. 64; *OR* 24, pt. 1, p. 143. Lt. Col. Henry C. Warmoth of McClernand's staff noted of the Widow Daniell and her

family, "The old woman and the youngs ones too, spitfires. Treated us very uncivily."

5. Diary of Charles A. Hobbs, Regimental Files, 99th Illinois, Vicksburg National Military Park.

6. George Crooke, *The Twenty-first Regiment of Iowa Volunteer Infantry* (Milwaukee, 1891), p. 55.

7. *OR* 24, pt. 1, p. 576. Bowen reported the action to his superiors in Jackson, after which he received the following telegram from General Pemberton: "In the name of the army, I desire to thank you and your troops for your gallant conduct to-day. Keep up the good work by every effort to repair damages to-night. Yesterday I warmly recommended you for a major-generalcy. I shall renew it."

8. Jerald H. Markham, *The Botetourt Artillery* (Lynchburg, 1986), p. 27. The ill-fated Baldwin was again surrendered at Vicksburg and was paroled. After his second exchange, he was killed in a fall from his horse at Mobile, Alabama, on February 19, 1864.

9. William P. Chambers, "My Journal," *Publications of the Mississippi Historical Society,* Vol. V (1925), pp. 262-263.

10. Edwin C. Bearss, *The Vicksburg Campaign, 2,* p. 357.

11. *The Pine Bluff Commercial*, December 17, 1904. Mrs. Shaifer was sister of then Confederate Col. Benjamin Grubb Humphreys of the Twenty-first Mississippi Infantry Regiment which served in William Barksdale's brigade of the Army of Northern Virginia, and her son was at Port Hudson with Company B, First Mississippi Light Artillery.

12. *OR* 24, pt. 1, p. 626.

13. Ibid., p. 678. The Confederate wings were separated by the deep and impenetrable valley of Centers Creek. All lateral movements or communications between the wings were via the junction of the Rodney and Bruinsburg roads, two miles west of Port Gibson. The roundabout distance of almost four miles took at least one hour for a marching column to travel.

14. Ibid., p. 591.

15. Letter, Francis G. Obenchain to William T. Rigby, July 4, 1903, Regimental Files, Botetourt (VA) Artillery, Vicksburg National Military Park. The other generals who died in defense of Vicksburg were: Brig. Gen. Lloyd Tilghman, killed at Champion Hill on May 16; Brig. Gen. Isham W. Garrott, killed on June 17; Brig. Gen. Martin E. Green, killed on June 27; and Maj. Gen. John S. Bowen, who contracted dysentery during the siege, died on July 13.

16. William C. Thompson, "From Shiloh to Port Gibson," edited by William R. Thompson, *Civil War Times Illustrated,* October 1964, p. 23.

17. Chambers, "My Journal," pp. 263-264; *OR* 24, pt. 1, p. 675.

18. Letter, Obenchain to Rigby, July 4, 1903.

19. *OR* 24, pt. 1, p. 602.

20. Bearss, *The Vicksburg Campaign,* Vol. II, p. 379; *OR* 24, pt. 1, p. 603.

21. *OR* 24, pt. 1, p. 603.

22. Chambers, "My Journal," p. 264. Grant arrived on the field around 10 o'clock, just in time to witness McClernand's successful assault. He then established his headquarters at the home of Caleb Perkins, situated 1,000 yards west of the Shaifer house. The Fifty-sixth Ohio claims to have captured the flag of the Botetourt Artillery, a claim that was denied by the Virginians. The record shows that the battery flag was surrendered at Vicksburg on July 4, 1863.

23. Letter, Francis G. Obenchain to William T. Rigby, July 16, 1903, Regimental Files, Botetourt (VA) Artillery, Vicksburg National Military Park.

24. Letters, Obenchain to Rigby, July 4, 1903, July 16, 1903.

25. Letter, Obenchain to Rigby, July 16, 1903.

26. *OR* 24, pt. 1, p. 589.

27. Letter, Obenchain to Rigby, July 16, 1903.

28. *OR* 24, pt. 1, p. 679.

29. Ibid., p. 680.

30. Letter, Obenchain to Rigby, July 4, 1903.

31. *OR* 24, pt. 1, p. 681.

32. Ibid., p. 659.

33. Ibid., p. 660.

34. Ibid., p. 673. The First Missouri was on detached duty at Coon Island Lake and the Second Missouri was left to man the Grand Gulf fortifications. Consequently, when Cockrell marched for Port Gibson he had only the Third, Fifth, and Sixth Missouri, 4 guns of Guibor's Missouri Battery (under Lt. William Corkery), and 2 guns of Landis' Missouri Battery.

35. Letter, Obenchain to Rigby, July 4, 1903.

36. *OR* 24, pt. 1, p. 659. At 2:00 p.m., Maj. Gen. James B. McPherson arrived at the Shaifer house with two fresh brigades led by Maj. Gen. John A. Logan. Although Grant insisted that McClernand had more troops than he could effectively deploy on his front, he ordered Brig. Gen. John D. Stevenson's brigade to support the attack up the Rodney road. Logan's other brigade, commanded by Brig. Gen. John E. Smith, was directed to bolster Osterhaus on the Bruinsburg road. From left to right, the brigades were commanded by Col. William Stone, Brig. Gen. Stephen Burbridge, Brig. Gen. George McGinnis, and Col. James Slack. Those in reserve were under Col. William Landram, Brig. Gen. William Benton, and Brig. Gen. John D. Stevenson.

37. Ibid., p. 612.

38. Ibid., p. 611.
    The four batteries were: Second and Sixteenth Ohio Batteries, Company A, Second Illinois Light Artillery, and Company A, First Missouri Light Artillery.

39. Ibid., p. 627; Bearss, *The Vicksburg Campaign*, Vol. II, p. 393 note. The four batteries were: Second and Sixteenth Ohio Batteries, Company A, Second Illinois Light Artillery, and Company A, First Missouri Light Artillery.

40. *OR* 24, pt. 1, pp. 612-613.

41. Ibid., p. 664; Robert S. Bevier, *The Confederate First and Second Missouri Brigade* (St. Louis, 1879), p. 180.

42. *OR* 24, pt. 1, p. 676.

43. Ibid., p. 660

44. Ibid., pp. 643-644, 653.

45. Ibid., p. 660.

46. Ibid., pp. 670-671.

47. Ibid., p. 681; Samuel C. Kelly, "A History of the Thirtieth Alabama Volunteers (Infantry) Confederate States of America," *The Alabama Historical Quarterly*, Vol. 9, Number 1, p. 135.

48. Letter, Obenchain to Rigby, July 4, 1903.

49. *OR* 24, pt. 1, p. 677; Bearss, The Vicksburg Campaign, Vol. II, p. 399. In a span of 27 hours, Baldwin's men had marched 8 miles to reach the battlefield, fought for seven hours, then marched 21 more miles to reach the safety of Bowen's camp. Historian Bearss states, "Stonewall Jackson's 'foot cavalry' would have been hard put to match such a performance."

50. Frederick D. Grant, "A Boy's Experience at Vicksburg," MOLLUS-New York, 3d Series,

pp. 89-90.

51. *OR* 24, pt. 3, p. 807.   There are no separate unit reports for Tracy's or Baldwin's brigades, incomplete returns for Green's brigade, and only one unit report from Cockrell's brigade.

CHAPTER FIVE
"Disaster and Disgrace":
John C. Pemberton and the Battle of Champion Hill

1. Diary (copy) of John A. Leavy, Diary Collection of Vicksburg National Military Park; Mary Loughborough, *My Cave Life in Vicksburg* (Spartanburg, 1976), p. 43.

2. Diary (copy) of Mrs. Emma Balfour, Diary Collection of Vicksburg National Military Park.

3. Ibid.

4. John C. Pemberton, *Pemberton: Defender of Vicksburg* (Chapel Hill, 1942), pp. 261-262.

5. Edwin C. Bearss, *The Vicksburg Campaign*, 3 vols. (Dayton 1985-1986), vol. 2, p. 637.

6. Michael B. Ballard, *Pemberton: A Biography* (Jackson, 1991), pp. 1-82, 84, and 86; Ezra Warner, *Generals is Gray* (Baton Rouge, 1959), pp. 232-233.

7. Ballard, *Pemberton*, p. 140; *OR* 24, pt. 3, p. 808.

8. *OR* 24, pt. 3, p. 859.

9. Bearss, *The Vicksburg Campaign*, vol. 2, p. 482.

10. *OR* 24, pt. 1, p. 215.

11. *OR* 24, pt. 3, p. 877.

12. *OR* 24, pt. 2, p. 125.

13. *OR* 24, pt. 3, p. 882.

14. *OR* 24, pt. 1, pp. 51-52.

15. *OR* 24, pt. 2, pp. 93-94; *OR* 24, pt. 3, p. 884.

16. *OR* 24, pt. 2, p. 75.

17. Robert S. Bevier, *The Confederate First and Second Missouri Brigades* (St. Louis, 1879), p. 186; Letter, William A. Drennan to wife, May 30, 1863, Mississippi Department of Archives and History, Jackson, MS.

18. Letter, Drennan to wife, May 30, 1863.

19. Ibid.

20. Letter, Alfred Cumming to Stephen D. Lee, November 3, 1899, RG 12, Vol. 12, Folder 15, Mississippi Department of Archives and History, Jackson, MS.

21. Joseph Bogle and William L. Calhoun, *Historical Sketches of Barton's (Later Stovall's) Georgia Brigade, Army of Tennessee* (Dayton, 1984), p. 15.

22. Letter John W. Johnston to William T. Rigby, June 14, 1902, Regimental Files (Botetourt Artillery), Vicksburg National Military Park; *OR* 24, pt. 2, p. 95; Letter, Francis G. Obenchain to William T. Rigby, July 14, 1903, Regimental Files (Botetourt Artillery), Vicksburg National Military Park.

23. Letter, Obenchain to Rigby, July 14, 1903.

24. Ephraim McD. Anderson, *Memoirs: Historical and Personal; including the Campaigns of the First Missouri Confederate Brigade*, edited by Edwin C. Bearss (Dayton, 1972), p. 311.

25. Ibid., p. 312.

26. Ibid., p. 313.

27. Letter (copy), James G. Spencer to Frank H. Foote, September 18, 1910, Regimental Files (First Mississippi Light Artillery), Vicksburg National Military Park.

28. Ibid.

29. *OR* 24, pt. 2, p. 77.

30. Ibid., pp. 82, 86, 93, 99, 112, and 120.

31. Leavy Diary; Samuel H. Lockett, "The Defense of Vicksburg," in Robert U. Johnson and Clarence C. Buel, eds. *Battles and Leaders of the Civil War*, 4 vols. (New York, 1884–1889), vol. 3, p. 488.

CHAPTER SIX:
"The First Honor at Vicksburg":
The 1st Battalion, 13th U.S. Infantry

1. Frederick H. Dyer, *A Compendium of the War of the Rebellion*, 3 vols. (New York, 1959), vol. III, p. 1713. The 13th U.S.I. was made up of seven companies comprising the 1st Battalion. Though authorized, a second battalion was not formed during the course of the war, hence, the "ist Battalion" is synonomous with the "13th U.S.I."

2. *OR* 24, pt. 1, pp. 438-440. In mid-March 1863, Admiral Porter with 11 vessels, planned to navigate a string of connecting waterways, heading up Steele's Bayou to Black Bayou, Deer Creek, Rolling Fork, the Big Sunflower River, and ultimately into the Yazoo River. Resistance at the Rolling Fork compelled Porter to begin backing down the narrow Deer Creek, all the while removing obstructions created by the Rebels. The Confederates nearly succeeded in capturing Porter's fleet, and might have, but for a rapid march by Col. Giles Smith's brigade, dispatched by Sherman in response to Porter's plea for assistance.

3. Ibid. pp. 254-255. Edward Crawford Washington was born in Virginia, but entered service from Pennsylvania. A clean-shaven, handsome man, Washington became a captain in the 13th U.S.I. on May 14, 1861. For service at Vicksburg, he was made brevet major to rank from May 20, 1863--the day he died.

4. *OR* 24, pt. 2, p. 255.

5. *OR* 24, pt. 1, pp. 51-53.

6. Ibid. p. 263.

7. Ibid. pp. 256, 263.

8. Ibid. p. 755; *OR* 24, pt. 2, pp 256, 263.

9. Letter from Frank Muhlenberg to William T. Rigby, July 9, 1902; Letter from W. W. Gardner to Dr. Levi Fuller, May 25, 1863; *OR* 24, pt. 2, 263, 267. Letters in Regimental Files (13th U.S.I.), Vicksburg National Military Park. All letters cited in this essay are in the Regimental Files (13th U.S.I.), Vicksburg National Military Park, unless otherwise noted.

10. Edwin C. Bearss, *The Vicksburg Campaign*, 3 vols. (Dayton, 1985-1986), vol. III, p. 741. A lunette is a two-sided outwork, usually crescent shaped, with an open or partially closed gorge. A redan is a three-sided, triangular work. The 27th Louisiana Lunette and the Stockade Redan were about 50 yards apart, and bridging the gap between the two

where the Graveyard Road entered the Confederate perimeter was a poplar log stockade made of sharpened posts 9"-12" in diameter, fronted by rows of abatis. The exterior slope of the Stockade Redan was 17 feet high, with a six foot deep ditch at its base.

11. *OR* 24, pt. 2, p. 257; Letter from Frank Muhlenberg to William T. Rigby, July 9, 1902.

12. *OR* 24, pt. 2, p. 267. Capt. P. P. Wood commanded Company A (6 guns), Capt. Samuel E. Barrett--Company B (6 guns), and Capt. Levi W. Hart--Company H (4 guns) all of the 1st Illinois Light Artillery.

13. Ibid, pp. 263-264; Letter from Frank Muhlenberg to William T. Rigby, February 25, 1903; Letter from Frank Muhlenberg to William T. Rigby, March 17, 1903. Companies A, B, C, D, F, G, and H were involved in the assault on May 19, 1863. Company H reported for duty on May 18, 1863. Company E did not join the battalion until June.

14. Ibid, pt. 1, p. 54; Letter from Frank Muhlenberg to W. W. Gardner, May 29, 1902; Letter from Frank Muhlenberg to William T. Rigby, July 9, 1902; Letter from W. W. Gardner to Dr. Levi Fuller, May 25, 1863; Letter from Frank Muhlenberg to William T. Rigby, March 11, 1903.

15. Letter from W. W. Gardner to Dr. Levi Fuller, May 25, 1863; Letter from Walter Wood to Frank Muhlenberg, extract on file at VNMP; Letter from David Wilson to Frank Muhlenberg, March 23, 1903; Letter from George Kaut to Frank Muhlenberg, extract on file at VNMP; Letter from James Kephart to Frank Muhlenberg, extract on file at VNMP; Letter from Frank Muhlenberg to William T. Rigby, January 21, 1903.

16. *OR* 24, pt. 2, p. 414.

17. Letter from Noble Warwick to W. W. Gardner, January 27, 1902; Letter from W. W. Gardner to Dr. Levi Fuller, May 25, 1863; Letter from Frank Muhlenberg to William T. Rigby, March 2, 1903; Letter from R. M. Nelson to W. W. Gardner, February 2, 1902; Letter from Joseph M. Richards to Frank Muhlenberg, extract on file at VNMP. Richards was the half-brother of Sgt. James Brown. Brown is interred in Section I, Grave Number 7796 of Vicksburg National Cemetery. The color guard consisted of 2 sergeants and 8 corporals, all of whom, except Sgt. R. M. Nelson, were either killed or wounded. Cpl. Slate died six days later, Warwick recovered from his wound.

18. *OR* 24, pt. 2, p. 264.

19. C. H. Smart, "Personal Recollections of Vicksburg, May 19, 1863;" Letter from Joseph C. Helm to Frank Muhlenberg, extract on file at VNMP.

20. *OR* 24, pt. 2, p. 267. Col. Thomas Kilby Smith's brigade consisted of the 55th Illinois, 127th Illinois, 54th Ohio, 57th Ohio, and the 83rd Indiana.

21. Letter from R. M. Nelson to W. W. Gardner, February 2, 1902. Although all was in confusion for the duration of the assault, command of the 13th U.S.I. initially devolved upon Capt. Charles Ewing, brother-in-law to William T. Sherman.

22. Letter from Frank Muhlenberg to William T. Rigby, April 13, 1903; Smart, "Personal Recollections of Vicksburg, May 19, 1863."

23. Letter from C. H. Smart to William T. Rigby, September 10, 1903. Smart states that the private was "a big recruit one who joined the regiment the day before--took up the flag and started up the hill with it after the last of the color guard was killed."

24. Letter from Frank Muhlenberg to William T. Rigby, March 11, 1903; Letter from W. W. Gardner to Dr. Levi Fuller, May 25, 1863; Letter from R. M. Nelson to W. W. Gardner, February 2, 1902.

25. Letter from Frank Muhlenberg to William T. Rigby, March 11, 1903; Letter from Joseph C. Helm to Frank Muhlenberg, extract on file at VNMP.

26. Undated letter from W. W. Gardner to Frank Muhlenberg, extract on file at VNMP; *OR* 24, pt. 2, pp. 267-268.

27. *OR* 24, pt. 2, pp. 281-282. Ewing's regiments were from left to right in line: 47th Ohio, 4th West Virginia, and 37th Ohio, with the 30th Ohio in reserve.

28. Letter from John W. Foreman to Frank Muhlenberg, April 18, 1903, extract on file at VNMP.

29. Letter from W. W. Gardner to Dr. Levi Fuller, May 25, 1863; Smart, "Personal Recollections of Vicksburg, May 19, 1863."

30. Letter from Joseph C. Helm to Frank Muhlenberg, extract on file at VNMP; Affidavit from W. W. Gardner, January 10, 1902, extract on file at VNMP; Letter from R. M. Nelson to W. W. Gardner, February 2, 1902. Nelson was able to retrieve the cord and tassel and led a wounded man to safety.

31. Letter from W. W. Gardner to Dr. Levi Fuller, May 25, 1863; Department of the Army, *The Medal of Honor of the United States Army* (Washington, D.C. 1948), p. 129. The Medal of Honor was awarded to Kephart on 13 May 1899. The citation reads: "Voluntarily and at the risk of his life, under a severe fire of the enemy, aided and assisted to the rear an officer who had been severely wounded and left on the field."

32. Letter from Frank Mullenberg to William T. Rigby, July 9, 1902; Letter from Frank Mullenberg to William T. Rigby, February 5, 1903.

33. Letter from Frank Mullenberg to William T. Rigby, February 5, 1903. Captain Washington was buried behind Confederate lines in an unidentified location.

34. Letter from W. W. Gardner to Dr. Levi Fuller, May 25, 1863; Letter from Frank Mullenberg to William T. Rigby, July 9, 1902. The building set afire was the Lynde house.

35. Letter from Joseph C. Helm to Frank Mullenberg, extract on file at VNMP; Letter from R. M. Nelson to W. W. Gardner, February 2, 1902; Letter from George Kaut to Frank Mullenberg, extract on file at VNMP.

36. Letter from R. M. Nelson to W. W. Gardner, February 2, 1902.

37. Letter from Noble Warwick to "My Dear General," October 25, 1906.

38. Letter from Frank Mullenberg to William T. Rigby, June 6, 1902.

CHAPTER SEVEN
"Spades Are Trump":
Siege Operations at Vicksburg

1. U.S. War Department, *The War of the Rebellion: The Official Records of the Union and Confederate Armies*, 128 vols. (Washington, D.C., 1890-1901), series I, Vol. 24, pt. 1, pp. 276-277. Hereinafter cited as *OR*. All references are to series I unless otherwise noted.

2. *OR* 24, pt. 3, p. 348.

3. Unidentified source, miscellaneous files (XV Corps), Vicksburg National Military Park.

4. Diary of Nathan M. Baker, Regimental Files (116th Illinois), Vicksburg National Military Park.

5. *OR* 24, pt. 2, pp. 312-131, 373.

6. Seth J. Wells, *The Siege of Vicksburg from the Diary of Seth J. Wells, Including Weeks of Preparation and of Occupation After the Surrender* (Detroit, 1915), p. 85.

7. *OR* 24, pt. 1, p. 283.

CHAPTER EIGHT
"Shut Up As In a Trap":
Citizens Under Siege

1. Peter F. Walker, *Vicksburg A People at War, 1860-1865* (Chapel Hill, 1960), p. 7.

2. Ibid, pp. 8-9.

3. Sara A. Dorsey, *Recollections of Henry Watkins Allen, Brigadier General Confederate States Army, Ex-Governor of Louisiana* (New York, 1866), p. 122.

4. *Vicksburg Weekly Whig*, November 14, 1860.

5. *Vicksburg Daily Citizen*, May 1, 1861.

6. *Vicksburg Weekly Whig*, May 1, 1861.

7. Diary of Mahala P. H. Roach, Southern Historical Collection, University of North Carolina, p. 50.

8. Ibid, pp. 103-105; Anne Harris Broidrick, "A Recollection of Thirty Years Ago," Southern Historical Collection, University of North Carolina, p. 12.

9. Jerry Korn, *War on the Mississippi*, (Alexandria, 1985), p. 16.

10. *OR* 18, p. 492; *Vicksburg Daily Whig*, July 1, 1862.

11. *Vicksburg Daily Whig*, July 11, 1862; Charles B. Allen, Plantation Book, Mississippi Department of Archives and History, p. 93.

12. City Council Minute Book, 1860-1869, City Hall, p. 177.

13. Stephen D. Lee, "Details Important Work by Two Confederate Telegraph Operators, Christmas Eve, which Prevented the Complete Surprise of the Confederate Army at Vicksburg," *Publications of the Mississippi Historical Society*, vol. VIII, pp. 53-54.

14. George W. Morgan, "The Assault on Chickasaw Bluffs," in Robert U. Johnson and Clarence C. Buel, eds., *Battles and Leaders of The Civil War*, 4 vols., (New York, 1884-1889), vol. 3, p. 467.

15. "A Woman's Diary of the Siege of Vicksburg," edited by George W. Cable, *The Century Magazine*, vol. XXX, p. 767; *Brokenburn: The Journal of Kate Stone, 1861-1867*, edited by John Q. Anderson (Baton Rouge, 1955) p. 162.

16. Mary Loughborough, *My Cave Life in Vicksburg* (Spartanburg, 1976), p. 16.

17. Diary (copy) of Emma Balfour, Diary Collection of Vicksburg National Military Park; Ibid, pp. 41-42.

18. Loughborough, *My Cave Life*, p. 42.

19. Diary of Emma Balfour.

20. "A Woman's Diary of the Siege of Vicksburg," p. 767; Ibid.

21. Loughborough, *My Cave Life*, pp. 56-57.

22. Ibid, p. 72.

23. Diary of Emma Balfour.

24. Loughborough, *My cave Life*, p. 79.

25. Ibid, p. 91.

26. Ibid., pp. 91-92.

27. Ibid, p. 131.

28. William W. Lord, "A Child at the Siege of Vicksburg," *Harper's Monthly Magazine*, CXVI-II (December 1908), p. 44.

29. Diary of William A. Drennan, Mississippi Department of Archives and History.

30. Loughborough, *My Cave Life*, p. 82.

31. Lucy McRae, "A Girl's Experience in the Siege of Vicksburg," *Harper's Weekley*, vol. LVI, June 8, 1912, p. 13; Diary of Margaret Lord, Manuscript, Library of Congress, Washington.

32. Loughborough, *My Cave Life*, p. 138.

33. "A Woman's Diary of the Siege of Vicksburg," p. 774; Ibid, p. 140.

34. Ida Barlow, manuscript, Mississippi Department of Archives and History; Kate Stone, *Brokenburn The Journal of Kate Stone 1861-1865*, edited by John Q. Anderson (Baton Rouge, 1955), p. 364.

CHAPTER NINE
"To Rescue Gibraltar"
Efforts of the Trans-Mississippi Confederates to Relieve Fortress Vicksburg

1. Joseph P. Blessington, *The Campaigns of Walker's Texas Division* (Austin, 1968), p. 250.

2. Norman D. Brown, "John George Walker," in William C. Davis, ed., *The Confederate General*, 6 vols. (New York, 1991), vol. 6, p. 88. Although popular reference sources such as Mark Boatner, *The Civil War Dictionary* (New York, 1959), p. 885, and Ezra Warner, *Generals in Gray* (Baton Rouge, 1959), pp. 319-320, omit reference to Walker's association with the 2d Virginia or list him as having served with the 8th Texas Cavalry, they are confusing the subject the subject of this essay with Capt. John G. Walker, a different officer altogether who did, indeed, serve in the 8th Texas Cavalry (Terry's Texas Rangers); U.S. War Department, *The War of the Rebellion: The Official Records of the Union and Confederate Armies*, 128 vols. (Washington, D.C., 1890-1901), series I, vol. 19, pt. 2, pp. 697, 703, 710, and 731. Hereinafter cited as *OR*. All references are to series I unless otherwise noted; Ezra Warner, *Generals in Gray* (Baton Rouge, 1959), pp. 319-320; Blessington, *Walker's Texas Division*, pp. 72-74; Edwin C. Bearss, *The Vicksburg Campaign*, 3 vols. (Dayton, 1985-1986), vol. 3, p. 1203.

3. Warner, *Generals in Gray*, p. 201; Bearss, *The Vicksburg Campaign*, vol. 3, p. 1204.

4. Warner, *Generals in Gray*, pp. 128-129; Bearss, *The Vicksburg Campaign*, vol. 3, p. 1204.

5. Mark M. Boatner, *The Civil War Dictionary* (New York, 1959), p. 678; Blessington, *Walker's Texas Division*, p. 250; Bearss, *The Vicksburg Campaign*, vol. 3, p. 1205.

6. *OR* 22, pt. 2, p. 828; Blessington, *Walker's Texas Division*, p. 79.

7. Blessington, *Walker's Texas Division*, p. 80.

8. *OR* 24, pt. 3, p. 846.

9. Samuel H. Lockett, "The Defense of Vicksburg," in Robert U. Johnson and Clarence C. Buell, eds., *Battles and Leaders of the Civil War*, 4 vols. (New York, 1884-1889), vol. 3, p. 488.

10. Richard Taylor, *Destruction and Reconstruction* (New York, 1879), p. 138.

11. *OR* 24, pt. 2, pp. 457–458.

12. Boatner, *The Civil War Dictionary*, p. 482.

13. *OR* 24, pt. 2, pp. 447, 458.

14. Blessington, *Walker's Texas Division*, p. 94.

15. *Ibid*, p. 96; Bearss, *The Vicksburg Campaign*, vol. 3, p. 1180; *OR* 24, pt. 2, p. 467.

16. Blessington, *Walker's Texas Division*, p. 96.

17. *OR* 24, pt. 2, p. 464; Bearss, *The Vicksburg Campaign*, vol. 3, p. 1182.

18. *OR* 24, pt. 2, p. 469. For further reading on the fighting at Milliken's Bend, see Norman D. Brown, ed., *Journey to Pleasant Hill: The Civil War Letters of Captain Elijah P. Petty, Walker's Texas Division, C.S.A.* (San Antonio, 1982). Petty, whose letters serve as the foundation for this work, was an officer in Waterhouse's 19th Texas Infantry.

19. *OR*, Series II, vol. 6, pp. 21-22.

20. *OR*, 24, pt. 3, pp. 589–590.

21. *Ibid*.

22. *OR* 24, pt. 2, pp. 471–472.

23. *Ibid*., p. 471.

24. *Ibid*., pp. 459–460, 465.

25. *Ibid*., p. 462.

26. *Ibid*., p. 469.

27. *Ibid*., pp. 462, 469.

28. Taylor, *Destruction and Reconstruction*, p. 139.

29. Bearss, *The Vicksburg Campaign*, vol. 3, p. 1203.

30. *Ibid*., pp. 1153, 1203.

CHAPTER TEN
"Triumph and Defeat"
Vicksburg Surrenders

1. John S. C. Abbott, *The History of the Civil War in America*, 2 vols. (New York, 1873), vol. 2, p.292.

2. *OR* 24, pt. 3, pp. 982-983.

3. *OR* 24, pt. 1, p. 283.

4. John C. Pemberton, *Pemberton: Defender of Vicksburg*, (Chapel Hill, 1942), p. 228.

5. Ulysses S. Grant, *Personal Memoirs of U. S. Grant*, 2 vols. (New York, 1885), vol. 1, p. 466.

6. Frederick D. Grant, "A Boy's Experience at Vicksburg," MOLLUS-New York, 3d Series, p. 98.

7. Pemberton, *Defender of Vicksburg*, p. 228.

8. Samuel H. Lockett, "The Defense of Vicksburg," in Robert U. Johnson and Clarence C. Buel, eds. *Battles and Leaders of the Civil War*, 4 vols. (New York, 1884-1889), vol. 3, p. 488; *Ibid*.

9. Grant, *Memoirs*, p. 467.

10. *Ibid.*; Bearss, *The Vicksburg Campaign*, vol. 3, pp. 1286-1287.

11. Diary of Capt. George Hynds (31st Tennessee), diary files, Vicksburg NMP; Diary of William Drennan, diary files, Vicksburg NMP.

12. William L. Foster, *Vicksburg: Southern City Under Siege* (New Orleans, 1982), p. 57.

13. Richard L. Howard, *History of the 124th Regiment, Illinois Infantry Volunteers* (Springfield, 1880), page unknown as only partial copy in library at Vicksburg NMP; Foster, *Southern City Under Siege*, p. 57.

14. Grant, *Memoirs*, p. 468.

15. *OR* 24, pt. 3, p. 460.

16. *Ibid.*

17. Lockett, "The Defense of Vicksburg," p. 492.

18. *OR* 24, pt. 1, p. 284.

19. Frederick Grant, "A Boy's Experience at Vicksburg," p. 98.

20. *OR* 24, pt. 1, p. 285.

21. *Ibid.*

22. Henry Steele Commager (editor), *The Blue and Gray: The Story of the Civil War as Told by Participants*, 2 vols. (Indianapolis, 1950), Vol. II, p. 677.

EPILOGUE

1. *OR* 24, pt. 2, p. 178. , Edwin C. Bearss, *The Vicksburg Campaign*, 3 vols. (Dayton, 1985-1986), vol. 3, p. 1311; Francis V. Greene, *The Mississippi* (New York, 1882), pp. 170-171.

2. *The Civil War Diary of General Josiah Gorgas* (University, Alabama, 1947), p. 55.

3. Mark M. Boatner, *The Civil War Dictionary* (New York, 1959), pp. 275-276, 558-559.

4. Dunbar Rowland, *Military History of Mississippi* (Spartanburg, 1978), pp. 196, 194, 264; Greer, "James Lockhart Autry," *Publications of the Mississippi Historical Society* (Jackson, 1916), Centenary Series, vol. I, pp. 457-462.

5. Ezra J. Warner, *Generals is Blue* (Baton Rouge, 1964), pp. 293-294.

6. William H. Leckie and Shirley A. Leckie, *Unlikely Warriors: General Benjamin H. Grierson and His Family* (Norman, 1984), p. xii.

7. *Report of the Adjutant General of the State of Illinois*, (Springfield, 1901), vol. VIII, pp. 54-57; Richard Surby, *Grierson Raids* (Chicago, 1865), pp. 178-181.

8. Biographical Files, Vicksburg National Military Park.

9. Warner, *Generals in Blue*, pp. 306-308; Lloyd Lewis, *Sherman, Fighting Prophet* (New York, 1932), p. 385.

10. Ezra J. Warner, *Generals in Gray* (Baton Rouge, 1959), pp. 118-119; *OR* 42, pt. 1, p. 852.

11. Warner, *Generals in Gray*, pp. 193-194; Richard N. Current (ed), *Encyclopedia of the Confederacy* 4 vols. (New York, 1993), vol. 3, p. 947.

12. Warner, *Generals in Blue*, pp. 441-444.

13. *Ibid.*, pp. 281-283.

14. Stewart Sifakis, *Who Was Who in the Union* (New York, 1988), p. 194; Roger D. Hunt and Jack R. Brown, *Brevet Brigadier Generals in Blue* (Gaithersburg, 1990) p. 282.

15. Mary Loughborough, *My Cave Life in Vicksburg* (Wilmington,1989), Introduction.

16. Diary (copy) of Emma Balfour, Diary Collection of Vicksburg National Military Park.

17. Warner, *Generals in Gray*, pp. 319-320.

18. *Ibid.*, pp. 161-162.

19. J. Franklin Jameson, *Dictionary of United States History* (Philadelphia, 1931), p. 206.

20. Samuel H. Lockett, "The Defense of Vicksburg," in Robert U. Johnson and Clarence C. Buell, eds. *Battles and Leaders of the Civil War*, 4 vols. (New York, 1884-1889), vol. 3, p. 492; Michael Ballard, *Pemberton: A Biography* (Jackson, 1991), p. 183; Warner, *Generals in Gray*, pp. 232-233.

21. Warner, *Generals in Blue*, pp. 183-186; Ulysses S. Grant, *Personal Memoirs of U.S. Grant*, 2 vols. (New York, 1885), vol. 1, dedication.

22. "The Gettysburg Address," delivered by President Abraham Lincoln on november 19, 1863; monument inscription, Pennsylvania Monument, Vicksburg National Military Park.

BIBLIOGRAPHY

MANUSCRIPTS

Ann Harris Broidrick, "A Recollection of Thirty Years Ago," Southern Historical Collection, University of North Carolina, Chapel Hill.

Ida Barlow, Mississippi Department of Archives and History.

Mahala P. H. Roach, Southern Historical Collection, University of North Carolina, Chapel Hill.

Margaret Lord, Library of Congress, Washington, D.C.

William A. Drennan, Mississippi Department of Archives and History.

NEWSPAPERS

The Pine Bluff Commercial, Pine Bluff, Arkansas, December 17, 1904.

Perry, Oran, "Perry Tells Story of the Siege of Vicksburg," *The Vicksburg Evening Post*, June 16, 1926.

Vicksburg Weekly Whig, November 14, 1860; May 1, 1861.

Vicksburg Daily Whig, July 11, 1862.

Vicksburg Daily Citizen, May 1, 1861.

Diaries and Journals, Vicksburg National Military Park

Nathan M. Baker, Regimental Files, 116th Illinois.

Diary of Emma Balfour.

C. A. Hobbs, Regimental Files, 99th Illinois.

Capt. George Hynds, 31st Tennessee

John A. Leavy, Surgeon, Green's Brigade.

LETTERS

Regimental Files, Vicksburg National Military Park

Alfred Cumming to Stephen D. Lee, November 3, 1899, RG 12, Vol. 12, Folder 15, Mississippi Department of Archives and History, Jackson.

C. H. Smart to William T. Rigby, September 10, 1903, 1st Battalion, 13th U.S. Infantry.

David Wilson to Frank Muhlenberg, March 23, 1903, 1st Battalion, 13th U.S. Infantry.

Francis G. Obenchain to William T. Rigby, July 4, 1903, Botetourt Artillery.

Francis G. Obenchain to William T. Rigby, July 14, 1903, Botetourt Artillery.

Francis G. Obenchain to William T. Rigby, July 16, 1903, Botetourt Artillery.

Frank Muhlenberg to W. W. Gardner, May 29, 1902, 1st Battalion, 13th U.S. Infantry.

Frank Muhlenberg to William T. Rigby, June 6, 1902; July 9, 1902; January 21, 1903; February 5, 1903; February 25, 1903; March 2, 1903; March 11, 1903; March 17, 1903; April 13, 1903, 1st Battalion, 13th U.S. Infantry.

George Kaut to Frank Muhlenberg, extract, 1st Battalion, 13th U.S. Infantry.

James Kephart to Frank Muhlenberg, extract, 1st Battalion, 13th U.S. Infantry.

James G. Spencer to Frank H. Foote, September 18, 1910, 1st Mississippi Light Artillery.

John W. Foreman to Frank Muhlenberg, April 18, 1903, 1st Battalion, 13th U.S. Infantry.

John W. Johnston to William T. Rigby, June 14, 1902, Botetourt Artillery.

Joseph C. Helm to Frank Muhlenberg, extract, 1st Battalion, 13th U.S. Infantry.

Joseph M. Richards to Frank Muhlenberg, extract, 1st Battalion, 13th U.S. Infantry.

Noble Warwick to "My Dear General," October 25, 1906, 1st Battalion, 13th U.S. Infantry.

Noble Warwick to W. W. Gardner, January 27, 1902, 1st Battalion, 13th U.S. Infantry

R. M. Nelson to W. W. Gardner, February 2, 1902, 1st Battalion, 13th U.S. Infantry.

W. W. Gardner, affidavit, January 10, 1902, 1st Battalion, 13th U.S. Infantry.

W. W. Gardner to Dr. Levi Fuller, May 25, 1863, 1st Battalion, 13th U.S. Infantry.

Walter Wood to Frank Muhlenberg, extract, 1st Battalion, 13th U.S. Infantry.

William A. Drennan to wife, May 30, 1863, Mississippi Department of Archives and History, Jackson.

BOOKS, ARTICLES, ETC.

"A Woman's Diary of the Siege of Vicksburg," ed. by George W. Cable, *The Century Magazine*, vol. XXX.

Abbott, John S. C., *The History of the Civil War in America*, 2 volumes, New York, 1873.

Anderson, Ephriam McD., *Memoirs: Historical and Personal; Including the Campaigns of the First Missouri Confederate Brigade*, ed. Edwin C. Bearss, Dayton, Ohio, 1972.

Ballard, Michael B., *Pemberton: A Biography*, Jackson, Mississippi, 1991.

Bearss, Edwin C., *The Vicksburg Campaign*, 3 volumes, Dayton, Ohio, 1985-1986.

Bevier, Robert S., *History of the First and Second Missouri Confederate Brigades, 1861-1865*, St. Louis, 1879.

Blessington, Joseph P., *The Campaigns of Walker's Texas Division*, Austin, 1968.

Boatner, Mark M., *The Civil War Dictionary*, New York, 1959.

Brokenburn: The Journal of Kate Stone, ed. John Q. Anderson, Baton Rouge, 1955.

Brown, Norman D., *Journey to Pleasant Hill: The Civil War Letters of Captain Elijah P. Petty, Walker's Texas Division, C.S.A.*, San Antonio, 1982.

Brown, Norman D., "John George Walker," in William C. Davis, ed., *The Confederate General*, 6 volumes, New York, 1991.

Chambers, William Pitt, "My Journal," *Publications of the Mississippi Historical Society, Centenary Series*, Vol. V, 1925.

Charles B. Allen, Plantation Book, Mississippi Department of Archives and History, Jackson.

City Council Minute Book, 1860-1869, City Hall, Vicksburg.

Commager, Henry Steele, editor, *The Blue and Gray: The Story of the Civil War as Told by Participants*, 2 volumes, Indianapolis, 1950.

Crooke, George, *The Twenty-first Regiment of Iowa Volunteer, Infantry: A Narrative of its Experience in Active Service*, Milwaukee, 1891.

Department of the Army, *The Medal of Honor of the United States Army*, Washington, D.C., 1948.

Dorsey, Sara A., *Recollections of Henry Watkins Allen, Brigadier General Confederate States Army, Ex-Governor of Louisiana*, New York, 1866.

Dyer, Frederick H., *A Compendium of the War of the Rebellion*, 3 volumes, New York, 1959.

Encyclopedia of the Confederacy, 4 vols, ed. Richard N. Current, New York, 1993.

Fiske, John, *The Mississippi Valley in the Civil War*, Cambridge, 1900.

FM 100-5 Operations, 5 May 1986, Headquarters, Department of the Army, Washington, DC.

Forbes, Stephen A., "Grierson's Cavalry Raid," Illinois State Historical Society, *Transactions*, Springfield, 1907.

Foster, William L., *Vicksburg: Southern city Under siege*, New Orleans, 1982.

Gorgas, Josiah, *The Civil War Diary of General Josiah Gorgas*, University, Alabama, 1947.

Grant, Frederick D., "A Boy's Experience at Vicksburg," *Military Order of the Loyal Legion of the United States-New York*, 3d Series.

Grant, Ulysses S., *Personal Memoirs of U.S. Grant*, 2 volumes, New York, 1885.

Greene, Francis V., *The Mississippi*, New York, 1882.

Greer, "James Lockart Autry," *Publications of the Mississippi Historical Society*, Centenary Series, Vol. 1, Jackson, 1916.

Grierson, Benjamin H., *Record of Services Rendered the Government, 1863*, privately printed, no date.

Hass, Paul H., "The Vicksburg Diary of Henry Clay Warmoth: Part II," *Journal of Mississippi History*, Vol.

XXXII, Jackson, Mississippi, 1970.

History of the Forty-sixth Regiment Indiana Volunteer Infantry, Compiled by Committee, Logansport, Indiana, 1888.

Howard, Richard L., *History of the 124th Regiment, Illinois Infantry Volunteers*, Springfield, 1880.

Jameson, J. Franklin, *Dictionary of United States History*, Philadelphia, 1931.

Johnson, Charles B., *Muskets and Medicine or Army Life in the Sixties*, London, 1917.

Jones, Samuel C., *Reminiscences of the Twenty-second Iowa Volunteer Infantry*, Iowa City, Iowa, 1907.

Joseph Bogle and William L. Calhoun, *Historical Sketches of Barton's (Later Stovall's) Georgia Brigade, Army of Tennessee*, Dayton, Ohio, 1984.

Kelly, William M., "A History of the Thirtieth Alabama Volunteers Confederate States of America," *Alabama Historical Quarterly*, Vol. IX, No. 1, Montgomery, 1947.

Korn, Jerry, *War on the Mississippi*, Alexandria, 1985.

Leckie, William H. and Shirley A., *Unlikely Warriors: General Benjamin H. Grierson and His Family*, Norman, Oklahoma, 1984.

Lee, Stephen D., "Details Important Work by Two Confederate Telegraph Operators, Christmas Eve, which Prevented the Complete Surprise of the Confederate Army at Vicksburg," *Publications of the Mississippi Historical Society*, Vol. VIII.

Lewis, Lloyd, *Sherman: Fighting Prophet*, New York, 1932.

Lockett, Samuel H., "The Defense of Vicksburg," in Robert U. Johnson and Clarence C. Buel, eds., *Battles and Leaders of the Civil War*, 4 volumes, New York, 1884-1889.

Lord, William L., "A Child at the Siege of Vicksburg," *Harper's Monthly Magazine*, CXVIII (December 1908).

Loughborough, Mary, *My Cave Life in Vicksburg*, Spartanburg, South Carolina, 1976, and the Wilmington, 1989 issue.

McRae, Lucy, "A Girl's Experience in the Siege of Vicksburg," *Harper's Weekly*, vol. LVI, June 8, 1912.

Markham, Jerald H., *The Botetourt Artillery*, Lynchburg, Virginia, 1986.

Morgan, George W., "The Assault on Chickasaw Bluffs," in Robert U. Johnson and Clarence D. Buel, eds., *Battles and Leaders of the Civil War*, 4 volumes, New York, 1884-1889.

Oldroyd, Osborn, *A Soldier's Story of the Siege of Vicksburg*, Springfield, 1885.

Pemberton, John C., *Pemberton Defender of Vicksburg*, Chapel Hill, 1942.

Porter, David Dixon, *Incidents and Anecdotes of the Civil War*, New York, 1885.

Report of the Adjutant General of the State of Illinois, Volume VIII, Springfield, Illinois, 1901.

Roster and Record of Iowa Soldiers in the War of the Rebellion, Vol. 4, Des Moines, Iowa, 1910.

Roth, David, "Grierson's Raid," *Blue & Gray Magazine*, Vol. X, Issue 5, Columbus, Ohio, 1993.

Sifakis, Stewart, *Who Was Who in the Union*, New York, 1988.

Smart, C. H., "Personal Recollections of Vicksburg, May 19, 1863," Regimental Files, Vicksburg National Military Park.

Surby, Richard, *Grierson Raids*, Chicago, 1865.

Taylor, Richard, *Destruction and Reconstruction*, New York, 1879.

The Story of the Fifty-fifth Regiment Illinois Volunteer Infantry in the Civil War 1861-1865, edited by Edwin C. Bearss, Huntington, West Virginia, 1993.

Thompson, William R. (ed), "From Shiloh to Port Gibson," *Civil War Times Illustrated*, October 1964.

Walker, Peter F., *Vicksburg: A People at War*, Chapel Hill, 1960.

War of the Rebellion: Official Records of the Union and Confederate Armies, 73 volumes, 128 parts, Government Printing Office, Washington, D.C., 1880-1901.

War of the Rebellion: Official Records of the Union and Confederate Navies, 31 volumes, Government Printing Office, Washington, D.C., 1895-1929.

Warner, Ezra, *Generals in Blue*, Baton Rouge, 1964.

Warner, Ezra, *Generals in Gray*, Baton Rouge, 1959.

Wells, Seth J., *The Siege of Vicksburg from the Diary of Seth J. Wells, Including Weeks of Preparation and of Occupation After the Surrender*, Detroit, 1915.

Wilcox, Charles E., "With Grant at Vicksburg, from the Civil War Diary of Captain E. Wilcox," *Journal of the Illinois Historical Society*, Vol. XXX, 1938.

Woodworth, Samuel L., "Grierson's Raid, April 17th to May 2d, 1863," pt. 1, *Journal of the United States Cavalry Association*, vol. XIV, No. 52, 1904.

INDEX